Race, Rights, and Recognition

Race, Rights, and Recognition

Jewish American Literature since 1969

Dean J. Franco

Cornell University Press
Ithaca and London

BP53

First published 2012 by Cornell University Press
Printed in the United States of America

Library of Congress Cataloging-in-Publication Data

Franco, Dean J., 1968–
    Race, rights, and recognition : Jewish American literature since 1969 /
Dean J. Franco.
        p. cm.
    Includes bibliographical references and index.
    ISBN 978-0-8014-5087-7 (cloth : alk. paper)
    1. American literature—Jewish authors—History and criticism.
2. Judaism and literature—United States—History—20th century.
3. Judaism and literature—United States—History—21st
century.   4. Jews—United States—Intellectual life.   5. Judaism in
literature.   6. Jews in literature.   I. Title.
    PS153.J4F66 2012
    810.9'8924—dc23   2011048712

Cornell University Press strives to use environmentally responsible
suppliers and materials to the fullest extent possible in the publishing of
its books. Such materials include vegetable-based, low-VOC inks and
acid-free papers that are recycled, totally chlorine-free, or partly composed
of nonwood fibers. For further information, visit our website at www.
cornellpress.cornell.edu.

Cloth printing   10   9   8   7   6   5   4   3   2   1

4/8/13

To Doris and David Franco

Contents

ACKNOWLEDGMENTS

Would you blame me if I said that I chose my topic at least in part based on the colleagues I wanted to read, debate, and share drinks with at hotel bars on the conference circuit? I chose wisely: This book has benefited from an ongoing four-year conversation with some of the brightest, nicest, most generous scholars I know. For instance, when my confidence flagged while I was writing on Cynthia Ozick, I emailed Ranen Omer-Sherman, whom I had never met, with a draft of the chapter attached. Ranen responded quickly with encouragement and help. Later, I presented a shaky version of the first chapter at a symposium at Penn State organized by the inimitable Ben Schreirer; Jeremy Dauber, arguably the star of the symposium, offered suggestions and kindly invited me to submit the essay for review at *Prooftexts*. I am grateful to Ranen, Ben, and Jeremy for their early generosity and encouragement. I echo the appreciation of many of my peers here by crediting Jonathan Freedman, whose work has always inspired me, and who is my imagined ideal reader for this book. Jonathan, along with Adam Newton, agreed to be on my MLA panel on Philip Roth and Race a few years back, and their support has been sustaining. More recently, Shaul Bassi, director of the Venice Center for International Jewish Studies, invited me to present work in progress, and our dialogue was both insightful and joyful.

And let's hear it for the authors: Lore Segal graciously provided personal information and encouragement, and Harriet Rochlin sat for hours and answered my questions about her life and work—and then fixed me lunch!

Closer to home, if further afield, Elizabeth Anker suggested I read Jacques Lacan on the Marquis de Sade while I was drafting the first chapter, and she later read portions of the book and gave me expert guidance. Much of what is interesting in this book is a result of her suggestions. At Wake Forest, Omaar Hena has been a constant sounding board for good and bad ideas (advising appropriately), a reading partner for some difficult theory, and a generous critic of nearly all the book's chapters. Call it friendship.

I have found friends and colleagues who work in other areas, even other disciplines, to be especially helpful readers and role models. Thanks go to Jarrod Whitaker, who was writing on early Vedic rituals while I worked on Jewish literature. His approach to his own book and his comments on mine illuminated for me just what a book should be. Likewise, Jessica Richard, Judith Madera, Gillian Overing, Melissa Jenkins, Scott Klein, Jennifer Raab, Susan Harlan, Adrienne Pilon, Scott Baker, and Beth Thompson have all read or discussed parts of this project at some point over the last four years, lending expertise, encouragement, and an enriched sense of audience. Wake Forest University is a great place to write a book. In addition to wonderful colleagues, I had the pleasure of working with terrific students, eager to learn, willing to help. Gratitude for research assistance goes to Arthur Nelson, Kara Solarz, Elizabeth Johnston, and Emily Young. And to Connie Green and Peggy Barret, sources of tranquility and humor, thank you.

Chapter 1 was originally published in *Prooftexts* 29, no. 1 (Winter 2009), by Indiana University Press; and chapter 2 was originally published in *Contemporary Literature* 49, no. 1 (2008), by the University of Wisconsin Press. I thank the publishers for their permission to reprint the articles here.

My wife Adrienne and my sons Ari and Gabriel are such a joy to be with, so as to make it very difficult to go into the office and get work done.

Only because they urged me on—occasionally by force—was I able to work. Finally, this book was made possible because of my parents, who encouraged and supported my interest in Jewish literature and history and who continue to share with me their interest in Jewish philosophy and culture. This book is dedicated to them, a small symbol of gratitude for their dedication to me.

RACE, RIGHTS, AND RECOGNITION

INTRODUCTION

The Politics and Ethics of Jewish American Literature and Criticism

In an early scene in Saul Bellow's novel *Mr. Sammler's Planet,* Artur Sammler, the elderly Holocaust survivor transplanted to New York, is invited to speak at Columbia University about his youthful acquaintance with the Bloomsbury circle.[1] The invitation comes from Lionel Feffer, a young Jewish acquaintance whose Marxist, Humanist, or Avant Gardist professions have a whiff of scam about them. First published serially in *The Atlantic* in 1969, the novel is set in 1968 and casts its revolutionary youth as a group of play-acting adolescents, foils to Sammler's role as a worldly, world-weary man of authentic experience.[2] During his lecture, while he is explaining George Orwell's disavowal of violence, Sammler is shouted down and finally denounced by a young radical in the audience: "Why do you listen to this effete old shit? What has he got to tell you? His balls are dry. He's dead. He can't come" (42). Sammler beats a hasty retreat, but, ever the intellectual, he meditates on the cultural meaning of his treatment. "What a passion to be *real*. But *real* was also brutal.... All this confused, sex-excrement-militancy, explosiveness, abusiveness, tooth-showing, Barbary ape howling" (43). It turns out that the audience had come expecting to hear a lecture on the radical philosopher Georges Sorel, whose advocacy of violence in support of social protest in the late nineteenth century anticipated and may have inspired SDS violence at Columbia in the spring of 1968, and Sammler seems to have stumbled into a live equivalent of an editorial debate of the time: Jewish liberals versus New Left Jews.

Sorel and Frantz Fanon and Jean-Paul Sartre were on the minds of many intellectuals and activists in the US in 1968, as violent protests and police counterviolence (or the other way around) occurred on several college campuses and urban areas throughout the country. SDS activists wanted the government out of Vietnam, while Black Panthers were demanding civil rights and cultural recognition. The National Council of La Raza and the Jewish Defense League, also founded in 1968, similarly parlayed violent rhetoric and tactics. As violence, political revolution, and ethnic identity became increasingly tangled, many intellectuals worried about the potentially fascistic implications. Writing in *The New York Review of Books* in February 1969, Hannah Arendt observed:

> Fanon, who had an infinitely more intimate experience of the practice of violence than any of its glorifiers, past or present, was greatly influenced by Sorel's equation of violence, life and creativity, and we all know to what extent this old combination has survived in the rebellious state of mind of the new generation—their taste for violence again is accompanied by a glorification of life, and it frequently understands itself as the necessarily violent negation of everything that stands in the way of the will-to-live.[3]

Later in the essay Arendt affirmed student violence as "rational" insofar as it is instrumental to legitimate student protest, but here she got to the crux of her concern, that violence as part of any political program feeds a swelling appetite for power. Bellow may not necessarily have shared Arendt's concern, but Sammler apparently does. For all his urbanity and mandarin intellectualism, Sammler has also bared his teeth, which the reader discovers later in the novel when Sammler reflects on his escape from a concentration camp and his killing of a German soldier. Sammler could have allowed the German to live, but he shoots him instead, and in doing so fans his own dying embers: "To kill the man he ambushed in the snow had given him pleasure. Was it only pleasure? It was more. It was joy. . . . When he fired his gun, Sammler, himself nearly a corpse, burst into life" (140). Decades later, in New York, Sammler once again encounters the thrill of the real, this time at his expense. Before shooting the German, Sammler could "see the soil already on his face," and he is similarly seen by the hostile crowd at Columbia as good as dead (140).

Sammler's equanimity with the students and his admission of his fascination with the real immediately precedes the most well-known, indeed notorious, scene from Bellow's novel: Sammler's encounter with the regal, black pickpocket on the Riverside bus. Sammler is fascinated by the pickpocket's clothing, demeanor, and refined methodology, and though Sammler weakly calls the police to report him, he is apparently conflicted and longs for a repeat encounter. He gets his wish shortly after leaving Columbia, but the pickpocket trails Sammler home and aggressively though mutely warns him off, by pinning him in a corner of his apartment lobby and exposing his penis. The animalistic metonymies for the pickpocket, from his "camel-hair" coat to his "elephant" penis, which he displays to Sammler as a mute sign of his power, have earned Bellow criticism for depicting post-rights African Americans as primitive, but the preceding scene at Columbia suggests that primitivism is in fact a self-conscious language deployed by an entire generation, an overt break from the liberal humanism of a prior generation (48–49). Moreover, Sammler appears to prefer the pickpocket's gesture to the hostile crowd's shouting. In contrast to the "Barbary ape howling" that forces him from the room, the pickpocket's phallic display is commanding: "No compulsion would have been necessary. He would in any case have looked" (49).

On the left and right, critics instantly collapsed the space between Bellow and Sammler, either criticizing or praising the novel's ostensible critiques of the New Left and urban African Americans and its seeming nostalgia for truth and beauty, but such readings require a series of binaries that do not necessarily hold within the novel: Europe vs. America, white vs. black, the prewar generation vs. the "voodoo primitivism" of the current generation (72). However, *Mr. Sammler's Planet* is neither for nor against civil rights, universal humanity, liberal civilization, feminism, or black power. Rather, the novel explores the superficial appearance and idiomatic performance of just these phenomena—and Sammler's attempt to get past that surface to the substantive meaning.

In this book I explore the work of recent Jewish American writers, including Bellow, who have engaged the themes of group-based rights and recognition in the United States, especially between 1969 and 1989. My argument is that these writers—Philip Roth, Cynthia Ozick, Allegra Goodman, Lore Segal, Tony Kushner, and Gary Shteyngart—explore, satirize, and experiment with the social values, political assumptions, and ethical commitments that underwrite the social transitions in post–civil rights America. Through their art, these writers expose the cynicism, limitations, blind spots, and conceptual aporias that nonetheless advance into mainstream political claims for group-based rights and recognition. In fact, they take us right to the edge of what can be thought and said when discussing these claims. In so doing, they test the ethical bases for the claims of multiculturalism. They also help us think productively about our current crises of global rights and recognition.

Let me be clear: I am not arguing that Jewish American literature simply attacks multiculturalism. Nor am I making the case that Jews ought to be part of an unreconstructed multicultural canon. This is not a book about blacks and Jews, and it neither deconstructs nor reconstructs the bases of multiculturalism. It does not argue for postethnic Jewishness, "critical post-Jewishness," or a more robust return to roots.[4] Rather, I am attempting to think along with Jewish American literature in an effort to understand how these writers have responded to the changing social regimes of racial recognition in the United States.[5] As I show, they ultimately come down somewhere between sympathy for an ethical basis for human recognition and criticism of recognition's expedient circuit into normative politics—the politics of naming groups, claiming rights, and shaming the perceived antagonists of social equality.

If "rights" and "recognition" are tied to individual and group-based empowerment, respectively, a third term emerges in the book that suggests a pragmatic first step toward new configurations of being and belonging: "proximity." All of the works I consider are about people from different ethnic or religious affiliations who find themselves in each other's paths. They are near enough to witness, sense, and experience each other. Indeed, proximity exposes group affiliation, subjecting it to scrutiny, because proximity is the (often anxious) occasion for thinking about one's relation to one's own group and for considering the salience or disposability of group-based identification itself. Proximity may lead to a politics of exploitation, as depicted in *Portnoy's Complaint,* or construct an ethics of effacement, as in *Her First American,* or provide the hinge between ethics and politics, as in *Homebody/Kabul.* I single out proximity here not to announce it as the master trope of this book but because it is what remains most real about our relations with others when all the knowingness, naiveté, sincerity, cynicism, universalism, or defensiveness over race, rights, and recognition is finally conceptually exhausted by this challenging body of literature. Who we are and what exactly that means may never be settled, but one thing is certain: we continually end up proximate to one another. The Jewish American literary contribution to thinking about intergroup relations is its many-sided and multilayered representation of and meditation on proximity—an "interruption" (borrowing from Lore Segal) of accepted ways of understanding interethnic relations.

Beginning with the term *rights* as used by Roth in *Portnoy's Complaint,* I am determined to delve into the phrases "civil rights" and "human rights," whose meanings are so ubiquitously conceded in literary criticism as often to go unquestioned. As historians of civil rights in the United States have pointed out, however, "rights" is not a fixed concept with a self-evident meaning.[6] Twentieth-century civil rights advances in the United States, including the right to vote and rights protecting minorities from unfair housing and labor practices, were thought to be a fulfillment of the Constitutional commitment, itself predicated on the Declaration of Independence, documents that simultaneously assume the self-evident status of man's freedom and elide or substantiate human subservience in the form of restrictions on women's rights and the support of slavery. If legislating civil rights in 1964 was the corrective to this historical wrong, it still remained the case that rights had to be secured through shifts in public behavior. Among the lasting social policies attending that effort was President Nixon's 1971 executive order directing federal agencies to make up for the underrepresentation of minorities in the pool of competitive bidders for government contracts and a series of public and private initiatives that inaugurated multiculturalism. Both practices continue to be politically controversial, often bringing forth knee-jerk reactions from critics and defenders, but it is worth recalling just what made and continues to make these social policies work in the first place: affirmative action is the supplement to civil rights, a social program that implicitly acknowledges that the self-evident status of "rights" and their legal guarantee lack pragmatic efficacy in the daily world of social prejudice and bigotry. This is the paradox of "rights": rights are inalienable to individuals but granted by the state; rights recognize individual worth but require group-based remedies in order for individuals to secure them. Such remedies presume a knowable group in the first place, predicated on biological "facts" of race and gender, and presume some social good beyond mere employment, namely public recognition and validation of a group's worthiness.

The coterminous threads of a deeply felt and honestly desired intervention for rights and recognition and a frequently cynical and often brutal politics of the same are knotted together in a tableau-scene in Bellow's novel. In a marvelous confluence of many of the themes and characters of *Mr. Sammler's Planet,* Sammler encounters the uncanny black pickpocket again, this time holding Feffer by the throat and trying to take his camera. Sammler has told Feffer about the pickpocket and Feffer has developed "an idea about him" and pursued him with a camera, hoping to "catch a criminal, sell a story to *Look.* Do a job on the police at the same time, and on [mayor] Lindsay...a triple killing" (123). Feffer's opportunism in the name of justice resembles Roth's eponymous hero in *Portnoy's Complaint* (the subject of chapter 1), and Bellow may have been after the same satire as Roth, but the struggle between the pickpocket and Feffer also bears the most serious humanistic drama of the novel. Among the crowd watching the brawl is Sammler's unbalanced Israeli son-in-law Eisen, and upon Sammler's command to "do something," Eisen begins to beat the pickpocket brutally over the head with a sack containing his own shop-crafted bronze Israeli ornaments, including a heavy Star of David. Horrified, Sammler declares Eisen's actions "the worst thing yet" and later ardently sympathizes with the pickpocket: "How much he would have done to prevent such atrocious blows" (290, 294).

Up to this point Sammler has been insulted and accosted, his daughter has stolen a scientific manuscript, his nephew has flooded his house and crashed his plane, yet this is the "worst"? Why is Sammler so shaken? Sammler's reaction is anticipated by an earlier conversation he has with his grand-nephew Wallace, in which he explains Tolstoy's faith that "you do not kill a man with whom you have exchanged such a look," a look that is a conscious appeal for life (188). Sammler longs for Tolstoy's truth to be universally true and not simply exceptional, but his own experience leads him to believe differently. Before he killed the German soldier, Sammler had also shared a look: "Sammler ordered the man to take off his coat. Then the tunic. The sweater, the boots. After this, he said to Sammler in a low voice, '*Nicht schiessen.*' He asked for his life" (139). The line suggests that the German's life is but one more object for Sammler to lift opportunistically, though the conflation of something simple like socks and a sweater with life itself suggests both Sammler's desperate need for the clothes in order to survive in the first place and his own undistinguishing, animalistic state of mind when he kills the German. This may explain Sammler's fascination with the pickpocket and his insistence on this other's *noblesse:* he is Sammler's hope, the one who lifts lightly, leaving life intact, and if not the warrant for Tolstoy's faith, he is at least a symbol of something true and real for Sammler. In contrast to all that he resists about the world, the pickpocket draws Sammler *out,* to observe, evaluate, judge, and witness in ways comparable to his visit to Israel during the Six-Day War: in the forest in Poland, in Gaza, and then on the Riverside bus, Sammler wanted to see something "real and true" (248). This book proceeds in this seam: between a belief in human recognition and the prospect of an ethics of responsibility and an awareness of how responsibility—"do something"—all too frequently yields "the worst yet," or catastrophic consequences.

While the pickpocket is fighting back against a reductive and exploitative portrait by Feffer, he is clobbered by an even blunter object of cultural reduction: Eisen's bronze sculptures. Bellow leaves the pickpocket mute to the very end, and in doing so he calls attention to two chords of Jewish discourse, the New Left's uneasy and at times opportunistic relationship to black rights and recognition and a cruder Jewish nationalism. Both are politically and morally inadequate in the novel, and the allegory fizzles out as the plot proceeds with Sammler's inarticulate humanism, but I press it into critical service here to say that as these very different kinds of Jews—charlatan New Leftist, Israeli nationalist, liberal humanist—contend with one another, all ignore the fate of the injured, perhaps dying, black pickpocket. Sammler flees the scene to attend to his dying nephew and patron Elya, shifting the plot to its more central social theme, a theme that dominates so much literary criticism, namely, generational impasse and the conflict between Old and New World Jews. Scholarship on Jewish American literary criticism has been overwhelmingly focused on diachronic cultural transmission or rupture: immigration, assimilation, or cultural betrayal; Jewish Oedipalism, feminist and queer Yiddishkeit revisionism; even geographical comparisons between Israeli Jewish and American Jewish cultures—all track currents of thought between generations of Jews but rarely and almost always insufficiently take account of the synchronic associations of Jews and the wider politics of race, rights, and recognition. Like Sammler himself, most critics at best only briefly contend with, and even then turn away from, the lateral social conflicts in their midst to attend to the ever-renewed subject of agonistic generational conflict. In the following chapters, I linger on the scene awhile, taking note of the proximity, contiguity, ventriloquism, and ultimately empathy that obtains between Jews and other minority groups, in view of a wider field of domestic and international concerns for race, rights, and recognition.

The first three chapters of this book examine works that explore the dilemma of the moral, ethical, or political conflicts that occur when individuals are also members of social groups. The second half is about global occasions for recognition and recognition's failure and the future of global recognition. Why conflicts? In the early twentieth century, sociologist Horace Kallen argued that no conflict exists when America recognizes the distinction between public and private spheres of life. For Kallen, in public we are individual agents, but our individual outlook, our moral orientation, and our social values are constituted by the cultural groups to which we belong.[7] Those groups exist in the sphere of our private lives: religious organizations, parochial schools, social clubs, language preservation societies, and periodicals. For Kallen, "America" was more than a place, it was an idea enacted when group-cultures harmonized through individual public practice in schools, work sites, or political forums. "Cultural pluralism" was the leading social goal for midcentury advocates of minority rights and equality, but at least since the 1960s, Kallen's thesis has been turned upside down: if racist discrimination occurs *in public,* then remedies for discrimination must be commensurately public. Consensus remedies including affirmative action—to prevent discrimination in labor, education, and housing and to undo centuries of exploitation—and multiculturalism—to promote public consciousness about the value of non-Anglo cultures—inaugurated a *politics* of identity. Identities became official public business after the late 1960s, so much so that attempts to sequester identity to the private sphere, by eliminating census questions about race, for example, are often regarded as reactionary.[8]

Jewish critics were wary of the public recognition of identity. As early as 1951, Will Herberg attempted to revise Kallen's thesis, arguing that the only salient "cultures" in America were in fact religious. In *Protestant, Catholic, Jew,* Herberg claimed that European ethnicities were atavistic and short-lived under the assimilative pressures of American mobility, and he viewed black American culture as the generally negative result of living under degrading and exploitative conditions and not an authentic culture in its own right.[9]

It is now easy to dismiss Herberg, along with later detractors of multiculturalism like Norman Podhoretz, but the question persists: just how deeply rooted and publicly relevant is culture? Beginning in the late 1960s, anthropologists like Clifford Geertz took up the argument that culture was rooted in human evolution, and was in fact constitutive of human beings.[10] If culture was fundamental to human beings, then it followed that public validation of culture was necessary to fulfill the promise of citizenship. In an influential essay defending multiculturalism, philosopher Charles Taylor explained that cultural validation was imperative for full-fledged citizenship, and he rooted his argument in Hegel's thesis on recognition. For Hegel, recognition is a dialectical phenomenon wherein one's own consciousness is alerted when it comes into contact with another consciousness. The encounter, allegorized by Hegel as the uncomfortable moment when two people look into each other's eyes and then break away in self-consciousness, permits individual self-consciousness at precisely the moment that one recognizes the consciousness of the other. Indeed, for Hegel, seeing the other see validates our own sense of self.[11] Taylor translates Hegel into a pluralist context by observing that "the discourse of recognition has become familiar to us on two levels: first, in the intimate sphere, where we understand the formation of identity and the self as taking place in a continuing dialogue and struggle with significant others" (37). This is the formation of identity in the private sphere, in familial, religious, and other intimate contexts. Second is "the public sphere, where a politics of equal recognition has come to play a bigger and bigger role" (37). Bigger, because of the post–civil rights reorientation of selfhood as a product of the public sphere in education, entertainment, politics, and consumer culture. If it is the case that selves are formed not only in the private home but also in the public sphere—the staple premise of the *bildungsroman*—then it is imperative for members of minority groups to find their cultures well represented and respected in the public sphere. This is the basis for Taylor's advocacy of multiculturalism as a means of conferring recognition of value to different cultures.

What Taylor does not account for, indeed the trap into which he falls in his own essay, is the way that the "discourse of recognition" is never value-free; rather, it is value-vexed, overwritten with cultural signifiers that construct the scene of recognition itself by providing a set of terms whereby recognition can take place. Taylor writes in the royal we, for example, but his point of view is masculine, educated, and above all liberal-individualist.[12] The problem is with the very conception of culture itself. A discussion of the "value" of multiple cultures means that culture has something like the status of an object that can be studied hermeneutically and appreciated objectively, with actual selves formed in relation to but ultimately separable from culture. But if selves are separable from cultures, are cultures truly necessary for the formation of selves? Or might "multiculturalism" be a way of fixing and surveilling the self, a technology for governing the messier tangle of difference (the experience of race, class, and gender) and historical narratives (the experience of migration and border crossing)? As far as Hegel is concerned, cultural perceptions and the visible signs of religious, racial, or ethnic difference surely mediate the gaze that passes between two people. The "look" that Sammler identifies in Tolstoy evades us when we live in a society hyperattentive to social differences.

Recognition that prioritizes social difference seems to swap ethics for politics. If no pure, unmediated gaze between differently marked selves is possible, a politics of social difference that names, validates, and advances minority groups by promoting cultural awareness or "celebrating diversity" would at least create a public sphere of tolerance for or even validation of minority cultures. However, though the discourse of multiculturalism ostensibly rejects the centering and privileging of any one culture, that centering takes place nonetheless, because multiculturalism is finally a discursive program, beholden to a logic of centers and margins. The discursive field of racial recognition can name only what it sees but also can see only what already has a name. Thus, when Bellow's Sammler reaches for a term to express his distaste for the sexual behavior of his younger generation of relatives, he calls it "sexual niggerhood" (162). The phrase offends if we presume that Sammler is naturalizing a stereotype of black sexuality and then appropriating that stereotype to critique his Jewish family members.

Of course, the phrase could be read precisely in the opposite way, that Sammler's critique *de*naturalizes the stereotype, unhinging the slur from any point of origin and granting it the free-floating capacity of language itself. It doesn't help that Bellow precedes the phrase with another ambiguous reference: "from the black side, strong currents were sweeping over everyone. Child, black, redskin—the unspoiled Seminole against the horrible Whiteman" (162). There are no Seminoles in the novel, and lumping together "child, black, redskin" in order to align Sammler's *Jewish* niece, daughter, and nephew with "the black side" seems an intentional conflation and a willful positing of linguistic ambiguity for Bellow. For Sammler, who otherwise thinks in long paragraphs, these metonyms of race seem to be just that: words pointing outward, unhinged from referential objects. I am not defending Sammler or Bellow here, merely suggesting that attention to the discursive field wherein difference is encountered, imagined, or recast significantly complicates and perhaps renders impossible the sort of recognition that Taylor seeks, for the signs for identity with which we would ostensibly honor cultures are in fact already in flux.

The instability of the discursive field of recognition in the United States may allow for the deconstruction of social difference, especially since cultural difference in the United States runs shallow compared to the cultural differences between nations in the Global North and the Global South or between dominant western economies and third-world labor. In the case of different nations, "difference" often does imaginative work on behalf of the reigning economic regime. For instance, in the United States the common liberal platitude in support of immigrant workers is that "they do the jobs Americans don't want to do." Independent of the veracity of the claim, the line suggests national differences organized by the capacity for labor, while the word *want* carries a liberal presumption of individual will, as if we do only those jobs we want to do and labor is a free choice. The ostensibly sympathetic platitude thus lodges difference as one more plank propping up exploitative labor relations between the United States and Mexico. This is what Elizabeth Povinelli calls "the cunning of recognition; its intercalation of the politics of culture with the culture of capital. We need to puzzle over a simple question: What is the nation recognizing, capital commodifying, and the court trying to save from the breach of history when difference is recognized?" (17).[13] Povinelli goes on to explain that the multicultural conferral of recognition on aboriginal peoples often originates from a cultural narcissism that imagines the aboriginal other as a version of ourselves before civilization or as the opening chapter in the story of colonization. Thought of in narrative terms, recognition requires aboriginal culture to play a static role in the drama of western advancement and development. We are familiar with this plot in American history, but this sort of asymmetrical recognition also pertains to contemporary neocolonial encounters, the subject of this book's final two chapters, where even the most liberal-minded Westerners struggle to arrive at an ethics or politics of respect for the radical difference between the liberal west and, say, Talibani Islam. Conservatives like George W. Bush have insisted that the love of freedom and the capacity for democracy is universal, while many non-interventionist leftists conceded that cultural difference dooms even well-meaning interventions abroad.[14] Tony Kushner and Gary Shteyngart, the writers discussed in the final two chapters, situate their characters between these two points of view, and both confront the sort of critique Povinelli has advanced, namely how to establish forms of recognition that do not simply recapitulate the global capitalist hierarchy.

"Jewish" "American" "Literature"

The writers I have chosen to examine in this book would not stretch the boundaries of anyone's definition of "Jew." All of the writers are self-identified Jews and "born" Jews, and the chosen texts are squarely Jewishly themed. But "Jewish" is nonetheless a term of art and ambiguity, and the literature examined in this book speaks productively about race, rights, and recognition precisely because "Jewish" signals multiple and perhaps contradictory commitments to identity. By now, readers of this book will be familiar with the vast body of scholarship and criticism that seeks to investigate just what a Jew is, first of all, and how the ambiguity of Jewish identity has made Jews at once pariahs of puritanical nationalists and exemplars of modernist nonbelonging. Labile Jewishness makes for productive criticism. Perhaps bucking a trend, in 2001 critic Michael Kramer argued that any discussion of Jewish literature necessarily depends on a racialist designation of "Jewish" for writers.[15] What else, Kramer wondered, would justify putting writers of different historical eras, linguistic traditions, national cultures, not to mention thematic interests under a common rubric if not an assumption that there was a single indelible commonality shared by Jews, namely race?

Kramer has a point. Closer to home, how can "Jewish American" capture commonalities between Cynthia Ozick and Gary Shteyngart? Philip Roth and Rachel Calof? While Calof and Shteyngart—eastern European immigrants—and Roth and Ozick—American-born—have much in common with each other, their life experiences, artistic influences, linguistic backgrounds, and religious commitments are significantly different. Why categorize them—and why categorize at all? The answer to this question and to Kramer's quandary is that categories only matter for the sake of academic argument. In practice, categories rarely matter to writers themselves, and to the vast majority of readers, ethnic categories only matter when writers are perceived to be significantly culturally different, and even then ethnic categories are often marketing gateways, flagging superficial semiotic differences on what is otherwise familiar literary territory. However, for teachers and scholars of literature, academic categorization may overemphasize identity, but that is a small tradeoff for the study and advancement of literature that would otherwise receive very little attention. Until the last three decades, it was a truism that there was no such thing as "Native American literature," and as many scholars of African American literature have observed, "writing" and "African" were once considered mutually exclusive.[16] In both cases, the identity category preceded the subcategorization of literature, and it is gathering the literature that revises our understanding of the culture, often cutting right into the core of racist histories and assumptions. However, Jews in America are no longer strange or exotic, nor does "Jewish" need recuperation from deliberate stereotypes. On the contrary, as Philip Roth discovered with the publication of *Goodbye, Columbus,* American Jews often believed they had more to lose than to gain through literature that deviated from the steady script of assimilation, success, and family strength.

So why categorize "Jewish American literature"? Perhaps commensurate with other ambiguities at the heart of "Jewish," organizing literature under that heading allows for a contingent way of reading that focuses on commonly assumed historical narratives, geographical allegiances, and affective cultural markers. Any of the authors in this book could and should be read under several different rubrics, and many have done so, but this book proceeds with the implicit question, what do we find when we line these authors up in this way? And pressing the question further, what happens when we read the literature *not* for a chronologically unfolding story of Jews in America but for the dynamic encounter with America itself?

In the end, it is "America" that links all of these writers. For each, Jewishness is an interface with American racial history; American social mechanisms of assimilation, acculturation, and class mobility; and the American struggle for domestic civil rights and global human rights. Jews have been active participants in changing the very meaning of "race" in American life, from Franz Boas's path-breaking anthropology in the early twentieth century that sought to denaturalize race to the activism of many Jews in the civil rights movement.[17] Meanwhile, the midcentury Jewish support for liberal rights has re-formed in some intellectual and political quarters as Jewish neoconservativism, which links Israel and the United States as embattled democracies whose commitment to liberal freedom is under assault from god-awful Islam and godless European socialism.[18] Because of American Jews' commitment to both the United States and Israel, Jewish writers and critics are particularly compelled to address international problems of national identification and global recognition and the paradoxes of human rights, especially following the U.S. wars in Iraq and Afghanistan and the subsequent instantiation of a class of enemies without rights. Jews are no different from other Americans, some of whom are outraged by the global war on terror and the concomitant domestic "state of exception" permitting the rollback of some basic civil rights, some who ardently support the promotion of democracy abroad and who subscribe to the Bush-era credo that freedom is the "gift from the almighty" delivered by the U.S. military, and probably a large plurality who take no interest in such matters whatsoever.[19] On the other hand, Jews may be unique in the twentieth century in that, as a group, they have transformed from a rootless cosmopolitan people—one recalls the "Jewish problem"—to a group identified with a modern nation, from an ambiguously racialized group to fully enfranchised white Americans. American Jews are not cosmopolitan per se, nor is the American Jewish diaspora as epistemically salient as it once was, but being Jewish in the United States may permit a measure of "epistemic privilege," as Paula Moya puts it, for understanding racial formation, while the debate over the equation of anti-Zionism and anti-Semitism directs Jewish consciousness toward international contexts for rights and recognition.[20]

It is difficult, not to mention unwise, to attempt sweeping claims about literature by Jews or any group of people, and this book's limited selection of texts should indicate the modesty of my project. Perhaps a better subtitle would be "*some* Jewish American literature since 1969." In any case, I do not mean to claim either that the predominant theme of U.S. Jewish writing is race, nor have I fooled myself into thinking I have covered a great deal of ground with my handful of authors. Indeed, in the final chapter and epilogue, I suggest that Shteyngart is only the most ostentatious jewel in the treasure trove of recent writing by eastern European émigrés in the United States, while the gesture to Harriet Rochlin's frontier saga and the New Western Jewish History movement only starts a conversation about a body of significantly underappreciated writing. Putting Rachel Calof's homesteading memoir in conversation with the novels by Shteyngart and Rochlin opens all three up to visions, revisions, and critiques of pluralism, multiculturalism, and the American geographical imaginary in the works that would not be evident investigating each work individually.

The seven literary authors I discuss do not stand for the whole of Jewish American literature, but they do write on the Jewish role during flash-points in the history of rights and pluralism in the United States: the development of the UN Human Rights Commission in the 1950s, civil rights policy in the 1960s, the "new pluralism" of the 1970s, and the globalization of culture from the 1990s to the present day. Some chapters draw on relevant Jewish contexts—Ozick's published writing on Jewish social and religious issues, for example—some on Jewish thematics—Goodman's exploration of multiple streams of Jewish history in America—and some on Jewish philosophical resources, including Derrida and Levinas, Kenneth Reinhard and Judith Butler, all of whom wrestle with biblical anteced-ents to approach postmodern problems of ethics. Finally, taking a cue from Jonathan Boyarin's *Thinking in Jewish,* I examine broad social phenomena *through* Jewish-identified authors and texts, situating debates about race, rights, and recognition within a local, contingent, and protean Jewishness.[21]

Methodology: Some "Multi," Some "Culture"

Questions about the power, meaning, and implications of difference, the cultural provenance of human rights, and the ethics of global multicultural recognition hearken response from both the humanities and the social sciences. Or at least they ought to. Too often, studies of race and ethnicity disparage or simply fail to attend to methodologies or insights across disciplinary lines, but the very term *multiculturalism* is nothing but a mashup of disciplinary directives. The very word *culture* has a proprietary foot in both literary and sociological methodologies. Matthew Arnold beat Franz Boas by a couple of decades, but both saw culture and social policy as imbricated.[22] Arnold was a poet and social reformer who characterized the drudgey working class of England as "Hebraic" and lobbied for more sweetness and light, which he characterized as "Hellenic." Through his advocacy of reform for English education, Arnold sought to improve English culture. For his part, Boas was a cultural anthropologist and literary muse. Both sought to reform the ways that culture interfaces with society. Boas's mentoring of literary writers, including Zora Neale Hurston, suggests that literature might be the companion to anthropology in the effort to apprehend culture. Or take Horace Kallen, nominally a philosopher trained under George Santayana and William James but best known for his work of social theory, *Culture and Democracy*. Kallen saw culture as a series of social facts that might be organized by a philosophically systematized democratic participation. In short, though the study of human rights, civil rights, and identity typically falls under the domain of the social sciences, the humanities have been and continue to be vital for explaining culture's interface with the social.[23]

The real disciplinary cleavage (aside from the ugly-sounding "ism") is "multi," a prefix more determinedly sociological or political, indicating a social landscape where differences cohabitate or clash. Political theory is especially good when it comes to the "multi," but less so on "culture," and the reverse seems true of literature study. Cultural affiliation is necessarily political when multiple cultures compete or collaborate for public recognition or for rights within a democracy. But the lived *experience* of culture, where culture is supple, dialogic, revisionary, heterodox; affective, mysterious, thrill-giving, or guilt-inducing; and ever-changing through contact with other cultures and through the interpenetration of various modes of religious engagement—all of it combine to make culture a very complicated, dynamic way of being in the world rarely accounted for in political theory's static depictions of cultures.

William Connolly's subtle and innovative work on pluralism is a rare exception, and he explains the difference between a dynamic and a static theory of culture in terms of becoming and being:

> By the politics of becoming I mean that paradoxical politics by which new and unforeseen things surge into being, such as new and surprising religious faith, a new source of moral inspiration, a new mode of civilizational warfare, a new cultural identity unsettling an existing constellation of established identities, a new collective good, or the placement of a new right on the existing register of existing rights. In highlighting the importance of becoming to politics, I do not disparage the importance of being, though I have learned through experience that some who focus only on being find it difficult to absorb a theory in which becoming and being are maintained in a relation of torsion. (121)[24]

Connolly's phrase "relation of torsion" suggests that cultures are under constant pressure, often from mutually opposing forces, and that change is the bend that does not break. I find Connolly's account more persuasive than the more frequently cited paradigm of Werner Sollors in which ethnicity is the product of "consent" and "descent," with individuals freely choosing and descent lines felicitously available from generation to generation.[25] Connolly, in contrast, explains that ethnicities, religion, cultures, and political identities exist in agonistic relation to one another or may be open to one another and, in either case, are in constant flux.

Connolly's insight is a useful starting point for this book, which seeks to understand the "relations of torsion" in Jewish American culture, as represented especially in literature. This is not a comparative book, but it presumes that Jewish writers have been significantly influenced by or have taken a strong interest in the social, political, and ethical problems associated with minority groups in the United States, including Jews, of course, but also the experiences of African Americans, Native Americans, Chicana/os, and Latina/os. The social activism of the latter three groups is not so widely disseminated as is the activism of African Americans, but the political philosophies, rhetoric of nationalism, and ethics of cultural recognition that underwrite Chicana/o, Latina/o, and Native American activism were in discursive circulation in the 1960s. Though the most prominent journal of Jewish American critique, *Commentary,* took a reactionary stance against communitarian cultural activism, Jewish literary writers represented cultural difference with significantly more complexity. There is no generic consistency to the texts included here, so I do not argue for the capacity of, say, the novel to trump political critique in terms of depth. Rather, literature's general attribute of putting the political *alongside* the ethical, of allowing for singular individualism *and* thick communal culture, and for reflecting people's ability to live *within* but *fail to understand* their social landscape allows literary writers to represent and re-envision the lived experience of culture. Indeed, what Connolly calls relations of torsion appears in literature as plot conflict, narrative complexity, and deep irony. Consider Cynthia Ozick's gun-toting Jewish rationalist Bleilip from her short story "Bloodshed." Though it is never clear why Bleilip has a gun, the story represents several kinds of conflicts, both diachronic and synchronic. Secular Bleilip is haunted by the memory of his dead, pious grandfather; resentful of the ostensible Jewish authenticity of Holocaust survivors in his family; and disdainful of the mystical practices of Hasidic Jewry. The story thus telegraphs the tension between several types of heterodoxy and a persistent Jewish authenticity. At the same time, the story's setting and context suggest several inferences for Bleilip's gun-toting: he may fear anti-Semitism or violent black nationalism, or he may be inspired by the armed Meir Kahane, founder of the Jewish Defense League, itself inspired by the Black Panthers.

Ozick's short story form compresses its conflicts into a space so tight as to sieve out sociology and to concentrate its primary themes, Jewish responsibility and covenant. In marked contrast but toward similar ends is Lore Segal's novel *Her First American,* set in the 1950s, about a Jewish war refugee and her "first American" love, an older African American intellectual. The context, from the Holocaust to the nascent civil rights movements in the 1950s, would seem to overdetermine the novel's plot, but Segal, a longtime friend of Ozick's, employs a different strategy for steering her plot around sociology, namely ellipses. Literally and figuratively, the text hearkens but then elides its social and political contexts, and while Ozick may be sincere in insisting that her work is *not* to be read as a representation of social reality, Segal's stylistic and narrative ellipses are best understood when the reader knows just what is being elided. In contrast, Roth's *Portnoy's Complaint* and Shteyngart's *Absurdistan* are both satires that depend on social context for their comedy. Likewise, Kushner's *Homebody/Kabul,* though far from a satire, dramatizes a contemporary global problem of cultural recognition. With all texts, understanding the social contexts and charting the literature's engagement with a broad discursive field of race, rights, and recognition seems necessary for understanding the political or ethical insight each has to offer.

While Roth was drafting his novel, black activism offered the loudest, most charged, and most salient critique and revision of race in the United States, and I draw on Eldridge Cleaver to draw out the racial critique at work in *Portnoy's Complaint*. Likewise, Shteyngart's conspicuous reference to Malcolm X suggests a way to get beyond *Absurdistan*'s otherwise all-encompassing reduction of culture to commodity. Of course, Malcolm X is not Shteyngart's contemporary, but his line "by any means necessary" appears prominently in *Absurdistan* and offers a telescoping view of the passage of black cultural nationalism into ameliorative multiculturalism and its final form as commodifiable "diversity" in the novel. More directly comparative is chapter 4's examination of Lore Segal's novel *Her First American* in relation to Horace Cayton's autobiography *Long, Old Road*. Cayton was intimate with Segal and was her basis for her character Carter Bayoux. Segal even lifts scenes and paraphrases dialogue from Cayton's work, but my aim is not to compare the two so much as to explore the discursive field wherein race exists for both authors and to measure how the politics of racial recognition torques each text's depiction of the relationship.

I know Cayton was the source for Segal's Carter because Segal told me so, in an email. Similarly, I know something about Harriet Rochlin's life and views on pluralism because she and I spoke at length in her home in Los Angeles. To understand more about Roth's satire of race relations in New York in the 1960s, I visited the Roth Collection at the Library of Congress. This book is by no means archival, but I have consulted original sources when I thought they would help me get past the prevailing critical paradigms for Jewish American literature. I presume that the writers discussed here are at least as interested in and influenced by the world around them as they are by the "world of their fathers," to paraphrase Irving Howe. Of course, these writers are interested in assimilation, second-generation cultural changes, the Holocaust, and Israel—themes commonly discussed in literary criticism—but these *Jewish* concerns are always intertwined with other social phenomena. When the characters in Segal's *Her First American* rush to the United Nations to observe a diplomatic meeting over an international crisis, it may be the Suez Canal crisis of 1956 or the decolonization of the Sudan, Morocco, or Tunisia, also of 1956. More to the point, Segal's elision of specific places and international actors and the broad concern shown by her Jewish, African American, and black African characters suggest how the Suez crisis and African decolonization were in fact one and the same event—and not separable according to black and Jewish concerns. Literally filling in the blank spaces in Segal's novel and figuratively reading behind and beneath the other texts with the support of contextual materials help situate the literature within a broader critique of the emerging multicultural consensus of the 1960s and 1970s.

Besides some peripatetic primary research, I also have three recurring theoretical tools in play throughout the book, though this book has no grand theoretical aspirations of its own. For obvious reasons, the first and last chapters draw on Freudian theories to discuss *Portnoy's Complaint* and *Absurdistan*—indeed, Roth and Shteyngart have great fun with Freudian theory. More relevantly, I proceed with the premise that there is a social drama playing out in the literature that remains understated, metonymic, or elliptical and that psychoanalytic theory is a useful tool in narrative analysis. Likewise, I attempt to draw out the implicit deconstruction of the language of identity within most of these texts and find in the work of Derrida and Judith Butler usable models of reading and critique. My archive of theorists is frequently Jewish: Freud, Derrida, Levinas, Butler, and Kenneth Reinhard. These five have expressly committed themselves to Jewish texts or contexts; Butler in particular has made a sharp turn toward Jewish philosophy in the last decade. I find that their Jewish sensibility matches this book's mode of critique, aiming to unravel the "white mythologies" of American Jewish identities, thereby opening space for a more engaged, productively critical way of "thinking in Jewish" about race, rights, and recognition in the United States.

On the other hand, two other frequently cited theorists, William Connolly and Slavoj Žižek, are most certainly not Jewish. An argument might be made—not here, not by me—that there is a whole "family" of theorists or theoretical occasions classifiable as "Jewish" that are responsive to the Jewish question of difference so prominent in post–Enlightenment era philosophy. Marx, Freud, and Derrida could hardly be more different as thinkers, yet the three share a common critique of post-Enlightenment rationality, property-based rights, and ontological as well as social self-presence. Theorists working under their influence necessarily return to the several Jewish questions—questions of Jewish national, racial, or moral being—present in western philosophy.

Ultimately, all of my sources including literature, criticism, and theory are present here in order to help think complexly about this book's main topic: how Jewish American writing (and writing that helps read Jewish American writing) can direct us to a more salient critique, a more expansive theory, and a more hopeful future for encountering race, securing "rights," and being open to forms of recognition that enable relations of responsibility and care between people and among groups of people. For this reason, I have sacrificed comprehensive coverage for what I hope are probing readings. Many more authors and texts should be discussed under a rubric like "race, rights, and recognition," and in fact I am confident that more and superior analyses are in print or on the way.

This book has two sections, "Pluralism, Race, and Religion," and "Recognition, Rights, and Responsibility." More prosaically, the first section could be said to be about what divides us and the second about ways of overcoming those divisions. Two other major topics, less divisible according to section, run through this book: literary accounts of diversity and multiculturalism and theorizations of civil and human rights. Most chapters speak to both topics, but readers particularly interested in Jewishness and diversity in America will appreciate chapters 2, 3, and 4. Chapters 1, 5, and 6 are especially focused on critiques and theorizations of discourses of civil and human rights. In the first chapter, I revisit Philip Roth's notorious 1969 novel, which so scandalized Roth's peers, to argue that Roth's satire of the limitations of "civil rights" is the true scandal. Drawing on Roth's manuscripts, notes, and research files archived at the Library of Congress, I examine how Alexander Portnoy's career as "Assistant Commissioner for the New York City Commission on Human Opportunity" is based on—and critical of—the actual New York City Civil Rights Commission. I compare Roth's novel with Eldridge Cleaver's prison memoir *Soul on Ice,* also published in 1969, to demonstrate how in both, even the sex is about race. In both works, civil and human rights are supplanted by a more malleable and potent quest for "rights of desire." Drawing on psychoanalysis and rights theory, the chapter concludes with a discussion of the radical potential in the portrait of "rights of desire." Though I do not attempt to push *Portnoy's Complaint* past its limits by claiming for it more ethical insight than it can bear, I do suggest that the novel's critique of "rights" opens up room for thinking about how other writers link rights with bodily enjoyment. I pick up on Roth's innovation in chapter 5, on Kushner's *Homebody/Kabul,* to argue that responsibility joined with an ontology of substitution—as in Levinas's "I live instead of another"—may yield a thesis of "rights" rooted in something outside of the political.

Chapter 2 recasts Ozick's theme of "Hellenism and Hebraism" as "Assimilation and Pluralism," with historical memory the rigorous check against glib American self-invention. Responding to the same social and political landscape as Roth, Ozick represents a more deeply rooted Jewish identity, constantly under assault from the secular or new ethnic social environment all around. I argue that Ozick's early fiction represents a "deep" multiculturalism in which "Jewish" is an essential, not a political or merely cultural, mode of being. Drawing on writing in *Commentary, Dissent,* and *The Jewish Annual Yearbook* for context and on political theorizations of multiculturalism and pluralism, I read Ozick's early stories, including "The Pagan Rabbi" and "Bloodshed," as underwritten by an implicit philosophical pluralism and her later novel, *The Messiah of Stockholm,* as a postmodern rebuke against sentimental cultural identification. Like Roth's, Ozick's early fiction ventures such a deep exploration and critique of the prevailing pluralism as to be unrecognizable to the mainstream of discourse on multiculturalism in its early formation.

Chapter 3, on Allegra Goodman's novel *Kaaterskill Falls,* explores how the author represents modern Yiddish, Hasidic, and secular Jews' relation to one another and the wider non-Jewish town where they visit for the summer. The novel exhibits a subtle anachronism: set in the mid-1970s, at the height of what political commentators called the "new pluralism," the novel folds the more recent problems of global religious diversity into its pluralist conflict, casting light on present-day American and global dilemmas of religious and cultural incommensurability. Read retrospectively, Goodman's fiction serves as a corrective to the critical neglect of pluralism in Ozick's work while representing a robust Jewish pluralism that is far more capacious than Ozick could or would allow. This chapter reads Goodman's novel in tandem with political theorist William Connolly's recent work on pluralism, religion, and secularism. Connolly's descriptions of successful pluralist encounters are borne out in Goodman's work, but Goodman gives us something Connolly cannot: a rich account of the turbulent tumble of people's contradictory responses to difference, where the sacred and the profane are constantly imbricated. This chapter concludes the book's first half, about pluralism and multiculturalism's challenge to Jewish commitments to political and cultural rights.

The book's second half extends the topic on civil rights and race to the international dimension of human rights and social recognition. Here my methodology shifts too, with longer, more comparative inquiries into the politics and ethics of recognition and into social theories of human rights and responsibility. Unlike in the first three chapters, where I find individual authors satirizing, evaluating, or otherwise critiquing 1960s- and 1970s-era social theories of racial and ethnic recognition, in the second half I argue that our writers may show us how to recuperate rights and recognition in our own global multicultural moment. Here I am not convinced that each of my authors is intentionally advancing a thesis on rights and recognition but am confident that the ethical and political scenarios they represent can be read against current events to imagine a recuperated notion of rights, responsibility, even pluralism (a new, new, new pluralism). Chapter 4 examines the under-studied novel *Her First American* (1985) by Lore Segal. Segal's novel, about a young Jewish war refugee and her romance with a cosmopolitan African American journalist in the 1950's, foregrounds several problems associated with ethical recognition important for the remaining two chapters. The two characters have deep-seated but asymmetrical experiences with dislocation, racial persecution, and American alienation. However, the novel quite literally elides their similarities and all other forms of political recognition, leaving gaps in the relationship and in the plot. These elisions seem symptomatic of a problem of political recognition itself, where political names are necessary for democratic recognition, on the one hand, but end up as straightjacketing "identities," on the other. As already mentioned, Segal's African American hero, Carter Bayoux, is based on Horace Cayton, a prominent sociologist and journalist, and I read his memoir *Long Old Road* (1965) in tandem with her novel to trace the fine line between effacing race and defacing the self through racial abnegation.

Chapter 5 explains how Tony Kushner's play *Homebody/Kabul* is a dramatic exploration of the ethics of cross-cultural recognition and responsibility. Notably, *Homebody/Kabul* received none of the popular acclaim and public affirmation that attended Kushner's earlier *Angels in America. Angels in America* gives us a beautiful vision of a politics to which we have already assented—the politics of pluralist coalitions—while *Homebody/Kabul,* in contrast, broaches an ethics about situations we've only just begun to glimpse: Western responsibility for globalization's reach and the difficulty of recognition across cultural and religious barriers. I analyze *Homebody/ Kabul,* a play about an upper-class London housewife who disappears into Kabul, in conjunction with *National Geographic*'s discovery and unveiling of their famous Afghan girl, Sharbat Gula. This chapter maps Kushner's play across the very same terrain as the celebrated *National Geographic* feature but finds in Kushner's play a complication of *National Geographic*'s teleology of loss and recovery, not to mention liberal feminism. I argue that though the play is laced with points of cultural incommensurability and misapprehension, it nonetheless models a vision of ethical responsibility for the other particularly suggestive for a post-9/11 comprehension of the world. Recalling the discussion of Roth's novel in chapter 1, I close chapter 5 with a fuller examination of what it would mean to live in a state of responsibility for the "enjoyment" of the other, and how an ethics of substitution—in contrast to the logic of sacrifice—thematizes Western responsibility for the postcolonial other.

Chapter 5 is unique in this book in that Kushner's play is not in any conventional way "Jewish." The characters, themes, and current events of the play are not coded as Jewish. Yet I read the play *Homebody/Kabul* as offering the most compelling Jewish analysis and vision for current global crises of recognition, first of all because Kushner's draw on Jewish ethics is so consistent and well known, and second, more germane to the chapter, because the play's ethical vision is deeply consonant with contemporary Jewish theoretical offerings by Derrida, Levinas, and Butler.

The final chapter, "Globalization's Complaint," takes the satirization of multiculturalism in Gary Shteyngart's novel *Absurdistan* as a challenge to the discussion of pluralist recognition of the preceding chapters. For Shteyngart's antihero, the Russian Jewish scion and practitioner of global multiculturalism Misha Vainburg, multiculturalism is the transcendent truth amid the commodification of everything under global capitalism. Misha derives his multiculturalism from his liberal arts alma mater "Accidental College," and Shteyngart's swipe at academia is the occasion for this chapter's discussion of how and why culture has become so venerated by some commentators and so discredited by others. Working toward a reconstructed *pragmatic* account of the efficacy of culture, I pause on Malcolm X's famous line "By any means necessary," which is ironically interpolated into *Absurdistan,* to consider what culture has meant and can come to mean again for Jewish American literature. Rethinking "culture" itself, I look backwards to a text with surprising parallels to *Absurdistan,* the memoir of the nineteenth-century Jewish homesteader Rachel Calof. Calof's Judaism is not "religion" exactly, and as culture it bears none of the contemporary anxiety about "memory" or "authenticity." Rather, Jewishness for Calof is simply a way of interfacing with the world. If that seems naive, I advance Calof's hint in a concluding epilogue, discussing the contemporary novelist and historian Harriet Rochlin, whose work on western Jewish history and interest in pluralism grew out of her experiences as a child in Boyle Heights, California, a mixed-race, politically progressive enclave of East Los Angeles. Rochlin's fiction evinces a pluralism in step with theorist William Connolly's thesis (from chapter 3), and Boyle Heights in particular suggests a model of pluralist recognition worth emulating in academia.

Rochlin is not a professional scholar, but I find her off-the-cuff views on pluralism as interesting and helpful as anything published by academics. Likewise, I find the writers under review here, in the end, more revealing than the theorists and critics I use to help read them. This is part of the genius of literature, its capacity for sustaining multiple, even contradictory points of view and epistemes, and its kaleidoscopic reward to readers willing to give texts a turn and look again and again. In addition, I credit literary writers' attention to the real world, in all its complexity and difficulty, with showing us what we already know to be true about ourselves and the many kinds of others in our world, and with pressing us through the force of creative urgency to recognize it.

Part I

Pluralism, Race, and Religion

1

Portnoy's Complaint

It's about Race, Not Sex
(Even the Sex Is about Race)

Early in Philip Roth's notorious novel *Portnoy's Complaint,* published in 1969, the adolescent Alexander Portnoy tells his parents that he will no longer attend synagogue on the High Holidays, for he is, he declares, not Jewish but a *human being: "Religion is the opiate of the people!* And if believing that makes me a fourteen-year-old Communist, then that's what I am, *and I'm proud of it!* ...I happen to believe in the rights of man, rights such as are extended in the Soviet Union to *all* people, regardless of race, religion, or color" (75).[1] Portnoy then strikes closer to home: "My communism, in fact, is why I now insist on eating with the [African American] cleaning lady when I come home for my lunch on Mondays and see that she is there" (75). On a roll, young Portnoy directs his rage toward his father Jack, a life insurance salesman whose clients include African American families in the Newark ghettos: "I tell you, if he ever uses the word nigger in my presence again, I will drive a dagger into his fucking bigoted heart! *Is that clear to everyone?* I don't care that his clothes stink so bad after he comes home from collecting the colored debit that they have to be hung in the cellar to air out. I don't care that they drive him nearly crazy letting their insurance lapse. That is only another reason to be compassionate" (74–75). Roth's satire of the Jewish family romance is transparent, but what is at stake in Portnoy's citation of the rights of man, communism, and the Soviet Union when he attacks his father? A conventional approach to the question would be to track the character's Oedipal rage: Portnoy overthrows his father by attacking his faith in America, including American racism. By aligning with the Soviet Union's promise of true liberation from race prejudice, Portnoy folds Cold War politics into his rebellion against his family's assimilationist agenda. However, this youthful utopian embrace of communism persists and matures beyond adolescent rebellion, becoming a politically trenchant position that is central to the plot; as an adult, Portnoy chooses a career as a civil rights attorney, eventually becoming "assistant commissioner" for the Mayor's Commission on Human Opportunity. It is well established that in *Portnoy's Complaint,* Roth was satirizing the midcentury Jewish family through the psychological templates of Oedipalism and sexual perversion. Here I propose to examine closely another point of satire, the Jewish American obsession not with sex but with race and rights.

By beginning not with the cooperation and conflict of black and Jewish civil rights activism of the 1950s but with the aftermath, including fear, skepticism, cynicism, and opportunism on both sides, this chapter initiates a significant theme for the book as a whole: Something went wrong. Between the conception of justice and its legal designation; between the success of Jewish ethnicity and its bowdlerization; between Jewish commitments to global human rights and the swap of "rights" for "intervention," Jewish American writers have found the grammar of race, the social implications of rights, and the narrative lacunae of recognition to be a rich seam for literary exploration. As Roth's novel makes clear, claims for rights and recognition necessarily pass through a politicized semantic field that has consequences for social policy, of course, but also for literature. In order to say something new about Jewishness, Americanness, and the Jewish American encounter with domestic and global multiculturalism, writers need to strip away, reimagine, or wholly reinvent the language of identity. Roth's novel is an appropriate starting point for examining this sort of literary intervention for its direct and often very funny and frequently very sad satirization of rights-talk.

Consider, for instance, Alexander Portnoy's phrase "collecting the colored debit," which is a reference to Jack Portnoy's door-to-door work in black neighborhoods, where he collects premium payments on life insurance policies. "The colored debit" is the amount of money owed, but the phrase suggests a debit, or debt, accrued by the fact of being black—the debt measuring their distance from a secure life in the racist America of the 1950s. Just who should pay this debt is a matter of dispute between Jack and Alexander Portnoy. Jack berates his clients for their supposed irresponsibility and lack of foresight. As an employee of Boston and Northeastern Life (insignia: the Mayflower), Portnoy's father is a model minority metonymically grabbing the wages of whiteness with one hand while, with the other, wagging a finger back at the "niggers" who "can think to leave children out in the rain without even a decent umbrella for protection" (10, 6). "Niggers" here refers to the failure to demonstrate the morally responsible behavior that Jack associates with the middle-class nuclear American family. At the same time, the intimacy of debt collection, including the fatiguing walk through the neighborhood and the door-to-door visits, results in Jack's figuratively collecting "blackness" in the sweat and stink of his clothes. Though Jack's hypocritically racist line suggests that blackness has rubbed off through contact, we recognize something more analogical at work. The underpaid, unappreciated labor, the physical hardship of the walk, and the impossibility of ever being promoted in his company—"my father...wasn't exactly suited to be the Jackie Robinson of the insurance business"—reveals the anxious proximity of working-class blacks and Jews in 1950s Newark (8). Jack uses the offending racial epithet as the distinguishing diacritic between black and white, anxiously occluding the contiguity of black and Jew, while Alexander affirms their common class position. Alexander Portnoy's tirade reverses the meaning of the phrase "the colored debit": the colored debit is precisely what the "colored" are owed. Portnoy assumes this debt by eating with the cleaning lady and scolding his father as a teenager and working for civil rights in New York as an adult.

The adult Portnoy holds the fictional equivalent of New York City's assistant attorney general for civil rights, and as I explain below, there is a clear line connecting the young Portnoy's commitment to international human rights with his later work in local civil rights issues. Portnoy's concern for rights is not just undermined by his obsessive sexual neuroses.

More than that, Roth has linked Portnoy's insistent sexual desire—what we might call "rights of desire," following the Marquis de Sade—with the normative framework of civil rights. That civil rights are tagged in this novel as "human opportunity" recalls the fact that U.S. civil rights laws correspond with the UN Treaty on Human Rights, while the UN framework is itself based on the Enlightenment-era document, *The Declaration of the Rights of Man and of the Citizen.* It was this 1791 French declaration that offered "tolerance" to Jews (among others), a foreign people in the midst of the republic, and Roth picks up on that tone—tolerance while holding one's nose—in Portnoy's defense of African Americans.[2] I mentioned Sade above because of the obvious resonance between Portnoy's exploration of desire and the same depicted in Sade's work, but Sade, too, is an interlocutor of the emergent discourse of "rights" in the French Republic. I develop this argument further, but for now I posit that as the Marquis de Sade's exploration of pleasure without limits is understood as a scandal to philosophy's promotion of "freedom" and "human rights," so, too, does Portnoy's pursuit of limitless pleasure engage with and scandalize the liberal civic virtue of "human opportunity."

Recall that the phrase "the colored debit" is linked to the broader issue of international human rights in Portnoy's rant and that human rights was the controversial filter through which many U.S. activists viewed the question of domestic civil rights. By declaring himself a communist in support of human rights, young Portnoy may tweak his father's patriotism, but Roth is doing more, as he is alluding to a significant controversy for American Jews. Jewish support for international human rights and domestic civil rights was a point of pride for many American Jews, and Jewish institutional support for rights was affirmed by both the American Jewish Committee and the American Jewish Congress in 1947. But there was a hitch. The rhetoric of "the rights of man" and of human rights was in use by communist sympathizers in the late 1940s and was taken up by leaders of the Soviet Union by the 1950s to critique American segregation. Indeed, young Portnoy declares himself a communist supporting human rights in 1947, the same year that the American Communist Party, the NAACP, and other black rights organizations petitioned the newly formed UN Human Rights Commission to investigate segregation and lynching in the U.S. South. Recognizing the legal merit in these petitions, Americans in the State Department and the Truman administration attempted to redirect the petitions themselves and then rewrote UN human rights treaties to appease southern states. The United States was at that time interested in leveraging the UN Human Rights Commission in its Cold War campaign against the Soviet Union, while the Soviets were eager to redirect the human rights lens on the Jim Crow South.[3]

Domestically, the war crimes trials at Nuremberg were routinely cited by human rights activists in the United States—including the NAACP, the American Communist Party, and the American Jewish Congress—as a fitting impetus for ending Jim Crow laws, at the behest of the United Nations if necessary. For the American Jewish Congress, assuming a leading role in the fight for civil rights in the United States meant spending some of the moral capital accrued from the Holocaust, another type of "colored debit." To do so without seeming sympathetic to communism, the American Jewish Congress specified its commitment to rights around particular issues of religious freedom and freedom from racial discrimination while aggressively celebrating American democratic ideals.[4] Arthur Goren phrases the dilemma this way: "Here was the snake in the garden: the agony and trepidation caused by the conspicuous presence of Jews among those accused of disloyalty and even espionage, and the presence of a marginal but vocal radical left within the organized Jewish community."[5] American Jewish organizations responded to McCarthyism and the persecution of left-wing Jews with a cautious, narrow, and liberal approach to human and civil rights.

Putting the topic of human rights at the center of Portnoy's tirade against his father is typical Roth mischief, poking at a sore spot on the border of Jewish public and private cultures. Though not as spectacular as the resurrected and sexually dynamic Anne Frank of Roth's *The Ghost Writer,* the subject of rights plucks at some similarly sensitive chords. Consider that the celebrated "black-Jewish alliance" breaks down—famously, not to mention painfully—over the very issues of communism, human rights, and support for American norms of democracy. Jewish American institutional support for human rights in the late 1940s would constrict to more firm and pro-American support for liberal democratic rights by the 1960s. I begin here with Portnoy's adolescent support for human rights to suggest that his interest in race and rights exists in tandem and in tension with a wider Jewish American current of thinking on rights and that through Portnoy, Roth satirizes the postwar Jewish commitment to liberalism. *Portnoy's*

Complaint is supremely a satire, and as such, it does not offer a positive or a normative model of rights—human, civil, or otherwise. Nor even does the novel model ethical relations between whites and blacks or blacks and Jews (or parents and children or men and women...). Instead, the novel's satiric representation of race, class, and gender relations amounts to a scathing critique of the biases and blind spots of postwar liberalism, especially among the ascendant third generation of Jews—a group unusually educated, politically active, staunchly liberal, and above all outspoken for civil rights in the 1950s and 1960s.

Writing that *Portnoy's Complaint* is "about race" is my attempt to call attention to the centrality of race to the novel.[6] Of course, sex is central also—central, that is, to the critique of race and rights. This chapter proceeds first by discussing the novel's depiction of race politics in New York during the 1950s and 1960s. I link *Portnoy's Complaint* to a perhaps unexpected parallel text, Eldridge Cleaver's *Soul on Ice,* also published in 1969 and also obsessed with sex, shame, and race.[7] Rather than treat sex and race as separate topics, I bring them together with the analytic of "rights." What is more, although I take *Portnoy's Complaint* to be a first-rate satire, I also argue that there is a deep and difficult critique of the idea of "rights" at work in the novel, but it is one that can only be accessed by analyzing how race affects the sex in the novel.

It's about Race

Published in 1969, *Portnoy's Complaint* was Roth's most polarizing novel to that point, satirizing what he has called the "folklore" of the Jewish American family—including the overbearing mother, the long-suffering father, and the pathologically good son—and hyperbolizing the Freudian war of id and superego in the character of Alexander Portnoy, the masturbation-addicted adolescent who grows up to be a highly respected civil rights attorney and who also happens to be a misogynistic sex addict.[8] Portnoy's mother is obsessed with purity and cleanliness, while Portnoy is committed to defilement, a dialectic internalized and performed in Portnoy's adult social and professional life as well. Portnoy pinpoints the origin of his sexual and social transgression in his mother, whose own Jewish body Portnoy both fears and longs to protect. But even here, between the mother and the son is the specter of race. The "primal scene" of the novel comes as a moment of discovery not of gender but of color, when Portnoy spies Sophie, his mother, washing utensils previously used by their black maid:

> Once Dorothy chanced to come back into the kitchen while my mother was still standing over the faucet marked H, sending torrents down upon the knife and fork that had passed between the *schvartze*'s thick pink lips. "Oh, you know how hard it is to get mayonnaise off silverware these days, Dorothy," says my nimble-minded mother—and thus, she tells me later, by her quick thinking has managed to spare the colored woman's feelings. (13)

As with Portnoy, Dorothy's "defilement" is policed and sanitized by his mother, and in retrospect her cause becomes his moral crusade to protect minorities from discrimination. At the same time, Portnoy does not relinquish the abjecting stereotype of Dorothy's racial otherness. This dynamic of internalization of and resistance to the mother's shame structures Portnoy's subsequent anxieties and excesses, which are likewise always marked by race.

Portnoy calls attention to the knife Sophie washes as the source of his castration complex—the hyberbolized maternal prohibition against masturbation—and it is precisely the knife's potential as an instrument of castration that establishes Judaism as a belated racial category for Portnoy.[9] Circumcision is the peculiar mark of Jewish racialization, the retroactive racialization of the Jewish male body that thereby folds the male child into the clan.[10] Circumcision thus supplements matrilineal genetic descent with cultural descent, with the mother ambiguously poised between race and culture. Portnoy's obsession with his mother—desire and repulsion—is analogous to his obsession with racial Jewishness—affirmation and rejection. At this point, a discussion of *Portnoy's Complaint* would typically proceed by analyzing the dynamics of generational conflict—how the second generation, which understood itself as more or less a "race," certainly a "tribe," clashes with the third generation, which has not only freed itself from the binding logic of race but has also so mastered its politics as to participate fluidly in race discourse.[11] This teleological and diachronic analysis is true enough, but it remains insulated from the lateral, contemporaneous social phenomena amid which it occurs. So instead of asking the question, "How did one Jewish generation react to the prior generation's self-identification as a race?" I pose this question: How is the political tension of racial politics in the late 1960s folded into *Portnoy's Complaint*? What sort of conversation about race does *Portnoy's Complaint* allow, not between the generations but within Roth's own generation? And how can we read Roth as responding to his present and not just the past?

Philip Roth did considerable research for his writing. His research dossier for *Portnoy's Complaint,* archived at the Library of Congress, contains, among other items, files on the New York City Commission on Human Rights (NYCCHR, or CCHR).[12] The NYCCHR, established in 1949 and charged with the oversight and enforcement of antidiscrimination policies in education and housing, was by the late 1960s beset by many of the tensions it sought to ameliorate: racial politicking, institutional racism, mistrust from black and white alike. During the 1960s, Jewish and African American political organizations consulted and collaborated with the CCHR. However, this coalition of interests was challenged in 1966 with the nomination of the first African American, William Booth, to the position of commission chairman. Booth was concerned with what he perceived to be a dearth of interest in black issues, and he increased the number of blacks on the commission and prioritized issues primarily affecting middle- and working-class blacks and Puerto Ricans. The focus on middle- and working-class social issues drew attention to the fact that in the late 1960s Jews played such a prominent role as figures of authority in black urban life, as schoolteachers and principals, building owners, and shopkeepers.[13] For their part, Jews resigned from the CCHR under Booth's leadership, perceiving that "Booth [was] using the agency for his own personal advancement" and that "the commission [had] become a black agency...[that] defined its constituency as the black militants."[14]

Roth acquired copies of several of the CCHR's official documents, including the commission's pamphlet "Law on Human Rights," which listed the commission's range of interests and policies, and a group of public relations pamphlets and reports.[15] His highlights and marginal comments on these documents—and their verbatim citation in the novel—illustrate his awareness of how the ideal of human rights is corrupted in its political implementation. For example, Roth's highlights of the pamphlet titled "50/50 Chance for All New Yorkers" singles out paternalistic and grandiose passages about "role models" and "problem-solving," and he gleaned information to highlight Portnoy's own hubris—his pride in being a minor

TV celebrity, for example, is sourced in the pamphlet's notice of a regular Tuesday evening prime-time broadcast called "Human Rights Forum." In both instances, black and Puerto Rican New Yorkers are cast as the helpless and passive recipients of white and Jewish intervention, while the masters of rights gain glory and status. Roth also underscored several passages on the African American experience with discrimination in labor, housing, education, and health care. One of his highlights from the CCHR's 1967 "Human Rights Report" communicates with epigrammatic force for the asymmetrical identification between blacks and Jews: "New York City is known throughout the world as an important center of banking and merchandising, yet employment opportunities in these industries traditionally have been negligible for Negro and Puerto Rican New Yorkers, *and in the executive level jobs for Jewish workers as well.*"[16] That same year, Martin Luther King would declare that "most whites in America...proceed from a premise that equality is a loose expression for improvement. White America is not even psychologically organized to close the gap—essentially it seeks only to retain it."[17] And to the extent that Roth establishes Portnoy's trajectory as paradigmatic of third-generation Jewish mobility and the transformation of one generation's commitment to the domestic family into the following generation's commitment to the American family, *Portnoy's Complaint* raises the question of whether or not Jewish liberals were likewise "psychologically organized" to see the gap in professed equality for African Americans and the breakthroughs in equality that had been made for their generation.

Even though by the time *Portnoy's Complaint* was published in 1969, the famous black-Jewish alliance was all but shattered, many Jews and non-Jews still considered it axiomatic that blacks had historically found Jews sympathetic, tolerant, brothers in common cause. In 1969, in his popular explanation of Jewish attitudes, *The Jewish Mystique,* Ernest van den Haag claimed that "Jews identify with the oppressed and deprived Negro treated by his white environment in a way all too familiar to them—a way which cannot but recall the memory of their own oppression, deprivation, and ghettoization. Now that they are successful, Jews feel they have an obligation to help those who suffer, as they did, from discrimination."[18] In fact, both the NAACP and the National Urban League counted a disproportionate number of Jews among their white supporters, and Jews were prominent as leaders of labor organizations premised on the equality of all workers regardless of race or ethnicity. However, historian Cheryl Green-berg concludes that this is a recent and not a longstanding identification. At the end of the nineteenth century, "few Jews or African Americans drew substantive connections between the experiences of their two peoples," and at the beginning of the twentieth century, "simultaneous cooperation and conflict characterized black-Jewish interaction, an unstable combination that remained at the heart of their relationship for the entire century to come."[19] Similarly, Nathan Glazer, in a 1964 essay in *Commentary* on the souring of the black-Jewish alliance, was quick to remind his readers that reports on the demise of that alliance stretch back to before the 1940s, though the tone of Jewish writing on the breakup is always one of histori-cal betrayal. However, by 1969 the tension between blacks and Jews was, Glazer explained, precisely the result of Jews' success at becoming white: "The 'white liberal' who is attacked as a false friend unwilling to support demands which affect him or his, and as probably prejudiced to boot, is generally (even if this is not spelled out) the white *Jewish* liberal—and it could hardly be otherwise, in view of the predominance of Jews among liberals, particularly in major cities like New York, Chicago, Philadelphia, and Los Angeles."[20]

As an example of the implication of the social upheaval in the novel's contemporaneous generational conflict, consider a letter Roth received shortly after the publication of *Portnoy's Complaint*. Lillian Cohen, a den-tist's wife from Syracuse, New York, wrote to urge Roth to "extend your-self further than 'what's in it for you' and help with a message to the young people who read you and yearn for guidance and direction."[21] Cohen wanted Roth to consider how Jewish families might break the chain of sexual neuroses handed down from parents to children. As inspiration for Roth, Cohen quoted Eldridge Cleaver's famous appeal: "the price of hat-ing other human beings is loving yourself less" [*sic*].[22]

Cleaver is not an obvious choice for propagating moral guidance to youth. After all, the Eldridge Cleaver of 1969 was an American radical, a black nationalist who had been implicated in violent antigovernment incidents. Released from prison in 1966, where he had been serving time for rape, he helped form the Black Panther Party shortly thereafter. He ran for president in 1968 on the Peace and Freedom ticket but fled to Algeria after a shootout between Black Panthers and the FBI. The Black Pan-ther Party and Cleaver in particular were not entirely positive figures for even the most progressive of American Jews due to their militancy and a recurring streak of anti-Semitism. In Algeria, Cleaver, who had previously pointed to Zionism as a model for black nationalism, attended a Fatah rally and openly promoted the PLO as an ally. Indeed, in an arrangement between Cleaver and Yasser Arafat, American Black Nationalists were invited to train at PLO camps.

Meanwhile, also in the late 1960s, many white ethnics were disavowing the pejoratives associated with whiteness. Taking cues from other ethnic nationalist movements, they championed a "new ethnicity," reviving Irish, Slavic, German, and Italian identities in American social life. For their part, the radical Jewish militants who formed the Jewish Defense League cited none other than Eldridge Cleaver as an influence in the formation of their nationalist movement, a point of interest that brings us back to Cohen's letter to Roth.[23] Cohen's citation of *Soul on Ice* may have suggested to Roth that, like Cleaver, he too was a "race man" working for the progress and liberation of his people from generations of mental colonization and cultural enslavement. At the same time, Cohen hinted at the underlying humanism and universality at work in Roth's satire. (Indeed, in another letter following the publication of *Portnoy's Complaint,* one fan called Roth "the Harriet Beecher Stowe of the Jewish people").[24] Cleaver would rally for nationalism, urging black Americans to take their fight for freedom to the streets of urban America. Roth, however, was after something at once less and more ambitious. His Jewish protagonist is neither a nationalist nor an assimilationist, but his cynical denunciation of society in the novel's conclusion suggests an equally radical revolutionary consciousness. Portnoy's final offense, "Up society's ass, copper!" may be read as lashing out against all the policing strategies of society, including the controlling categories designating race and class that would situate people as insiders and outsiders, winners and losers in a contest of capital accumulation (274). That the denunciation is couched in terms of mock-aggressive and homophobic sexual violation does not undermine the sentiment so much as speak to the impossibility of finding a discursive space outside social designations.

Even the Sex Is about Race

Alexander Portnoy's obsession with "shikses"—non-Jewish women who physically embody alien whiteness—places most of the protagonist's action in a virtually segregated white world: the ice-skating rink, college

campuses, and midwestern middle-class homes. Whiteness is ubiquitous to the point of invisibility but for the fact that it is the object of Portnoy's obsession. He explains, "Through fucking I will discover America.
Conquer America—maybe that's more like it. Columbus, Captain Smith,
Governor Winthrop, General Washington—now Portnoy. As though my
manifest destiny is to seduce a girl from each of the forty-eight states. As
for Alaskan and Hawaiian women, I really have no feelings either way, no
scores to settle, no coupons to cash in, no dreams to put to rest—who are
they to me, a bunch of Eskimos and Orientals" (235). Portnoy's casual dismissal of postcolonial Americans is explained by the overall logic of the
passage. In the first instance, nothing is gained—no "coupons to cash in"—
for Portnoy with "Orientals" because, as he explains elsewhere, "to them
we are not Jews, but *white* ... just some big-nosed variety of WASP!" (90).
Black women are hardly a part of Portnoy's "American dreams": no coupons to cash suggests how racial mobility is tied to class mobility, while
blackness, seemingly immutable and socially immobile in the early 1960s,
is more an object for appropriation than the subject of transformation.
Black and Puerto Rican women are certainly not absent from the novel,
nor do they escape Portnoy's objectification. As with white women, blacks
and Puerto Ricans are signs for "race," though as objects of his liberation
rather than of his conquest. If this seems an incoherent pairing of "conquest" and "liberation"—where the processes of both terms seem naturally
at odds—the effect is obviously to undermine the integrity of each, indeed
to show how "liberation" is, in fact, the rhetorical rationale of conquest.

Portnoy's behavior stands out as an interesting illustration of Cleaver's
aphorism that "the price of hating others is loving oneself less." Portnoy is
not so much "hating" others as using them for his own social gain, though
he does garner shame and self-loathing for his efforts. To complicate matters further, Cleaver's line comes at the end of the first chapter of his memoir, *Soul on Ice,* where he explains how he ended up in prison for raping
white women (36). His desire for white women, monstrously rapacious in
twentieth century stereotypes, was indeed a monster, installed, he believes,
by white supremacy itself, and he describes the thrall he felt for white
women as "the Ogre" and its conquest, "*my Moby Dick*" (24, 32). Reversing
the myth of sexual predation, Cleaver sees himself justified as a potential
victim rather than perpetrator. Interracial *desire* and not its suppression
is the monster for Cleaver, and he set out to kill it off. His rejection of

white colonization amounts to a rejection of his own desire, a destructive masochism that takes as its symbol white women. Rape, which Cleaver calls an "insurrectionary act," is his attempt at mastering the Ogre, but it transforms *him* into the monster, as he attacks not white *supremacy* but white *women* (33).

Cleaver's metaphor of the Ogre signifies the process of racialization: through the thrall of white woman he experiences blackness as feminine passivity and vulnerability to violation (these are Cleaver's terms). Active sexual domination—rape—structurally reclaims masculinity. Moreover, for Cleaver blackness is rescued from white supremacy by a performance of domination, thus re-instantiating blackness as aggressive hypersexuality. That is, gendered sexuality—active or passive sex—allegorizes race. Cleaver defines whiteness as control of the sexual economy, and blackness is precisely the sexuality in need of control. Redefining blackness, therefore, can only occur as a claim upon whiteness.

This peculiar mix of desire and shame appearing in Cleaver's metaphysics of sexuality reads very startlingly like the diagnosis of "Portnoy's Complaint"—the medical condition named after Portnoy by his psychoanalyst Spielvogel: "A disorder in which strongly-felt ethical and altruistic impulses are perpetually warring with extreme sexual longings, often of a perverse nature...neither fantasy nor act issues in genuine sexual gratification, but rather in overriding feelings of shame and the dread of retribution."[25] The simultaneous attraction and repulsion across racial lines follows what Kathryn Stockton calls the "pretzel logic" of miscegenated desire, but it can only trip up our analysis if we believe race is indelibly fixed on the body.[26] Cleaver may have believed this to be so. Roth's protagonist, however, sees race as a site of play and a kind of game. More liberated from biological constraints than Cleaver, Portnoy views race as strictly sociological: he is disgusted with anyone who accepts his or her racial assignment uncritically. Still, in *Portnoy's Complaint,* the idea of racial difference does not wither under Portnoy's scorn. Rather, the social facts of race provide the necessary hurdles over which Portnoy may pass and thus chart his gaining ground on America. The problem he finds in crossing these barriers, however, is that his skin is always whiter on the other side. Visiting the home of his farm-raised midwestern college girlfriend, for example, Portnoy senses a home redolent of Christianity ("There! Is *that* it, is that Christianity I smell, or just the dog?"), and he fears even to sit on their toilet seat, lest he contract something spiritually infectious (225). Among Jews, Portnoy feels predictably on the margins, but upon "conquering" non-Jewish white women he finds himself in the alien corn of WASP America.

As in *Soul on Ice,* in *Portnoy's Complaint* sexuality presumes and also produces racial subjects. In both, desire and taboo are racially coded insofar as object choices are not only gendered but also raced bodies. Roth's novel is comedic, but it relies structurally on the same symbolic economy of race and sexuality as Cleaver's justification for his crime. Like Cleaver, Portnoy longs for white women and becomes aware of his own racial distinctness through contiguity. Also as with Cleaver, Portnoy's desire is masochistic, bringing him moral "pain." And finally, again like Cleaver, Portnoy turns that masochism outward, deflecting it or displacing it onto the women he ravishes.

A paraphrase of Freud's theory of "moral masochism" is conspicuously evident throughout the novel. Locating masochism as the unconscious of sadism, Freud explains,

> Conscience and morality have arisen through the overcoming, the desexualization, of the Oedipus complex; but through moral masochism morality becomes sexualized once more, the Oedipus complex is revived and the way is opened for a regression from morality to the Oedipus complex.... Masochism creates a temptation to perform "sinful" actions, which must then be expiated by the reproaches of the sadistic conscience.[27]

It is worth noting that *Portnoy's Complaint* is narrated from a psychoanalyst's couch, with the protagonist frequently citing Freud to the silent analyst as he rants about his parents' controlling behavior yet acknowledges the pleasure he finds in that control. The psychosexual dynamic is thus not the "hidden message," nor even the latent structure for the reader to discover. Rather, psychosexual processes are the internal allegory of the novel's themes of social identity. The "desire" punished is Portnoy's racial transgression, a fact that makes him a spectacular but not original member of his generation of American Jews.

Between 1950 and 1970—just before the social solidification of multicultural identities—young Jews experienced tremendous social mobility, including the freedom to step out of Jewish history. The sorrows of Jewish assimilation were contemporaneously chronicled in lugubrious articles in *Commentary* and the *Jewish National Yearbook* as well as in fiction by such writers as Cynthia Ozick and Saul Bellow.[28] *Commentary* was especially prolific in its paternalistic (and gloomy) forecast of the end of Jewish culture in America at the hands of this new generation (Irving Howe's famous statement that Roth had a "thin personal culture" captures the general tone), while Bellow's protagonist Artur Sammler "doubted the fitness of these Jews for this erotic Roman voodoo primitivism" (*Mr. Sammler's Planet* 59). Roth's Portnoy may have crossed barriers and ventured into social terrain previously unavailable to American Jews, both in his career and in his sex life. However, Portnoy lacks the revolutionary vision of Cleaver, as he courts rather than disables paternal disfavor.

Portnoy's erotics of social transgression are evident in a chapter recounting his first night with his girlfriend, Mary Jane, a West Virginia coal miner's daughter who is willing both to dominate and submit. Her willingness is precisely Portnoy's fantasy, and he projects a commensurate fantasy that she must be having of him. At the moment that he is literally prostrate, sexually servicing her, he imagines that she is dreaming of "the gentle fire burning, the book-lined living room of our country home, the Irish nanny bathing the children...[and] her husband whom People Are Talking About, The Saintliest Commissioner of the City of New York...seen here with his pipe and his thinning kinky black Hebe hair, in all his Jewish messianic fervor and charm" (163). Her fantasy (at least as he imagines it) of class rescue is the basis of Portnoy's thrill of sexual slumming.

However, the persistent racial metonym—"Hebe hair"—dislodges Portnoy's racial position at the very moment at which he would install himself securely in Mary's class fantasy. The racial instability amplifies into anxiety and then paranoia: "Suddenly I *knew*—some big spade was going to leap out of the closet and spring for my heart with his knife....Was she a call girl? A maniac? Was she in cahoots with some Puerto Rican pusher who was about to make his entrance into my life? Enter it—and end it, for the forty dollars in my wallet...?" (160). And then the fear repeats: "Here he comes, I thought, my *shvartze,* out of the closet,—eyes, teeth and razor blade flashing!" (161). The episode presents a telling triptych of the location of race in Portnoy's moral masochism. Like that of the moral masochist, his erotic fulfillment is undercut by fear and shame, the knife-wielding antagonist being entirely a negative fantasy projected by Portnoy onto the scene. What is more, the repetition of the fear three times describes Portnoy's shame in increasingly narrow terms. The first reference to the black man as a "spade," a term that appears nowhere else in the novel, reads as a cultural borrowing of a widespread racial epithet. Fear of the "spade" in collusion with this white woman suggests the generalized fear by white men over the loss of their singular social power—white supremacy—amid the tectonic shifts in social roles in the 1960s. The second repetition specifies the fear of the Puerto Rican, locating the menace closer to Portnoy's personal experience as human opportunity commissioner. The final epithet, fear of the *"shvartze,"* cites the Yiddish pejorative for black men and locates Portnoy as little more than another Jewish victim, suffering simultaneously from wily women and black marauders. The return to Jewishness in this moment underscores the fear, planted in him as a child, that his ascension to white power as a civil rights attorney will be undercut precisely through an intimacy with the black and Puerto Rican citizens he is supposed to represent.

As a complication of Cleaver's already complex binaries of race and sexuality, Portnoy associates blackness with physical and moral threat, whiteness with access and privilege, and Jewishness with passivity and victimization. In this particular fantasy, the endpoint of this collusion of blackness and female agency is an off-white Jewishness that is sexually violable. David Savran explains how masochism, so central to twentieth-century American masculinity, allows the white male to shift gender and racial roles in order to fulfill the fantasy of the victim: "[The] slippage between sexual and racial differences is one reason why masochistic fantasy has such enormous psychic power.…It allows the white male subject to take up the position of victim, to feminize and/or blacken himself fantasmatically."[29] White men, in particular, learn a vocabulary of "injury," explains Jennifer Travis, "through which to articulate and claim a range of emotional wounds."[30] Roth's character does not assume blackness or femininity per se but expresses his injury as sexual victimization and passivity—the socially structured corollaries of racial symbolism. Consequently, Jewishness functions as both white and off-white, as it enables access and agency in the material world and retreat and abashedness in the psychic. The phenomenon that Savran reads as "fantasmatic slippage" in sexual and racial identities is satirized by Roth as ludicrous posturing. But make no mistake, this posturing, diagnosed as a "complaint," is not a malady impeding erotics so much as eroticism itself. How else to explain the very length of the complaint, a single psychoanalytic session enduring over more than 250 pages, but for the erotic pleasure it brings the complainer, Portnoy? This is not so much the "erotics of talk," described by Carla Kaplan as the narrative courting of the ideal feminist reader, as it is the erotics of re-signification, the controlling thrill of renaming social designations of race—black, white, and Jewish—against the reader's expectations.[31]

Portnoy's sexual episodes can be understood not as erotic in themselves but as occasions of and for re-signification. The novel's offense or humor (depending on the reader) is the result of the preposterous reversal of racial positions. This is evident in Portnoy's relationship with Sally Maulsby, the daughter of an aristocratic Connecticut family and, for Portnoy, precisely the embodiment of gentile privilege and beauty against which he measures his own Jewish outsider status. Portnoy becomes particularly offended when Sally, who is otherwise sexually willing, is reluctant to perform oral sex on him. He imagines that it is her Protestant aversion to his Jewishness that inhibits her, and he links her resistance to his father's failure to gain promotion after decades as a life insurance salesman for a Boston-based company—both examples for Portnoy of the East Coast Brahmin aversion to Jews. Portnoy's attempt to coerce Sally to perform oral sex is consequently tinged with aggression and vengeance. After her first effort, she panics and tells him, "I'll suffocate," to which Portnoy replies:

"Not if you breathe you won't."
"I can't with that in my mouth."
"Through your nose. Pretend you're swimming."
"But I'm *not*."
"PRETEND!"

When she surfaces seconds later in tears, Portnoy tells her for the first time, "I love you," while internally realizing that "there could never be any 'love' in me for The Pilgrim. Intolerant of her frailties. Jealous of her accomplishments. Resentful of her family.... No, Sally Maulsby was just something nice a son once did for his dad.... A little bonus extracted...for all those years of service and exploitation" (240–41). Portnoy's admission that his satisfaction is in Sally's humiliation recalls Cleaver's "insurrectionary" rapes of white women; for both writers, white women are, like Moby Dick, objects of longing, loathing, and vengeance.

The erotic satisfaction for Portnoy results from his ability to manipulate not just women but also the very narratives that would seem to control and structure his relationship with them. Wildly importing his father's story into the story he tells about Sally would seem to smack of paranoia but for the fact that it gives Portnoy the fantasist's chance to change the ending. It is as if Freud, famously smarting all his life because of his childhood perception of his father's subaltern status, finally got the chance to knock the hegemon on his keister.[32] This strategy rivals Cleaver's for its strange offensiveness, but Roth sustains the satire through comic absurdity, including a chiasmatic allusion to Shakespeare's *Othello*. As Sally casually tells Portnoy about her debutante facility, from dressage to table etiquette, he thinks, "What skills she had learned in far-off Connecticut! Activities that partook of the exotic and even the taboo she performed so simply as a matter of course: and I was as wowed...as Desdemona, hearing of the Anthropapagi [*sic*]" (237). The analogy at once highlights the relationship as interracial while re-signifying the racial status of each. Portnoy equates the Connecticut-born Sally with the Semitic Moor Othello, installing himself in the analogy as the swooning, doomed Desdemona. Othello's story of the man-eaters, transposed onto Sally, recalls Cleaver's association of white women with the man-eating Ogre. In each instance, the one who is actually sexually aggressive—Portnoy and Cleaver—refigures himself as passive, seduced, or preyed upon. With Portnoy, the reversals are yet more shocking, for white Sally becomes not only black but also a Semite, like Othello, while the Semitic Portnoy becomes the fair and natural-born Christian. Portnoy initially diagnoses his relationship with Sally in historical terms, linking up with prior generations' experience with anti-Semitism, while the subsequent racial re-signification highlights his status as a foreordained victim.

Kant with Sade, Roth with Cleaver

We return now to Portnoy's employment title, assistant commissioner for the City of New York Commission on Human Opportunity (107). As noted above, Roth used the real-life title of the commission—New York City Commission on Human Rights—in all drafts of the novel until the final copy.[33] His switch of *Rights* to *Opportunity* stands out amid the mass of names, titles, and events associated with the actual commission that he did not change. What could this mean? Perhaps the shift from *Rights* to *Opportunity* gets us closer to, rather than further from, the heart of liberal human rights thinking, for the way it emphasizes individual agency and choice. Opportunity returns to the more Lockean foundation of rights, rooted in property, where freedom means the opportunity to buy and sell one's own labor. Opportunity, following this logic, is the right to buy and sell things unimpeded, the right to self-improvement and self-cultivation, and the freedom from constricting social designations that would limit opportunity—caste or class barriers. Opportunity contrasts *rights* in the sense that rights, though presumed to be inherent for all at the individual level, require structural change in a social system for their guarantee, along with the threat of possible intervention by some superseding authority. Rights claims always reveal a paradox: though rights are putatively located in a person's a priori status as a human or a citizen, making a claim for rights or claiming that one's rights have been violated indicates how rights are in possession of the state, which in turn "gives" rights through legislative intervention and oversight.

In Roth's novel, opportunity is spoken of with a huckster's tone, suggesting the opportunism of Portnoy himself, as his civil rights work primarily secures *his* opportunity to be a white liberal rather than a Jewish victim. This is clear when he takes Mary Jane to "equal opportunity night" in the Bronx, a town hall–style meeting where black and Puerto Rican denizens speak out to Portnoy about the debased conditions of their tenements. However, Mary Jane sees Portnoy's opportunism at work:

> "All those poor Puerto Rican people being overcharged in the supermarket! In Spanish you spoke, and oh I was so impressed! Tell me about your bad sanitation, tell me about your rats and vermin, tell me about your police protection! Because discrimination is against the law! A year in prison or a five-hundred-dollar fine! And that poor Puerto Rican man stood up and shouted, 'Both!'...Big shit to a bunch of stupid spics....Human opportunities! *Human!* How you love that word! But do you know what it means, you son of a bitch pimp!" (142)

These citizens comprise a tableau with which Portnoy can establish his own humanity as a compassionate, tolerant pluralist. Having written the law, he gives the citizens their voice, a gift he values more than any actual remedy for discrimination. The event itself, "equal opportunity night," suggests that opportunity is not inherent but is doled out by those who write the laws. Opportunity becomes contingent on time and space (a "night," a given room) and is hierarchically designated. Indeed, "equal opportunity night" resonates rather remarkably with the modern neologism "free speech zones"; in either case, the "opportunity" for voicing complaints is constrained. In the case of *Portnoy's Complaint,* it is the careerist lawyer who parlays discrimination into his own prestige and would-be moral *Bildung.* Not exactly Othello's "Anthropophagi," the Bronx residents tell their own story, but it is framed through the human rights lens and usurped for Portnoy's glory.

If the history of "rights" seems to reach its nadir in Alexander Portnoy's appointment to the commission, we still have not fully contemplated the implications of the conflation of opportunism and rights at work in his sexual and social transgressions. Portnoy is, after all, chiefly the advocate for sexual opportunity, and his quest for "rights of desire" may be read as the underside to his role as a human rights advocate. Rights, in their most basic formulation, are the rights to pleasure: "life, liberty, and the pursuit of happiness" is such a memorable phrase that we may fail to take stock of the verb *pursuit*—the active seeking of happiness, which surely authorizes the emergence of private desire into the public domain. This is also at work in the French *Declaration of the Rights of Man and of the Citizen,* which declares, "Liberty consists in the ability to do whatever does not harm another; hence the exercise of the natural rights of each man has *no other limits* than those which assure to the other members of the society the enjoyment of the same rights."[34] The challenge inherent in such a formulation is that "freedom to do everything" may quite easily run into the injunction against injury. The advocacy of "no limit" is immediately qualified: my limitlessness may not impose upon your limitlessness. We notice that "no limits" is sustained, but the obvious paradox of rights—that if I follow through on all my desires, I will likely impose on your freedom in some way (the freedom not to be bothered by me)—is inevitable and duly noted. I should pause here to remark that though a discussion of the 1789 *Declaration of the Rights of Man and of the Citizen* may seem to be quite a detour from the topic at hand, it was this declaration that eventually led to the emancipation of Jews in France, yielding their status, for the first time in European history, as citizens of the nation of the first order, but at a cost: "the obliteration of Jewish culture, after the obliteration—which is a euphemism—of the Jew within the citizen."[35] Jewishness was the corrupt, vestigial expression of a people suffering centuries of oppression, according to eighteenth-century French apologists. Liberating the Jew meant precisely liberating him from Jewishness. Without forcing an analogy, we should nonetheless note the resonance between the promise of emancipation through deracination for the Jew in France and the mid-twentieth-century American attempts to free African Americans from their "slave mentality." Norman Podhoretz's infamous declaration that African American culture is nothing but a stigma may be particularly ugly, but it was somewhat typical of the liberal project of rights for blacks in the 1950s and 1960s.[36] Indeed, the black-Jewish alliance may be said to have split precisely over the question of individual rights—"you are free to be individuals"—versus collective cultural recognition—"we are free to be black"—which brings us back to the question of opportunity. The promise of opportunity and liberal rights meant in some quarters the obliteration of the Negro within the citizen, or cultural genocide.

Arguing that *Portnoy's Complaint* is "about race," I have demonstrated that the novel is deeply interested in racialized Jewishness and that Jewishness is a social and psychological condition fraught with sexual anxiety. By placing his Jewish characters in close proximity to blacks and Puerto Ricans, Roth reveals the anxiety of Jewish racial instability. The hierarchical ordering of race—whites on top, blacks on bottom, Jews in between—draws from Roth's keen powers of observation but also his dossier on the NYCCHR. At the same time, Roth transparently satirizes the opportunism and expediency of liberalism for white ethnics by assuming a private ethnicity and a public corporate citizenry. Though there are no three-dimensional black or Puerto Rican characters in this novel, their marginalization—despite their putative centrality to Portnoy's professional life—exposes how little liberal tolerance has to offer.

But in arguing that even the sex is about race, I want to go one step further, to suggest how Roth's representation of the expedient politics of rights, imbricated with Portnoy's outlandish sexuality, teaches us about the very nature of freedom. Though I do not mean to suggest that *Portnoy's Complaint* is a philosophical novel, or even, à la Sade, "philosophy in the bedroom," Roth's representation of Portnoy's "rights of desire" necessarily shades his representation of civil rights. The eruption of Port-noy's ostensibly private desire into public—his public masturbation, for example—appears to be perversion, but we should note that private desire has a public outlet all the time. Every person, every citizen, knows that the desire of the other can be policed when it encroaches on our own desire at any time. This is what Jacques Lacan means when he states that the rights of man "are reducible to the freedom to desire in vain"; insofar as desire (limitlessness) is policed by the prohibition of injury to the other's desire (self-limitation), desire and failure are mutually constitutive.[37]

What would prompt such a lugubrious conclusion from Lacan, and how might rights of desire or civil rights "be in vain" in Roth's novel? Lacan explores the link between sexual liberty and human rights in his influential essay "Kant avec Sade" (Kant with Sade).[38] The essay places the two contemporaneous writers, Immanuel Kant and the Marquis de Sade, in the context of emergent rationalist explorations of the meaning of "rights" and the limits of freedom following the *Declaration of the Rights of Man and of the Citizen.* Kant's contribution to a philosophy of rights is well known. His philosophy of reason established the reasoning human as the universal basis for human freedom. He limned freedom with his in-novative categorical imperative, stating that the good is truly good when a reasoning person recognizes its universal applicability as *good for all.* The Marquis de Sade, the famous libertine author of *Justine* and *Philosophy in the Bedroom,* plumbed the limits of the good in his exploration of a pleasure beyond contemporaneous religious and social moralism.[39] In Sade, plea-sure is attained and extended through the exploitation of another and with the explicit understanding of the submission of the self to the pleasure of the other—a universalization of the rights to pleasure. Lacan reads Sade and Kant alongside each other to arrive at a paradox at the heart of lib-eral conceptions of human freedom. The imperative to do right, derived from Kant, is conjoined with a necessary absolute freedom—itself a good, pursued in the twentieth and twenty-first centuries under the banner of "human rights." Lacan insightfully interprets Sade, especially *Philosophy in the Bedroom,* as similarly motivated by an ethics of freedom, the impera-tive to pursue the "rights of enjoyment": "I have the right of enjoyment over [*le droit de jouir de*] your body, anyone can say to me, and I will exer-cise this right, without any limit stopping me in the capriciousness of the exactations that I might have the taste to satiate."[40] Lacan's paraphrase of

Sade here posits the subject—"anyone can say to *me*"—as parenthetical and passive, available for, even responsible for, the other's pleasure. This is a radical freedom indeed: everyone is free to take pleasure in me. For Lacan it points out the Catch-22 of liberalism: "It is because no man can be the property of another man, nor in any way be his privilege, that he cannot make this the pretext to suspend the right of all enjoyment over him [*droit de tous à jour de lui*], each according to his taste. The constraint he would undergo would not be so much one of violence as one of principle."[41] That is, precisely because I cannot compel another to abdicate his freedom, I cannot deny him his right of enjoyment over me. This is where politics comes in to police desire. Freedom from the other's freedom is not a right inherent in my humanity, endowed in me by the creator. Rather, it is a political construct that easily becomes exploitative where social hierarchies occur: "I, or my group must be free from the presence of you or your group." In Roth's novel, renaming rights as opportunity suggests at once that opportunity is potentially exploitative and that opportunity—unlike rights, premised on universal reason—is competitive.

Returning to Roth's novel, the Sadean scenarios are hard to miss. Portnoy is constantly searching for opportunities to fulfill his desire, and he often coerces the women he sleeps with—indeed, it is only when the coercion or submission is absent that Portnoy becomes bored in his relationships. Portnoy's coercion of oral sex from Sally Maulsby is one of several instances in which he attempts to exercise his own rights of desire over and against the self-determining choices of his sex partners. But it is also notable that at least as often, Portnoy desires to be in the position of submission, to give oral pleasure. Indeed, giving and receiving oral sex are his chief pleasures, while iterations of copulation are the least fulfilling. We recall Lacan's insistence that "there is no such thing as a sexual relationship" in the comedic description of Portnoy's much anticipated three-way session with an Italian prostitute and Mary Jane: "Boy was I busy! I mean, there was just so much to do" (137).[42] It's either my pleasure, or the other's pleasure, but one has to be renounced for the other.

We find ourselves with an inverted paraphrase of Cleaver's solipsistic aphorism. If the price of hating others is loving yourself less, the price of loving yourself fully seems to be paid by the other. Cleaver's solution to this dilemma is to eliminate same-other distinctions and thereby eclipse the self. After establishing the biological dichotomy between black and white (body versus mind), Cleaver theorizes a black sexual essence in the final chapter of *Soul on Ice*, "To All Black Women from All Black Men." The totalizing title suggests that Cleaver is speaking for *all* black men and *all-black* men, a fundamental essence that eclipses individuality. Speaking in "the voice of the Black Man," he aspires to the liberation of black men from the dominance of "Omnipotent Administrators"—those, like Portnoy, who rule the system with their brainpower rather than their powerful bodies. Next, he predicts the reunification of the "black eunuch" with his "Balls" through his reunion with his "Black Queen" (236, 241). Despite the sentiment of liberation, Cleaver's sexual solidarity is no more ethically satisfying than Portnoy's concluding rapacious quest for the "messianic Jewish hole" in Israel (268). Cleaver's memoir, radical as it is, betrays its reliance on old myths of racial essence, patriarchal dominance, and dichotomous power struggle. Meanwhile, *Portnoy's Complaint,* though aiming to satire just those hangups, would seem to be as wedded to them as *Soul on Ice.*

What happened to human rights, civil rights, and the sexual revolution for which we famously recall the 1960s? Is it possible that *Portnoy's Complaint,* this seemingly transgressive, liberating, boundary-breaking novel, in fact arrives at the lugubrious conclusion that liberation is a ruse? Kenneth Reinhard notes that "for Lacan the sixties did not signal the libido's momentary liberation from the constraints of repressive cultural ideals, but the construction of yet one more line of defense against the disturbing impossibility of intersubjective sexuality, the inconsistency in the symbolic order that materializes as a *factum,* or 'Thing' whose concealment, according to Lacan, both defines human relations and marks their limit."[43] Likewise, as *Portnoy's Complaint*'s twinning of libidinal and social liberation makes clear, the new lexicon of civil rights, formalized in the law and embedded in a raft of social programs, commissions, and civic policies, shuffled the terms by which we understand race, without significantly liberating us from the concomitant politics of inequality built into racial discourse. Portnoy's fixations are the objects of satire—the Jewish family, assimilation, structures of power—but Portnoy himself is as well. He is so folded into the machinery of race and class in America that nothing he says escapes the narrative's ironization.

Portnoy's Complaint satirizes this system, but in the final pages it also offers a clear-sighted critique. Departing from the parade of characters who succumb to Portnoy's verbose pummeling, the novel presents Naomi, the Israeli woman whom Portnoy attempts—and fails—to seduce in Israel. Her critique is perhaps the novel's most accurate diagnosis of "Portnoy's Complaint":

> "Pardon me, but I must speak the truth: you think you serve justice, but you are only a lackey of the bourgeoisie. You have a system inherently exploitative and unjust, inherently cruel and inhumane, heedless of human values, and your job is to make such a system appear legitimate and moral by acting as though justice, as though human rights and human dignity could actually exist in that society—when obviously no such thing is possible." (262)

Remarkably, Naomi's idealistic critique echoes Portnoy's own adolescent rant against his parents, cited at the beginning of this chapter. That democracy masks segregation and racism and that competitive capitalism requires social inequality are the fundamental premises of the young Portnoy; that he is on the receiving end of his own lecture marks the failure of his *Bildung* and the eclipse of his idealistic quest for a humanism that transcends ethnic and national divisions. When Naomi calls him a "self-hating Jew," he responds, "maybe that's the best kind," again, a twisted echo of his adolescent renunciation of Judaism in favor of humanity at large (265). The line comes without insight, of course, but it suggests finally what is potentially at stake—if never realized—in Portnoy's activity of racial resignification: the cancellation of racial identification itself. The best kind of Jew is certainly *not* self-hating, but self-abnegation, or categorically being for the other without insisting on reciprocity, is surely better than cynically manipulating the lexicon of race while maintaining power and control, and better than Cleaver's weird Manichean nationalism. Naomi calls Portnoy "self-hating," but nationalist self-love creates its own peculiar walls. A third option returns us to Lacan. As Reinhard reads "Kant with Sade," the ethical conjunction of Kant and Sade is the responsibility for the enjoyment of the other: "For the sadist, everyone but me is entitled to this freedom . . . the Sadian moral maxim enjoins that we serve the *jouissance* of the Other."[44] To submit for the other's enjoyment—Portnoy as the object of Mary Jane's fantasy—or to renounce the symbolic privilege of differential race relations—as Portnoy intuits as an adolescent—is finally the radical potential hinted at, though surely not realized, in the novel. To paraphrase from Reinhard, the moral imperative on the horizon at the end of *Portnoy's Complaint* is to be the *opportunity* of the other.

Satirizing the self-hating Jew puts Roth in the same conversation about group identity as Cleaver, but it doesn't necessarily follow that—as with Cleaver—Roth is after a yet more committed, robust generation of Jewish-identified Jews. The Jewish nationalist Naomi may get off the best straight lines of the novel, and they surely echo Cleaver's critique of racist America (she all but calls Portnoy an "omnipotent administrator" of the system). But the novel's conclusion, framed as a commencement, is apocalyptic and not a call to arms. "Up society's ass, copper!" Portnoy screams, and "society" is best understood as the society he has internalized: all the mechanisms of group identification, status, and hierarchy (274). None of this is replaced by a new model or even a new identity. Rather, we have the end of language, or signification itself. Portnoy closes with a five-line scream: "Aaaaaaaaaaaaaaaaaaah...." (274). What follows is simply an invitation, finally, to interpret, critique, and ultimately reconstruct the disastrous regime of social identification that has produced Portnoy in the first place, as the psychoanalyst speaks for the first time in the novel, "Now vee may perhaps to begin, yes?" (274). Hating others may mean loving yourself less, but the primal scream at the novel's end obliterates the lexical barriers that cordon off "self" and "other," and this linguistic apocalypse may permit new modes of social understanding.

Clearly the novel never transcends satire, and the psychoanalyst's injunction to begin analysis is marked as a punchline. Yet it remains the case that Roth would subsequently investigate the double binds of identity categories in his novels, including *The Ghost Writer, The Counterlife,* and *Operation Shylock,* while *The Human Stain* addressed the landscape of race, rights, and recognition, including the failed promise of group-based recognition.[45] If Roth never answered Mrs. Cohen, the dentist's wife from Syracuse who asked for advice for all the young people who read him, the novel's final gesture is an invitation "to begin" and quite possibly a beginning for Roth himself.

Roth's subsequent fiction has been described by Ranen Omer-Sherman as a "lamentation" for the overwhelming hold of "identity" upon American Jews, who remain obsessed with the meaning of Jewish ethnicity and Jewish loyalty and the tension between diasporic location and their Zionist commitments (191).[46] Roth's Zuckerman novels especially read as a deconstruction of the self-evidence of the identity, "Jewish," and *The Human Stain* in particular reaches beyond Jewish identity to explore human existence beyond the social and political overlays of identities. That novel's hero, Coleman Silk, commits himself to living outside the givens of social identity, but narrator Nathan Zuckerman reveals that we always live out our lives pinned down by the group-based presumptions of others. Nonetheless, well after Coleman has been pilloried as a racist and murdered by an anti-Semite, Nathan gives Coleman a gift of narrative recognition, placing him in a space beyond all social frameworks, the space of moral abjection itself. At his nadir, isolated from his family, scorned by his former colleagues, the subject of scandalous rumors and accusations of racism and sexism, Coleman takes on a pariah status that, in Nathan's imagination, affords him a space beyond social locations and leaves him available for a truly human recognition. Echoing "up society's ass," Coleman's lover Faunia tells him to throw out all the social ways of knowing the world and to hold off all social conventions and to give in to a moment of bare-naked, scarred, stained, human submission to the recognition of another.

To recognize the precarious life of another, to know that you share in that precariousness, and to submit to the other's vulnerability is the ethical hint at the end of *Portnoy's Complaint,* taken up in *The Human Stain* thirty years later. But if *The Human Stain* is Roth's lament for the deleterious detour of identity politics since 1969, Tony Kushner's play *Homebody/Kabul,* the subject of chapter 5, takes on the challenge of recognizing the socially abject other in a vastly more complicated geopolitical context. If we missed Roth's insight within his satire in 1969, Kushner's play, about Western responsibility for Afghanistan, comes just in time.

2

RE-READING CYNTHIA OZICK

Pluralism, Postmodernism,
and the Multicultural Encounter

The decades-long consistency of Cynthia Ozick's commitment to Jewish moral concerns and her concomitant iconoclasm in defense of human over material and even aesthetic values has led to a critical consensus that Ozick's great topic is the dichotomous values of Hebraism and Hellenism.[1] Ozick herself has often framed the competing cultural impulses inhabiting the Western mind in just these terms, in essays ("Preface," "Metaphor and Memory"), stories ("The Pagan Rabbi," "The Dock-Witch") and novels (*The Cannibal Galaxy, Heir to the Glimmering World*).[2] In her early fiction, writer-protagonists self-flagellate over their covetousness for fame, and some of her best stories represent how a devotion to literature above and against real life turns into a self-cannibalizing venture for authors. And in her novels, her heroes and heroines are often caught between their attraction to the spontaneity of their inventions and their commitment to tradition and memory. In Ozick's intellectual worldview, echoed in the predominant critical interpretation of her works, the spontaneous, ahistorical, creative, aesthetic impulse—which is also chauvinistic, bigoted, anti-Semitic, soulless, and pagan—is Hellenistic. Memory, tradition, covenant, empathy, and ethics are Hebraic.

Evidence for the critical consensus seems present in these lines from Ozick's first published story about moral persuasion, "The Pagan Rabbi":

> "What are they like, those people?"
>
> "They're exactly like us, if you can think what we would be if we were like them."
>
> "We are not like them. Their bodies are more to them than ours are to us. Our books are holy, to them their bodies are holy." (12)[3]

The holiness of the text, vehicle of God's word and epistle of moral rectitude, contrasts with the epicurean pleasure of the body. At a first glance, the symmetry of books and bodies suggests a neat homology between the sacred and the profane, Jews and gentiles. That's one way of looking at it. However, in Ozick's writing, nothing is ever so tidy, for moral paradox and quandary lie at the crux of her work, as they do in real life.

The question preceding the answer offers another perspective. The question, posed by Sheindel, wife of the suicide "Pagan Rabbi" of the title, presumes the most basic sort of difference. Indeed, in 1966, the year "The Pagan Rabbi" was published, "What are they like, those people?" might well have been a banner question limning all sorts of cultural encounters between people of different cultures, ethnicities, and religions. Edged with suspicion, curious without being generous, and quick to judge, scrutiny of the other was the gritty corollary to the dominant politics of recognition that emerged in the 1960s. The scrutiny might occur between whites and blacks, Protestants and Catholics, Jews and gentiles, beats and squares, communists and capitalists. Identity refraction may not have been on the character's mind, but for the intellectual denizens of mid-1960s New York, such as Ozick, it was inescapable. The subsequent emergence of minority authors into the literary mainstream, combined with the academic valorization of multiculturalism and ethnicity, would render the study of the "other" a moral imperative. To draw the story out just a bit further, by the 1980s the enfranchisement of academic multiculturalism and the popular marketing of newly empowered ethnic authors ended up leaving many Jewish authors, critics, and scholars on the sidelines, simultaneously resentful and envious of a multicultural literary movement with little place for Jewish Studies. Returning to the early formation of ethnic and multicultural studies, and—beyond intuition—placing Ozick's work at the beginning of this formation may give insight into how it happened that Jewish authors—the celebrated ethnic group of the 1950s—were found to be incompatible with the new vogue of difference by the end of the twentieth century.[4]

Like Roth, Ozick depicts the madness in the social solidification of ethnic identities, but while Roth's satire drains the life out of social identity, Ozick pushes past what she deems the idolatry of identity and toward what she considers essentially true about Jewishness in particular: moral seriousness and covenant. For Ozick, Jewish difference is real, has a historical legacy, and has moral and spiritual implications. In contrast, for Ozick ethnicity is mere faddishness, sentimentality, and political gamesmanship. Ozick's difference from Roth notwithstanding, her early fiction cooperates with *Portnoy's Complaint* as an examination and critique of the new social regimes of identity that emerged in the 1960s. For both, Jewish proximity *and* marginality to increasingly enfranchised identities yield a rich source of ambiguity and paradox, a basis for their ironical literature. However, in contrast to Roth's humor and absurdity, as well as his hints at a universal ethics of being for the other, Ozick's fiction is deadly serious, often intimating violence, hostility, and fear, precluding even the détente and mutuality of contemporaneous schemes of ethnicity and multiculturalism in public life in the 1970s. Roth's fiction would become increasingly illuminating on the fraught *human* and not simply Jewish or ethnic condition, a universalizing theme capacious enough to capture both the Jewishness of *Operation Shylock* and the interracial scenes of *The Human Stain*. Ozick's fiction, in contrast, consistently depends on Jewish moral distinctiveness and militates against universalizing modes of recognition. Proximity in Roth yields exposure; in Ozick, retrenchment, a position that, ironically, is the starting point for multiculturalism.

Pluralism and Postmodernism

If we do not typically think of Cynthia Ozick as "multicultural," it is precisely because she has created a literary world where social identities are either comedically sent up or, in the case of her most scathing critique of identity, *The Messiah of Stockholm,* smoked out and incinerated. Indeed, *The Messiah of Stockholm,* a novel about a middle-aged book reviewer named Lars who believes he is the son of the great Polish writer Bruno Schulz, employs a postmodernist suspension of reality in order to disrupt all logic of identity.[5] All identities in *The Messiah of Stockholm* are suspected forgeries, dependent on the pliability of history. This is perhaps why *The Messiah of Stockholm* is Ozick's least Judeo-centric novel, even though it is also clearly her "Holocaust novel." Identifying with history—rather than studying history or respectfully mourning history—turns history's subjects, people, into things and identities into idols.[6] *The Messiah of Stockholm* narrates Lars's ethical choice to sacrifice his claims on Holocaust history, and it amounts to Ozick's own sacrifice of an immediate relation to the past as fodder for her literature. In contrast to so many of her contemporaries—Toni Morrison, Leslie Marmon Silko, and Edwidge Danticat come to mind—who narrate the resonating and haunting presence of the past in contemporary life, Ozick holds history at arm's length. The novel mythologizes Schulz but condemns its own mythologization. This novel's self-reflexivity may be postmodern, but it is a postmodernism of a different order than the sort of aesthetic free play that Ozick has condemned in the past. Early on, Ozick was suspicious about literary gestures that flew free of the laws of moral gravity, and she condemned such efforts by Barth, Barthelme, and Pynchon as idolatrous. With *The Messiah of Stockholm,* however, Ozick singled out the postmodern melancholy of traumatic history's subjects—those who would calcify an identity around the event of traumatic loss—and mirrored it with a postmodern, self-unraveling tale.

Nonetheless, the immolation of identity in *The Messiah of Stockholm* signaled the depth of Jewish selfhood in Ozick's work—a concern present at the outset of her writing career. During the period when Ozick was building her literary reputation (1965 to 1975) and was involved in her most formative and formidable disputations about art, culture, and Jewish identity, she participated in the ongoing Jewish response to the new politics of identity and cultural recognition in public policy and the reorientation of literature and the academy toward ethnicity and multiculturalism.[7] During the 1960s and early 1970s, when institutional Judaism and Jewish intellectuals were wrestling with new social policies and multicultural developments in the arts and the academy, Ozick was a regular contributor to journals like *Commentary, Commonweal,* and *Midstream,* journals central to understanding—even producing—the relationship between Jewish American interests and the New Left, the New Ethnicity, and multiculturalism. Indeed, it is in these journals that some of Ozick's feistiest stories and most contentious reviews and letters initially appeared. *Commentary* was a particularly appropriate venue for Ozick's reflections and polemics on art, culture, and the social and moral obligations of writers. *Commentary,* the journal of politics, art, and ideas published by the American Jewish Committee, began a skeptical response to ethnic nationalisms and multiculturalism as early as 1964; by 1969, when Ozick's first story appeared in its pages, the journal had established a clear defense of liberalism against group-based claims for rights and began attacking the politics of radical multiculturalism and ethnic nationalism. Ozick's essays and letters sit alongside those of Norman Podhoretz, Nathan Glazer, and Robert Alter, all three of whom argued that liberal individualism underwrites culture and ethics, at a moment when liberalism was being rejected in the struggle for cultural rights and recognition by African American social rights organizations. In contrast, the claims of black nationalism and subsequent Chicana/o, Native American, and other post–civil rights and postcolonial cultural movements were philosophically communitarian, oriented not around the freedom of the individual to express his or her culture but around the belief that, after so many decades of official government policies of colonialism, enslavement, and white supremacy, the individual can only be liberated through the freedoms gained on behalf of the group. For ethnic nationalists, arts that promoted group identity were thought to promote freedom of consciousness for the group's citizens.

By the late 1960s, as a consequence of the philosophical and political impasses between Jews and other ethnic groups, the Jewish proponents of liberalism were marginalized from organizations to which they were once central and spoke a language of humanism that no longer held currency with the radical new left.[8] In turn, Jewish intellectuals furiously critiqued the philosophical underpinnings of ethnic nationalism. Podhoretz attacked affirmative action, Alter critiqued the new Ethnic Studies departments, and Glazer limned his studies of the "new ethnicity" with critiques of ethnic nationalism. As a regular contributor of essays, fiction, and letters to *Commentary,* Ozick is literally "on the same page," but that tells only half the story. Ozick's writing echoes but also interrogates the premises of these writers' views and allows readers to explore the double bind of cultural commitments. Ozick's oft-stated disgust for the politics of "ethnicity" resonates in common with her contemporaries' critiques of the politics of identity and anticipates her postmodern unraveling of identity itself in *The Messiah of Stockholm*. However, a closer look at her early fiction reveals that she is after something more rather than less Jewish in her study of group identity. I suggest that the default critical paradigm for Ozick, "Hebraism and Hellenism," useful as it is, overlooks how her complicated aesthetics are embedded in a concomitant politics. What we now call "essentialism" Ozick assumes as a premise in her fiction about the ineluctable differences between Jews and gentiles. In Ozick's fiction, assimilation is not only *not* inevitable, it is *impossible*. Characters, even whole communities, are embedded in a politics not of individual resistance but of cultural incommensurability. Though the stories I'll discuss below, published between 1966 and 1976, are all about Jews, their investigation of cultural pluralism, including the limits of radical pluralist separatism, parallels and is responsive to ideas prevalent in ethnic separatist movements, and the dilemmas of separatism described in her fiction resonate with those described by political theorists such as Charles Taylor, Will Kymlicka, and William Connolly.[9] Political theory has had to address multiculturalism in relation to liberalism primarily because of the intransigence of minority cultures resistant to assimilation in the post–civil rights and postcolonial era. Meanwhile, Jewish religion and culture, if recognized at all, are regarded as firmly a part of the mainstream of western culture. Looking back on Ozick's early fiction, however, we find a compelling presentation of Jewish religion and culture that imagines Jews as radically outside the mainstream, in the margins with the usual multicultural suspects.

Cultural Pluralism and Its Others

A glance at the front covers of Jewish journals from the late 1960s confirms that Ozick's fiction is gathered up in the rising alarm and response to the new politics of ethnicity and race. Consider, for example, Ozick's acclaimed story, "Envy; or, Yiddish in America," published in *Commentary* in November 1969.[10] 1969 stands out as the year *Commentary,* like other Jewish reviews, became increasingly concerned over both the "crisis" of identity in Jewish American cultural life and the growing hostility and prevalence of black anti-Semitism in mainstream society.[11] In the January issue, Earl Raab wrote on "The Black Revolution and the Jewish Divide," and in March Milton Himmelfarb wrote a piece asking, "Is American Jewry in Crisis?" April's edition featured Nathan Glazer's essay "Blacks, Jews, and Intellectuals," a companion to Raab's piece, and in September Theodore Draper wrote a long historical essay on "The Fantasy of Black Nationalism." Ozick's "Envy" appeared in the next issue. Does this contiguity suggest any common theme? Clearly Ozick, like nearly everyone else writing for *Commentary,* was meditating on Jewish identity in 1969. However, a close reading of "Envy" demonstrates that the story's conflicts and plot development result from and turn on questions of liberal identity, ethnic nationalism, and the cramped middle ground of cultural pluralism—the very topics highlighted in *Commentary* and other Jewish and national journals in the late 1960s.

In "Envy," the forlorn Yiddish poet Edelstein, desperate for English translation and American fame, represents the conflicted nature of pluralism: he views Yiddish culture as unchanging and properly antimodern but with something to say to a modern world. Such a pluralism appeals to a market of readers who look to Jewish culture for old-world wisdom. This is the sort of pluralism where ethnicity is "celebrated," diversity is commodified and purchased, and culture becomes either static or, worse, produced by the very market that would consume it. If the Jewish artist is obliged to produce a market-driven Jewishness for a non-Jewish readership, does this redefine Judaic authenticity for ordinary Jews? Are they likewise obliged to perform and produce as "Jewish" a culture that looks back and draws from the Old World? If Jewish Americans invent a new culture, one that is responsive to the American experience, how can it be understood as "Jewish"? Such questions are the common boilerplate of intellectual symposia and academic conferences, not to mention rabbinical sermons, but they are also at the crux of debates about the viability of pluralism around the time Ozick was writing: is culture something organic and intrinsic to a "people"—and if so, how does it change?—or is it contingent on environment and ever in flux—in which case, why *not* change? Edelstein wants it both ways, resisting cultural evolution while still seeking market success, and he courts a young translator, begging her to recall her duty to the culture of her ancestors: "Hannah, youth itself is nothing unless it keeps its promise to grow old. Grow old in Yiddish, Hannah, and carry fathers and uncles in the future with you" (74). Edelstein eventually admits that he is not offering Hannah the prospect of progress through traditional continuity but rather death or, more precisely, the choice between death by assimilation and death by cultural stasis. In his view, not only should there be no evolution of Jewish culture in the United States, but contemporary Jews are obligated to devote themselves to old-world Yiddishkeit. What is more, a Yiddish culture of fathers and uncles is, for a young woman, a culture of servitude and not innovation. Hannah's response is bilious: "Die.... Die now, all you old men" (95, 97), a rejoinder that confirms Edelstein's two choices, death or death. In either case, there is no continuity, only rupture, metaphorized by death.

When Edelstein offers the metaphor of death, he invites Hannah to mourn a history of suffering, including the Holocaust. However, for Hannah, the death of the preceding generations is the only way to be free from the claims they make upon her. This bind of culture is summarized effectively by Walter Benn Michaels, who asks:

> What makes Jewish history your history unless your grandparents were Jews? And although culture seems a more promising criterion of Jewishness—to be Jewish is simply to do what [Isaac] Berkson called "Jewish things" (57)—it's equally difficult to see how the reduction of Jewish identity to the doing of "Jewish things" can underwrite the desire to avoid assimilation, the "loyalty" to an "ethnic community" (103) that Berkson plausibly presents as the crucial feature of cultural identity. For if your grandchildren do not do the things that you have done, and if your culture is nothing more than what you do, how can they be understood to have lost *their* culture? To what "community" have the assimilated children been disloyal? (138)[12]

Michaels concludes, finally, that cultural pluralism is an oxymoron, because "culture" cancels the sense of individual free choice inherent in "pluralism." Though Michaels limits his range of understanding by sticking to "assimilation" as the only alternative to cultural loyalty, thereby ignoring the possibility of evolutionary cultural history, the presence of irony in culture, the dialectics of cultural archives, and, most importantly, affective responses to culture (for many of us, that our grandparents did "Jewish things" is a very emotionally compelling reason to do them too—some of us love our grandparents), he succinctly establishes how certain forms of cultural pluralism presume a never-changing static culture.[13] Edelstein pleads that "whoever forgets Yiddish courts amnesia of history," but the alternative would be to step out of the present and join with history, effectively become history, which yet again, in Edelstein's eyes, amounts to cultural death (74).

The critical conflation of modernism with Judaism raises the question, how can the Jewish writer address the modern world from a Jewish point of view, where "Jewish" is not the cipher for, and thus superfluous to, modernity? Writing about Kafka as a Jewish artist for *Commentary* the year before "Envy" appeared, Robert Alter explains: Kafka "could envision the ultimate ambiguities of human life in general with a hyperlucidity because he had experienced them in poignant particularity as a Jew. Out of the stuff of Jewish experience which he himself thought of as marginal, he was able to create fiction at once universal and hauntingly Jewish" ("Jewish Dreams" 54)[14]. Alter writes not to defend the term "Jewish literature"— "there is something presumptuously proprietary about the whole idea of sorting out writers according to national, ethnic, or religious origins," he begins—but to insist that writers are Jewish only on an individual basis: "One must always attend to the particular ways in which Jewish experience impinges on the individual, and this impingement is bound to differ in small things and large, from one writer to the next" (48, 54). Alter's concession to ethnic categorization sustains individuality and refuses the embeddedness that Ozick explores through her poet Edelstein. Indeed, if we grant that Edelstein is, according to Elaine Kauvar, based on the Yiddish poet Jacob Glatstein, then we can see that just as Glatstein wrote from the "diminished imperative," as Michael Galchinsky puts it, expressing the particular tragedies afflicting Yiddish, which were by no means universalizable to a wider modernist condition, so too is Edelstein committed to a Yiddish expressive exclusively of the Jewish experience of exile (Kauvar 58, Galchinsky 243).[15]

"Envy," like several of Ozick's stories, ends with a peculiar apocalypse that suggests the limitations of both pluralist and universalist approaches to culture and identity. Edelstein misdials a public pay phone and ends up speaking to a hostile and anti-Semitic Christian evangelist who preaches universalism and the end of "abnormal" Judaic culture: "Everyone you come into contact with turns into your enemy. When you were in Europe every nation despised you. When you moved to take over the Middle East, the Arab Nation, spic faces like your own, your very own blood-kin, began to hate you. You are a bone in the throat of mankind" (100). The raving anti-Semitism, including the suggestion that Jewish culture is deservedly debased by history, is an attack on the very idea of "culture," with reasoning startlingly like that of Michaels: why should you continue doing what Jews always have done, speaking as they have always done, believing as they have always done, remaining unresponsive to what is new?

Edelstein thinks the interlocutor may be black, and indeed at one point he paraphrases mid-1960s black nationalist rhetorical appropriations of the Holocaust: "You people were cowards, you never even tried to defend yourselves," an echo of Stokely Carmichael's declaration that "if white America decides to play Nazis, we're going to let them know that Black people are not Jews" (quoted in Sundquist 318). Read as an echo of Carmichael, the caller's Holocaust reference accuses Jews of being both too exclusive and not exclusive enough, and certainly it was this sort of provocative public statement that contributed to the Jewish fears of black anti-Semitism. However, there is a double standard for ethnocentrism in both Carmichael's line and in the complaint of Edelstein's interlocutor: your ethnocentrism is rooted in depravity and weakness, ours in truth and strength. We might be inclined to read Ozick's scene as cultural defensiveness against the threatening claims of black and ethnic nationalisms. It comes as a surprise, then, to compare the logic of Edelstein's anti-Semitic interlocutor with a similarly reasoned cultural attack, written by none other than Norman Podhoretz, against black nationalism. Podhoretz, in his 1964 *Commentary* essay "My Negro Problem—and Ours," questions why black Americans would work to maintain a separate culture of their own, given what he perceives to be the state of black cultural life: "When I think about the Negroes in America and about the image of integration as a state in which Negroes would take their rightful place as another of the protected minorities in a pluralistic society, I wonder whether they really believe in their hearts that such a state can actually be attained, and if so, *why* they should wish to survive as a distinct group.... What does the American Negro have that might correspond to [Jewish culture]? His past is a stigma, his color is a stigma, and his vision of the future is the hope of erasing the stigma by making color irrelevant" (387). Podhoretz roots his antipathy in his childhood scraps with black boys in his neighborhood and ends with a yearning that things be different, that the "man I now have a duty to be" can override the sentiments of "the child I once was," but his psychological rhetoric misconstrues the political and economic substance of the ethnic conflicts of the 1960s (387). Podhoretz's essay reveals what is often missing from theories of cultural pluralism, a vocabulary (not to mention programs and policies) of cultural recognition *and* group-based remedies for historical and ongoing race-based injustice, where the end of racism is guaranteed by more than one man's choice to tolerate or forgive. Ozick knows the double binds of pluralism. In an argument similar to Podhoretz's claim that the hope of the black American is the erasure of the stigma of color, Edelstein's interlocutor proffers "Christianity [as] Judaism universalized" and offers to free him of "Judaic exclusivism" (99). Ozick shows the bite in such offers, as the interlocutor rails, "Even now, after the good lord knows how many years in America, you talk with a kike accent, you kike, you Yid," to which Edelstein responds, "On account of you I lost everything, my whole life! On account of you I have no translator!" (100). Edelstein's closing accusation is not directed at the anti-Semitism per se that precludes translations but at a universalism that requires Jewish history to operate as *prehistory* to the present, always a stigma or stain that the "enlightened" (read Christian, assimilationist, or modern) age would rather forget.[16]

Ozick's challenge of cultural pluralism stabs at an idea deeply embedded in Jews' thinking about the role of Jewish culture in American social and political life. The term *cultural pluralism* was first coined by Horace Kallen in 1907 to describe a democracy sustained by contributions from different cultures to the whole of American social and democratic life, where no one cultural group was dominant or central (Whitfield xxxi). Rejecting prevailing race-based descriptions of the ideal American, Kallen argued pragmatically that the *experience* of being American, including the experience of immigrating, settling, mingling with other immigrants from different countries, and participating in the American experiment in democracy and personal liberty conferred American identity (Kallen 98). Cultural pluralism is rooted in Kallen's pragmatism and Franz Boas's sympathetic and contemporaneous thesis of cultural relativism and environmental cultural development.[17] Contrary to many social commentators of his day who responded to the "rising tide of color" with either nativist policies or programs for assimilation, Kallen believed that there was no centrally American culture either in need of protection or fit to promote assimilation.[18] Rather, "America" amounted to a "harmony" of peoples, with each culture contributing to the whole with its own unique accent (Kallen 96). The nation was under no obligation to assimilate immigrants, nor did it have the right or reason to demand assimilation, for the nation exists to guarantee the liberty and pursuit of happiness to individuals, and culture—whatever the culture—is the means through which Jewish, Irish, Italian, or African Americans experience these virtues.[19] Later advocates of cultural pluralism, including midcentury advocates for black and Jewish social advancement working through the American Jewish Committee and the NAACP, appealed to liberalism—the social priority of the individual—as the basis for social integration and tolerance, rather than pointing to the rights of a cultural group qua group. An individual's cultural practices are his or her own business, pluralists contend, and can be a basis neither for discrimination nor for special treatment.

Keeping faith with cultural pluralism, Jews labored through the 1940s and 1950s to negate identity as a discriminatory factor in employment, university admissions, and political appointments and subsequently were prominent in opposing affirmative action policies perceived as exclusionary quotas. As a political strategy, pluralism was highly effective for Jews because it eliminated the racial basis for discrimination while allowing Jews to operate in the political sphere as individuals. Indeed, Will Herberg recast cultural pluralism along religious lines in his 1955 book *Protestant, Catholic, Jew,* arguing that the only enduring cultures in America were not race-based but deeply embedded in religious traditions and practices.[20] Karen Brodkin explains it this way: "Ethnic Pluralism gave rise to a new construction of specifically Jewish whiteness. It did so by contrasting Jews as a model minority with African Americans as culturally deficient. Ethnic pluralism also gave rise to a new, cultural way of discussing race" (144).[21] Brodkin gives Nathan Glazer the dubious intellectual credit for the implicit racism in later versions of the thesis, but she also associates the general development of the white Jew as model minority with the New York intellectuals, a diverse group whose one common link would be an association with Jews and whiteness and a commitment to liberal pluralism.

Jews, Ethnicity, and the Jewish Moral Self

Ozick consistently refuses pat political or sociological readings of her literature as direct commentary on social issues of the day. For example, in a reply to Ruth Weiss on the role of the artist as a social chronicler, Ozick explains, "'the sociological reality'...is what the imaginative writer is least interested in, and sets out, in fact, to bypass" ("Letter" 8).[22] She further claims that her fiction is not even about the real world: "The poetry of fiction may take up ideas, may resemble ideas—but not 'real' ideas, i.e., ideas about reality; like, say, an idea about a political conflict, or a pattern of immigration, or the exact geographical location of a 'traditional Jewish environment.'...All writing is fabrication, including criticism," because essays *and* fiction are both "made up, invented; both are, in the most serious sense, dreams" (9). Ozick's readers will be familiar with the privilege reserved for the writer in these lines, but here we also find a recurring paradox in Ozick's simultaneous commitment to serious, even liturgical, literature and a literature that is entirely the stuff of dreams. Ozick reminds Weiss of her now-notorious 1971 essay calling for a "New Yiddish" in which she rejects the rising fad of postmodern literature as a mere language game not fit for Jewish writers. Instead, borrowing from Ortega y Gasset, Ozick explains that "it is above all the Jewish sense-of-things to 'passionately wallow in human reality.' Covenant and conduct are above decoration" (165).[23] If the essay was then an experimental piece and now obsolete, it nonetheless stands as exploration of how cultural values—what Ozick calls the "Jewish-sense-of-things"—enter into the public domain. Decoration is a pejorative associated with postmodernism for Ozick, indicating an art that copies reality but lacks the soul of human moral concern. To write "Jewish" by drawing on stock yiddishisms, comic domestic scenes, or standard second-generation rebellion dramas would amount to so much sociology for Ozick, what in another context she calls a "prefabrication" ("Literary Blacks and Jews" 108).[24] To the extent that it is a fabrication, ethnicity is worse than epiphenomenal: It is antihuman, prioritizing the superficial above the real, the corporate group identity over the one that emerges through moral rectitude.

Despite Ozick's subsequent misgivings, her call for a "New Yiddish" and her attempts at writing a liturgical literature fall within the most progressive versions of cultural pluralism. Indeed, her emphasis on language especially evokes the agendas of contemporaneous black nationalist and Chicana/o nationalist cultural and language rights movements and would link her with the language-based multicultural politics animating Canada beginning in the 1970s.[25] In "Toward a New Yiddish," originally given as a talk at the Weizman Institute in Israel, Ozick explores the dialectical and at times paradoxical problem of Jews being universally dispersed but maintaining a fundamentally Jewish moral identity and the relation of that identity to a universal ethics. Ozick takes as her foil George Steiner, the artist and critic, who, like many other modern Jews and non-Jews, declares that diaspora is the central condition of being Jewish. Ozick agrees yet argues that to be a Jew in the diaspora means living in resistance to the assimilating or absorbing tendencies of a dominant culture. The lures of secularism, paganism, or nostalgia need to be beaten back with a rigorous reaffirmation of Jewish values that emerge from and exist despite or perhaps flourish in diasporic marginality and contingency. At stake is not the banal concept of "Jewish identity" but the Jewish moral self, which Ozick views as a vehicle of moral truth in the world. Acknowledging that for individual Jews this is an idiosyncratic and possibly autodidactic venture, Ozick nonetheless holds out for a specific prescription on the necessity of a Jewish artistic activity. The Jewish artist is, by definition, one who judges the culture around him or her. "If he does not judge what he finds, if he joins it instead, he disappears" (166), a banner statement that could easily limn the "disappearance" of nearly all of Ozick's assimilationist characters, from the suicidal pagan rabbi to the gun-toting Bleilip of "Bloodshed."

The New Yiddish is not an expression of ethnicity (as the old Yiddish has become for popular culture) but aims to be a liturgical language. "Touched by the covenant," Jewish-English will be an English thoroughly inhabited with Jewish ethical concerns (175). Written for public instruction, the New Yiddish will be an explicitly pluralistic language, philosophically in concert with Kallen's "American Idea," where a plurality of cultures meet and compete, inform, critique, and ultimately strengthen one another in the public sphere. Ozick calls for just such a linguistic scenario, explaining that English might broadcast Jewish ideas, and presumably ethical care, to a wider English-speaking world. Ozick is not, however, advocating that Jewish culture become integral to an American culture, in contrast to Kallen. Kallen believed that "once the wolf is driven from the door and the Jewish immigrant takes his place in American society a free man (as

American *mores* establish freedom) and an American, he tends to become rather the more a Jew" (Kallen 104–5). In Kallen's philosophy, Jewish culture is strengthened by its liberation from the margins of society in Europe to the center of American democracy, but Ozick considers it vital that Jews and Jewish culture remain marginal rather than central. Put another way, Kallen was adamant that there be no central American culture at all, while Ozick's thinking depends upon it. Her claim, "Diaspora, c'est moi," explicitly rejects liberalism by insisting on the metaphysical and cultural condition of diaspora and the enduring historical and geographical asymmetry with the rest of American culture: culture is not just what we do, it is what we are (155). In fact, the plausibility of a New Yiddish is secondary to Ozick's hope that American Jews cease living like "envious apes" and become "masters of our own civilization" (177).

Ozick's New Yiddish amounts to a theory of Jewish culture in America sympathetic to what we now call multiculturalism. Not the corporate multiculturalism in which diversity is blandly celebrated and all cultures are presumed to be on the same plane of value, without attention to historical and legal contingencies and the American phenomenon of racialization. Rather, Ozick flirts with the radical proposition that different cultural values require separate public and political sanctioning. This "strong" multiculturalism, as theorized in recent years, holds that America hosts many different cultural groups whose life experiences, cultural values, religion, and language are different from the mainstream and worthy of protection and maintenance by the state (O'Neill 222, Kymlicka 22).[26] Ozick's New Yiddish is oddly situated among other proposals for ethnocentric renewal and even ethnic nationalism, somewhere between contemporaneous black separatism, the Chicana/o *Moviemiento,* and the "American Indian Movement," on the one hand, and the more accommodating goals of the New Ethnicity on the other. Compared to contemporaneous ethnic nationalist movements, which bundle language rights (Spanish, Black English, and Native languages) with demands for control over land, schooling, and housing policy, Ozick's new Yiddish lacks a material correlative, yet her diasporism is more akin to exile than the immigrant-formed ethnicities that enjoyed revival by Slavs, Germans, Poles, Italians, and Irish in the early 1970s. Ozick's diasporism and its frosty reception in the early 1970s is symptomatic of the location of Jewish culture in relation to the trends in institutional multiculturalism developing at that time: lacking a theory of place and claims on material rights—theories and claims that Jewish intellectuals and critics are only now beginning to articulate—Jewish literature and culture has struggled to sustain a conversation with both white ethnic cultures and with institutional "multi-cultures," including African American, Asian American, Native American, and Chicana/o cultures.[27] Indeed, diasporic-oriented cultural advocacy, which is distinct from both nationalism and ethnicity, lacked a theory of culture through the 1970s and early 1980s until the developments of postcolonial theory. Even now, attempts to imagine Jewish culture in a postcolonial and postnational theoretical context are undercut by persistent and important debates about the very category "Jewish culture," the relationship of diaspora Jews to Israel, and institutional notions about race in American that do not include Jews.[28] In place of a Jewish American "nation" in Ozick's early fiction, we have Jews who are prominently and even spectacularly marginal to the mainstream, either as immigrants, Holocaust survivors, or Hasids—all three in "Bloodshed." Ozick is not herself a Hasidic Jew, nor an immigrant, for that matter, but by depicting these people, especially in cultural conflict, she demonstrates the values and limits of quasi-nationalist group identity.

From Pluralism to Multiculturalism

Ozick's early story "The Pagan Rabbi," first published in 1966, most starkly depicts the author's view of the difference in cultural values between Hasidic Jews and those derisively described as "Puritans"—white American Protestants—at the beginning of the story. The narrator of the story is a former Torah scholar, now a secular Jew, who is puzzling over the unaccountable suicide of his old friend and former colleague, the illustrious young rabbi Isaac Kornfeld. Visiting Isaac's widow, the narrator finds himself scrutinized as an exotic emissary of secular American culture. Sheindel, Isaac's wife, has discovered that her husband had become devoted to Romantic philosophy and literature and held the pagan belief that the material world is animated by a godly spiritual force. In fact, in what is a cross between a suicide note and a modern midrash on monotheism, Isaac explains his death as an attempt to find everlasting liberty for his soul in the material world, where it might reside cordially with the dryads and naiads of the forests and streams. Has the rabbi gone mad?

Has he, in his immersion in Romantic poetry and the Greek classics, lost sight of the boundaries between stories and real life? Importantly, both Sheindel and the narrator treat Isaac's belief in pantheism not as madness but as misdirection: the world of magic, spontaneity, and a plethora of gods may exist, but this is no place for a Jew. For her part, Sheindel is not so much mournful or even shocked over her husband's death as bitter that he would scale "the fence of the law" and succumb to the temptations of the non-Judaic world (25). This belief in the plurality of truths generates the story's tension and anxiety right to the end. Sheindel has thrown out all her plants—"they are like little trees"—and when the narrator returns home he likewise purges his apartment of plants, a confirmation of Isaac's declaration that "Great Pan lives" but also a warning: this is not for Jews (15, 17).

The plurality of worlds—monotheistic and pantheistic—exists for a plurality of people, Jews and gentiles both. Sheindel explains this to the narrator in a moment of mockery, cited at the beginning of this chapter. She has not yet disclosed her husband's secret, and in a veiled attempt to learn more about non-Judaic culture, she asks her interlocutor, "What are they like, those people?" and he replies, "They're exactly like us, if you can think what we would be if we were like them" (12). The narrator's lame answer is peculiarly tautological but in no way out of step with the cultural politics of white ethnicity in the 1960s, where the difference difference makes does not add up to all that much. Jews and gentiles are mutually ethnic, according to the narrator's formulation, different from each other, but not so different as to be beyond the reach of the imagination. Sheindel's response, "We are not like them," echoes Ozick's sense that Judaism and anything that can be properly called Jewish culture belongs to moral conscience and memory, while the non-Judaic or Hellenic cultures are materialistic and self-aggrandizing. "We are not like them" means that the differences are essential.

In "The Pagan Rabbi," Isaac's encounter with the dryad forces him to confront the possibility of plurality. But Ozick does not make it easy. For Isaac, the choice is not between Judaism and pantheism, for in fact his Jewish soul has already made that choice for him, according to the dryad. In his journal, which runs right up to the moment of his death, Isaac explains that his growing interest in Romanticism convinced him of the plausibility of an animate materialism—paganism—and he sought out confirmation, calling on a nymph from the woods to come and free his soul from his body. One such nymph responds and complies with his request. Isaac is initially joyous, believing that his expansive and spontaneous soul is finally to be liberated from his narrow, limited, confining body. He is shocked, then, when the nymph points out his soul to him, in the form of an old scholar:

> "'He passes indifferent through the beauty of the field. His nostrils sniff his book as if flowers lay on the clotted page, but the flowers lick his feet. His feet are bandaged, his notched toenails gore the path. His prayer shawl drops on his studious back. He reads the Law and breathes the dust and doesn't see the flowers and won't heed the cricket spitting in the field.'"
>
> "'That,' said the dryad, 'is your soul.'" (35)

The soul is Jewish through and through, from its resistance to worldly seduction to its devotion to the law. The nymph abandons Isaac at this point; in a desperate attempt to join her, Isaac hangs himself from her own embodiment, a nearby oak tree. The story's moral is clear enough: we are not like them, and attempts at assimilation are deadly.

Indeed, this may be the moral of several of Ozick's stories. At the end of her novella "Usurpation," the Jewish Hellenistic poet Shaul Tchernichovsky resides in heaven, a self-hating soul cavorting with the "Canaanite idols [who] call him, in the language of the spheres, kike" (178).[29] Similarly, as we saw earlier, Edelstein, the pathetic Yiddish poet of the story "Envy, or Yiddish in America" clamors for fame and desperately converses with an anti-Semite who calls him a "kike" (100). And as we will see, Bleilip, the protagonist of "Bloodshed," is a secular Jew who carries a gun out of unspoken fear for his own annihilation. The dryad concludes, "I do not like that soul of yours.... *It denies all our multiplicity,*" but Ozick consistently acknowledges multiplicity (34, emphasis added). The narrator's final act of flushing the plants down the toilet suggests less a refusal to believe in the pagan world than an affirmation of the segregation between the Hebraic and the pagan. As the story notes in closing, the plants journey through the sewers to the small bay cradling the park where Isaac died, where they will find good company with Isaac's former consort (37).

The story asks not only whether Jews and non-Jews are like each other in some fundamental way but also, whether they *can* be like each other.

Are the differences culturally constructed and historically derived? Or are they in some way more essential? The narrator's response to Sheindel's question is perhaps intentionally inane because it suggests a formula for assimilation, which Ozick vehemently rejects as an annihilation of a people for the putative sake of anemic democracy. To assimilate, after all, literally means "to make one thing like another," and Ozick not only resists that formulation but regards it as impossible. If you can imagine yourself like the other, either you *are* really like the other, in which case you do not need to use your imagination, or you are not like the other, in which case your imagination will fail you or, worse, falsely and dangerously lead you to see sameness where there is really difference. Isaac's suicide is less an act of despair and more a desperate attempt at assimilation. He no longer wants to be a Jew committed to Hebraic denials of a wider sphere of corporal pleasure but instead to be liberated from a self-limiting culture, free from history, free to enjoy the religion of "all-of-a-sudden" (33). With Sheindel's dismissal of such a facile assimilation, Ozick anticipates Artur Sammler, protagonist of Bellow's *Mr. Sammler's Planet,* who likewise "doubted the fitness of these Jews for this erotic Roman voodoo primitivism. He questioned whether release from long Jewish mental discipline, hereditary training in lawful control, was obtainable upon individual application" (59). In Bellow's novel Sammler realizes that he is an anachronism in modern New York City, but his suspicion that his younger Jewish relatives are also unfit for the spontaneous adoration of the body and the degradation of tradition and propriety through endless experimentations with whatever is new matches Sheindel's simple declaration that "their bodies are more to them than ours are to us" (12). Of course, Jews have suffered the failed promise of emancipation before. European assimilation may be the limit case, but for Ozick it indicates how deep the differences between Jews and non-Jews through Western history run, so much so as to make the wider goal of assimilation—to be like and to be liked—never fully achievable.

One of my aims here is to argue that for Ozick, ethnicity is homologous with assimilation: both rely on self-absorbed and self-aggrandizing pretensions to universality only lightly hinged to a mostly irrelevant pastiche of history. But if it is not an ethnicity, what can "Jewish" be in America? The dramatic tension of "Bloodshed" results from the challenge to the very term *Jewish* posed by the encounter of very different sorts of Jews, the religious Jews living in a Hasidic enclave and the ethnic Jew, Bleilip. Bleilip, the protagonist of "Bloodshed," is a comfortable, secular, progressive Jew, "a lawyer though not in practice, an ex-labor consultant, a fund-raiser by profession" (59). "Fund-raiser" suggests that Bleilip works for one of several Jewish institutions, flush with money and moral support after the Six-Day War, and we may infer that he proceeds from a career in left-wing politics to Jewish institutional retrenchment, a trajectory paradigmatic of Jewish institutional involvement in public policy at large, reduced from a wider role in progressive coalition politics to the inward-facing task of raising money for charitable Jewish organizations. Describing the turn inward with enthusiasm for *Commentary* in 1969, Earl Raab explained, "The Black Revolution is spurring the Jewish community—and America—into a renewed understanding of pluralistic politics. The fresh Jewish stirrings are not primarily a backlash reaction.... There is most significantly a real turning inward; in a real sense, a *regrouping*" (32). Through Bleilip's contrast with Hasidic Yussel and Toby, Ozick considers if the turn inward is a self-strengthening or in fact a solipsistic idle. For Bleilip, the regrouping means confronting different ways of being Jewish, his own cosmopolitan version juxtaposed against the seeming provinciality of his Hasidic cousin. He is thrown for a loop, however, when he realizes that his own Jewish roots are uncomfortably and uncannily similar to the Hasidim he comes to visit. Indeed, the story's comedy occurs as we see that the further out of the city Bleilip travels, the more provincial he discovers himself to be. Though initially he sees himself as properly Jewish in the Alfred Kazin style and his formerly secular and now Hasidic cousin Toby as a "convert," by the end of the story he is forced to question the nature of Judaic group boundaries and just where he fits within them.

The story's conclusion inverts Bleilip's and the Hasidim's presumed positions of insider and outsider, respectively, as we learn of Bleilip's increasing sense of alienation from society at large, thus prompting his visit to Toby and Yussel. At the story's end, the rebbe orders Bleilip to "disgorge" his pockets, revealing that Bleilip carries with him two guns, one a toy and one a real weapon. Why Bleilip carries a gun and harbors a vague paranoia is not immediately evident, but it may symbolize the anxiety inherent in Jewish American pluralism around this time. If Jews were inspired by African Americans, as Raab reports, they were also fearful of black anti-Semitism and the threat of black anti-Semitic violence.

Reflecting on the social tensions of 1969—two years before Ozick wrote "Bloodshed"—a commentator for the annual Jewish Yearbook remarked that American Jews may be paranoid about anti-Semitic violence, but "we come by our paranoia honestly," citing the increasing hostility of blacks toward Jews who worked in civil and social institutions directly involved in black cultural life (86). Bellow in *Mr. Sammler's Planet* checks this paranoia by representing blacks and Jews as equally menacing, with each using different symbolic tools; the notorious black pickpocket of Bellow's novel silences and controls Sammler with his serpentine penis, while Sammler's son-in-law brutalizes the pickpocket with kitschy Israeli art. Read against these depictions of the tools of cultural menace, we may say that Bleilip's great error is that he wields such a nondescript tool. The gun signals how lost he is to Jewish culture, not because it is a tool of destruction but because it is so culturally insipid.

In contrast to Bleilip's isolated secularism, Ozick's Hasidim represent a radical pluralist alternative for being Jewish in America. Ozick probably modeled the story's new and growing Hasidic town on the village of New Square in upstate New York, home of the Skver Hasidim who moved from Brooklyn to the countryside in the late 1950s, or perhaps on the village of Kiryas Joel, settled by the Satmar in the early 1970s. Though Hasidic Jewry in Ozick's fiction is typically understood as an interrogation of secularism, we should also note that Hasidic communities like the Skver and Satmar challenge liberal Jewish conceptions of the place of cultural difference in a liberal democracy. Both Hasidic towns are communitarian, and as such they are discomfiting to American liberals, Jewish and gentile alike. The social values of these Hasidic villages are not based in increasing property values, bigger houses, the pastoral distance between neighbors, or even diversity but on proximity, contiguity, homogeneity, and an interest in profit for the sake of study and worship. The Satmar of Kiryas Joel were the defendants in an important Supreme Court hearing in 1994 on the constitutionality of the state of New York providing special funds to Satmar schools so that special-needs Hasidic students would not have to endure the trauma of mixing with non-Hasidic children in already established special-education schools outside of Kiryas Joel. The Supreme Court case turned on questions of the character and meaning of "identity" for Hasidic communities. If these communities are "ethnic," then, according to logic of diversity, it is a virtue for Hasidic children to mix with non-Hasidic ones. If they represent an instance of liberal pluralism, than public-private distinctions obtain, and the state is not responsible for maintaining Hasidic cultural values in a public forum. However, Jonathan Boyarin argues that the Satmar and groups like them are governed by an internal, Judaic *nomos,* a legally recognizable culture of conduct unique to diaspora, where Jews' survival as Jews requires that they regard themselves as a culture apart from the mainstream (116).[30] This interpretation naturally poses problems for democratic pluralism, and the case of Kiryas Joel turned precisely on the question of whether a group like the Satmar could be good stewards of democratic state power. Complicating the question of radical cultural difference is the fact that Hasidic communities are at once ethnic as well as religious and genealogical communities, making their Jewishness at once subject to and moot for the Constitution's Establishment Clause delineating the government's protection of religious freedom.

Boyarin discusses the genealogical nature of the Hasidim literally, taking note of their large extended families and the subsequent cultural priorities for multifamily housing and close housing proximity, but we may also understand genealogy as a racializing metaphor that would encompass Jews in general. Indeed, Ozick's "Bloodshed" begins with genealogy: Bleilip comes to visit Toby, his cousin by both his parents, who are also cousins, but this intimate connection seems to Bleilip severed by her joining the Hasidim (55). When the rebbe challenges Bleilip, he asks, "Who are you, what do you represent, what are you to us?" (66). The question already excludes Bleilip from the community, and the way he frames it—"our practices are well known since Sinai"—suggests that Bleilip is estranged from Judaism itself (66). Bleilip replies, "A Jew. Like yourselves. One of you," but the story furnishes no logic of identification, be it cultural, religious, or racial, to justify the claim.

The reversal of Bleilip's expectations is irony enough, but Ozick goes one step further in her conclusion, putting Bleilip and the rebbe in a difficult and tense scene of mutual identification, forcing readers to figure out just what the two can be said to have in common as Jews. Put another way, Ozick is challenging the very notion of cultural pluralism, asking, "What is culture?" and "What comprises the pluralities themselves?" Kallen's idea of cultural pluralism harbors a peculiarly unresolved tension between the freedom of individuals to continue adhering to their cultural traditions and a set of traditions that are unchanging, even binding for individuality. William Connolly credits that tension with rending the fabric of tradition and enabling "creedal ventilation," the opening up of tradition to mystery, doubt, and new experience (61). Ozick's Bleilip provokes this tension when he is challenged by the rebbe to identify himself as anything other than an enemy or an apostate. The rebbe presumes a difference where Bleilip insists on sameness and, moreover, affiliation—"one of you." But Bleilip resists more—"this was not the sort of closeness he coveted"—and attempts to separate himself from the rebbe and his followers, challenging the Rebbe's desire to resurrect the bloody temple rites of ritual slaughter (59). The rebbe asks Bleilip if he is not at least occasionally a believer, and Bleilip wavers before answering yes (72). The phrasing of Bleilip's response and its consequences for thinking about the nature of group and community identity are comparable to a similarly phrased moment in Bernard Malamud's 1958 story "Angel Levine."[31] In Malamud's story, the protagonist is asked if believes that a black Jew named Levine is in fact an angel sent from God: "Believe, do not, yes, no, yes, no.... 'I think you are an angel from God,'" he declares finally (55). The joyous conclusion, affirming the universality of Jewish compassion, is the protagonist's declaration, "Believe me, there are Jews everywhere" (56). In Ozick's paraphrase, however, the universalist denouement is eschewed for something more narrow and difficult, the struggle with God that characterizes Judaic covenant. The rebbe asks if, besides his disbelief, Bleilip sometimes also believes: "'No' Bleilip said; and then: 'Yes'" (72). It is the doubt as much as the belief that links Bleilip to the rebbe, and rather than folding him into a universal community of Jews, Bleilip is declared "bloody as anyone," phrasing that refers to the ancient temple rite of the scapegoat, a scenario of ritual slaughter where otherness is required for the sake of authenticity and purity. To be a Jew is to take responsibility for the otherness of the Jewish community and necessarily requires concomitant outsiders. The gun and the goat both suggest a non-Judaic wilderness, the source and repository of threats to the community.

As a response to Raab's enthusiasm for Jewish American "regrouping," the end of "Bloodshed" replaces institutional Jewish collectivism with a vision that runs much deeper. Picking up on Boyarin's motif of genetics as the *nomos* of diasporic Judaism, we might conclude that whatever Bleilip has in common with the rebbe as a Jew, it is his difference from— signaled by his fear of—the wider world out there in the wilderness. The

hyperbole of the trope of blood in this story, from Bleilip's parents to potential bloodshed in defense of cultural values, suggests that though Bleilip
and the rebbe may have little in common as they go about their daily lives
in America, they are bound together by past suffering and the potential for
future cataclysm. Though I do not mean to suggest that Ozick is currently
a multiculturalist, the strong barriers she draws between Jews and gentiles
and the price her characters pay for crossing those barriers illustrate a Jewishness that is neither an ethnic, nor merely a religious, choice. Rather, it is
an identity of blood, or at least it is so thick as to require the essentializing
metaphor of blood. Thinking about blood in this story, the rejection of the
lures of easy universalism in "Envy" and the compelling representation
of "multiplicity" in "The Pagan Rabbi," we find in Ozick's early fiction
recognition of multiple cultures thick in value and deeper than the vogue
of ethnicity. Multiculturalism, especially in its academic and institutional
forms, presupposes at least an equal plane of value upon which people
from different groups might encounter and learn about one another, but
with Ozick, no such plane exists, and in fact multicultural encounters are
more fundamentally clashes about the value and depth of cultural continuity. Crucially, in Ozick's early fiction, liberal prescriptions for cultural
practice are undercut when characters discover that their individuality is
already underwritten by, or embodied in, a preexisting cultural being.

Until now, scholars of Ozick's fiction have described the cultural divide
running through her work as the historical incongruity of Hebraism and
Hellenism. Without disputing the interpretive efficacy of this dichotomy,
I have shown here that cultural divisions and conflicts also have local and
contemporaneous roots in the America of the author's present. Moreover,
we see that Ozick is attentive to the explicit political arguments about pluralism and multiculturalism of her peers and that her fiction explores with
greater imaginative depth the consequences of liberal and communitarian propositions about race and identity. Precisely because Ozick took a
strong stand on the incommensurability of cultural identities, her work is
virtually unknown among scholars of African American, Native American, Asian American, and Chicana/o literature. Here, I have attempted to
establish a critical perspective for reading Ozick in a multicultural context,
but returning to the formation of multiculturalism itself. I close with the
question, what might we say about Jewish literature in general if we re-
trieve this multicultural encounter?

3

The New, New Pluralism

Religion, Community, and Secularity in *Allegra Goodman's* Kaaterskill Falls

A Ship in a Bottle

During a moment of crisis in Allegra Goodman's novel *Kaaterskill Falls,* Elizabeth Shulman, a Hasidic Jew who has pushed against the boundaries of the *kehilla,* or religious covenant, a little too daringly, muses on the gathering shame and curiosity developing around her: "What a contortionist she must seem to her Kaaterskill neighbors, making a business in Hamilton's back room. What a marvelous object she is to them. A ship in a bottle. How did she get in there? How could she get out?" (237).[1] Elizabeth's metaphor instantly captures two aspects of her quandary, for she is at once subject to scrutiny and trapped. At issue is her decision to open a kosher market in the back room of an existing town store, Hamilton's, in Kaaterskill Falls. The town is decidedly non-Jewish throughout the year, though it reluctantly gives way to Jewish vacationers fleeing the summer heat of urban New York. Elizabeth's desire to open a kosher market is pragmatic, if a bit singular, and at first she receives guarded permission from her clan's rabbi. However, her choice to sell food that is certified kosher from a different clan's rabbi causes a scandal, and her permission is revoked. Suddenly, she goes from being a subject in her own right, a member of the community in good standing, to an object of curiosity and rebuke. An insider, she is transformed not so much into an outsider as a person not fully accepted by the community, the very definition of the word *inappropriate*. As with a ship in a bottle, her community first marvels at her achievement, then pauses to consider the trickery and deception at work in her placement.

It is telling that at the peak of her shame, Elizabeth does not cry out to god, does not fall to her knees in prayer, does not even run for shelter in the space of her traditional domestic duties (though she does, eventually) but instead produces a *metaphor* with which to contemplate her changed state of relations with her community. In fact, it is precisely her literary and artistic bent that consistently sets Elizabeth off from her community, and *Kaaterskill Falls* uses art, literature, and theater to cleave the alluringly profane world from Elizabeth's world of sacred duty. The sons of the clan's head rabbi, Rav Kirshner, are as different as Esau and Jacob, with Jeremy being a literature professor who shares his father's wide-ranging intellect but not his dedicated spiritual heart, in contrast to Isaiah, the drudgey, religious good son who eventually inherits the position of head rabbi when his father dies. For her part, Elizabeth never doubts in god nor wavers in her faith—in contrast to Jeremy—but her interest in Shakespeare, Victorian novels, and Romantic art necessarily lead her to contemplate a secular world with sufficient clarity and closeness as to pique her desire for greater encounter with the secular. Never doubting her own religiosity, she nonetheless doubts the prevailing opinion that the sacred has nothing to learn from the secular. What saves Elizabeth all along is her presumption that there is in fact a distinction between the sacred and the secular, that she knows just where the dividing line lies and what each must mean. Though she may peek over the "wall" of the Kehilla, she is determined never to scale it.

The metaphor of the ship in the bottle also humorously captures the spatial dynamics of Elizabeth's transgression—a "ship in a bottle," "a shop in a shop"—though putting it in these terms reveals more about insider-outsider boundaries than she may presume. The metaphor suggests how boundaries operate like a Möbius strip, where something outside is folded into the inside and the inside line soon becomes the outside. Thus Elizabeth's kosher shop is in the back room of Hamilton's secular sundries store. Though literally an insider, the location of her store marks her quite clearly as an outsider. Ironically, when Elizabeth's customer traffic massively outpaces Hamilton's, he is temporarily the outsider, as bewigged and befrocked Jewesses march past his counter, ignoring him on their way to Elizabeth's. It's a neat trick indeed, but with consequences that push well beyond the claims of insider-outsider status commonly made on behalf of Jewish American ethnicity. Like the ship in the bottle, Elizabeth's store is at once remarkable and inappropriate. What distinguishes her inside position is not the typical Jewish American ethnic trait of self-fashioning and class ascension but rather of a contortion of the dimensions of religiosity to fit within the secular, which nonetheless seem to permit the fullness of the religion. Put more simply, what matters most is not the traversal of boundaries between inside and outside but that qualitative difference of each, where the secular world—Hamilton's store, the "the bottle"—contains, delimits, but remains unaffected by the sacred within, namely Elizabeth, "the ship."

Right away, the status of boundaries between sacred and secular and the enchantment of the secular world through art and literature put Goodman's novel on the same ground as Cynthia Ozick's early fiction, including the stories discussed in chapter 2. Notably, too, Goodman's novel is set during roughly the same time period as Ozick's, the early 1970s, when the politics and public practice of multiculturalism were beginning to sort out into the then tense, now ameliorative compromise of multiculturalism. We recall that Ozick disparaged "ethnicity" and wrote instead about the conflicting values of sacred and secular life, appearing as Hebraism and Hellenism. Goodman's novel addresses "ethnicity," however, by exploring and exploding even that fundamental dichotomy. In her novel, Goodman returns to the 1970s, with seeming naiveté, in order to refract Jewish ethnicity into a distinct spectrum: religion, history, culture, and a disposition toward life that Ozick depicts as essentially spiritual but Goodman demonstrates to be historically contingent and even faltering in the modern world. In *Kaaterskill Falls,* American Judaism, even Orthodox Judaism, is not a bastion of sacred observance in a sea of secularity but is troubled by its facile adoption of that very binary. Goodman's heroine Elizabeth Shulman suffers censure not because she has been led astray by an extant secular world but because her own Jewish community invents, believes in, and fears such a world in the first place.

As with other texts discussed in this book, especially *Portnoy's Complaint* and *Homebody/Kabul, Kaaterskill Falls* locates the conceptual contradictions and political contortions inhering in the social experience of race and ethnicity, and the novel inscribes a potentially richer, more complicated if harder to articulate version of intersubjective recognition. Goodman's motif for this exploration is deceptively simple: Victoriana and Victorian-era separate spheres for men and women, in public and private, in relation to the sacred and the secular. In fact, Goodman, herself a trained scholar of Victorian letters, traces her characters' dilemmas through a conventionally Arnoldian distinction between spontaneity and invention, on the one hand, and law and habituation, on the other. In contrast to Ozick's use of the Hebraism/Hellenism dichotomy, however, Goodman does not naturalize it as the given state of 1970s American celebrations of hedonism, grimly checked by a minority of the morally serious. Instead, Goodman places the dichotomy at the problematic core of American Judaism itself. Different from Roth's satire or Ozick's retrenchment, Goodman depicts a robust plurality of ways of being Jewish and augurs pluralism into a monological orthodoxy.

Kaaterskill Falls refuses to permit sacred and secular to exist as knowable and essentially different categories. Rather, the sacred and the secular in *Kaaterskill Falls* are not only imbricated but also mutually constitutive. The mutual constitution of the sacred and the secular is indeed one of the topics of this chapter. Here I suggest the point only by returning once more to the ship in the bottle. What surprises us about this object of curiosity is the incongruence and seeming impossibility of these two objects in space and time: "A ship? In a bottle?!" But we must also account for the fact that the object status of each is contingent upon the other. The bottle, a utilitarian instrument, is suddenly enchanted by the presence of the ship. The ship, a child's toy connoting fantasy and freedom, is interesting precisely because it is radically constrained and delimited. So, too, are the distinctions of "sacred" and "secular" most visible and perhaps even only existent when put in relation to one another. A kosher grocery store, after all, is hardly a sacred space—at least not until one is slipped into the back of Hamilton's. Yet, more than a differential construction, the sacred and the secular establish their boundaries in opposition to the other, to create semiotically different spaces and different social realities.

The sacred-secular distinction at work in *Kaaterskill Falls,* especially as it is bound up in the politics of nascent multiculturalism, bears the pressures of another tension as well, the distinction between public and private, especially regarding religious and cultural practice and expression. The public practice of religion by Hasidic Jews is in tension with America's prevailing Protestant-derived virtue of religion sequestered to the private sphere. Indeed, the very term *religion* speaks to a mode of worship and practice that sorts public and private. If there is "religion," then there is something that is not religion, which we typically call the secular, but for Hasidic Jews as well as for many other faith communities—and, importantly, non-belief-identified communities and individuals—this distinction of different realms does not apply. As Ozick's "pagan rabbi" learns when he speaks to his "soul," the enticing world of the secular is not only a damnable temptation, it doesn't even really exist. This moral paradox reads as typical contrarian quandary in Ozick, but interpolated into Goodman's novel, the point speaks more to the false distinction between public and private, sacred and secular.

The other sleight-of-hand of *Kaaterskill Falls* is the novel's purposeful conflation of several chronotypes. Within the novel, Victorian-era conventions of domesticity and public culture, not to mention the influence of Victoriana on Elizabeth, coexist with the post-Holocaust, proto-Zionist, and multicultural sensibilities of several different characters. More unusual, the novel's setting in the mid-1970s places all of its meditations on the place of Jewish values in public life squarely in a moment when conflicts over public pluralism were finally resolving into the compromise we now call "multiculturalism." Multiculturalism—be it the command to "celebrate diversity" or the generalized promotion of the dubious virtue of "tolerance" for difference—is an imaginary framework wherein cultures are presumed to be internally coherent and unchanging. At the dawn of the era of multiculturalism, we were taught to value *knowing* about cultures but also to presume that we could never *be* members of cultural groups we are not born into. In the late 1960s and early 1970s, advocates of radical separatism, including political leaders of black, Chicana/o, and Native American coalitions, provoked worried response from advocates of assimilation and liberal pluralism, including many Jews. Advocates of liberal pluralism insisted that while individuals had the utmost freedom to cultural and religious practice within private spaces—the home, a site of worship, a private school—the public sphere, including public schools, hospitals, prisons, and public works projects, must remain free of sectarian cultural or religious expression. Beyond the rhetoric was a raft of policy questions: what holidays should be recognized, what languages spoken, and what cultural histories, religious practices, or dress codes permitted or enforced in public institutions? Radical activists for ethnic separatism argued that public cultural practice was a necessary aspect of decolonization, with some political and educational theorists claiming that cultural recognition in the public sphere was necessary to recuperate the dignity of historically oppressed minorities in the United States. At the same time, the vogue of ethnicity in 1960s and 1970s, combined with the guilt-induced dis-identification from whiteness by many white ethnics, allowed for the compromise ethos of multiculturalism, or the "celebration of diversity," to cite the popular mandate. When it comes to commodifiable cultural objects, *we're all different.*

"Boutique multiculturalism," to use Stanley Fish's term, answers the demand for cultural recognition with a marketplace of consumable culture.[2] Culture, once thought to be a deep-seated way of life, the visible sign marking the boundaries of insiders and outsiders, became instead a sign of credit, purchasing insider status, or just plain obliterating social dividing lines (recall the phrase "it's a black thing—you wouldn't understand" and its subsequent spinoffs. It would be hard to imagine such an unironic assertion of group boundaries today). Simply put, multiculturalism has brought us culture as a series of objects that can be purchased and consumed, including food, music, clothing, flags, film, and tourism. The salutary effect of this transformation is the opportunity for cross-cultural experimentation or the decoupling of "culture" from the idea of "authenticity." At the same time, the marketplace consumption of culture situates national attention about culture strictly to the public sphere, sublimating or outright ignoring residual or emergent cultural practices that exist amid longstanding as well as newly arrived cultural groups in the United States. Culture has come to seem merely *political* and not necessarily personal or involved in the construction of ethics. A truly remarkable aspect of this transformation of culture is the seeming separation of culture from the lived experiences of its adherents. Specifically, in the marketplace of consumer culture, culture's origins in social class, religious difference, and histories of arrival in the United States are elided.

Twenty-five years ago, Werner Sollors argued that "ethnicity" was merely a semiotic expression of difference with no internal content.[3] His insights pertaining to literature were true enough, but only half right when applied to the lived experience of culture. Cultural difference—what we mean by "ethnicity," finally—does perform semiotically in the public sphere but has spiritual, psychological, and affective ramifications in the private. Immediately, this suggested "doubling" of culture as both a public and private phenomenon forces the question: if culture—or religion, or belief, to return to *Kaaterskill Falls*—has a private locus as well as a public performance, how can there ever really be a divide between public and private? The pluralist dictum of the early twentieth century, to be a citizen in public and a Jew, an Irishman, an Italian (and so on) at home, makes no sense, not because identity is corporate or communally held, as many separatist activists argued. Rather, the public/private distinction is thwarted by individually held adherence because individuals are indivisible along public and private lines.

My reference to Ozick above is not incidental, as the prior chapter should have made clear. I argue that Ozick's early fiction from the late 1960s through the mid-1970s is startlingly in step with the more strict versions of pluralism insofar as it represents the failure of any form of Jewishness that is less than essentially covenanted and skewers assimilation or any sort of joining with the non-Jewish crowd as fatal. A perhaps perverse history of Jewish American literature would note Ozick's early stories as the last best shot at Jewish literature's inclusion in the multicultural canon, for third-generation Jewish American writers throughout the 1980s and 1990s represented the intangibility and not the robustness of Jewish identification, in contrast to so much celebrated identitarian writing by Native American, Chicana/o and Latina/o, and African American writers during the same period. Read against this development, Goodman's anachronism is political. Goodman sets her novel during the formation of multiculturalism but grants Jewish life far more particularity and dynamism than is generally recognized in our current multicultural moment. Goodman's pluralistic novel depicts a dynamic Jewishness far from settled or even internally coherent when it comes to issues of history, observance, or Zionism. The novel, then, returns to the moment formative of consensus but brings to it a scene of fundamental dissensus. Doing so, *Kaaterskill Falls* appears to depict what social theorists in the 1970s called the "new pluralism" but in fact interpolates insights from current political theories that challenge the very bases of the new pluralism.[4] Goodman's complex use of time and space and the multiple historical registers affecting her Jewish characters cast considerable doubt on the very premises of multiculturalism.

Kaaterskill Falls is set in the town of Kaaterskill Falls in the Catskill mountains between 1976 and 1978. The town is the summer retreat for several groups of Jews of varying degrees and styles of religiosity, including the fictional Kirshner Hasidim. The novel's central character, Elizabeth Shulman, is a Kirshner, living a conventionally facile religious life with her husband and five daughters, deeply embedded in and entirely at ease with the observance of Jewish law and custom. Indeed, "observance," with its connotation of a subject-object split, mischaracterizes Elizabeth's religiosity. As we learn early in the narrative, "For [Elizabeth] religion is such a habit, ritual so commonplace, that she takes it for granted....Her religious life is not something she can cast off; it's part of her. Its rituals are not rituals to her; not objects, but instincts. She lives inside them and can't hold them up to look at" (54, 57). This simplicity and habit are significant for the outcome of the novel and its meditation on the ethos of pluralization. So habitual is Elizabeth's religiosity that she feels no anxiety over different styles of religion or even secularism. Rather, it is secularity itself that intrigues Elizabeth, who perceives it as a mysterious object for investigation. Indeed, responding to a naive and potentially scandalous comment from her secular neighbor Beatrix, Elizabeth thinks, "Cecil and Beatrix cast a kind of spell. All the rules are different with them," so different that "she doesn't even disapprove of them" (24). This pluralism, supported by a pragmatism—different rules for different people—makes Elizabeth an especially appealing character. Certainly she would be tolerant of us, whatever our professions of belief.

However, Elizabeth's facility with religion is revealed as her blind spot by the novel's end, for she is one of the rare Kirshners who cultivates this ethos. Following an impulse for entrepreneurship, Elizabeth secures permission from the elderly Rav Kirshner to open a small market in Kaaterskill Falls. After a surprisingly successful beginning—the result, ironically, of high demand from visitors in the wake of the Rav's death—the market venture is closed by the succeeding Rav—his son Isaiah—when Elizabeth admits to selling food certified kosher by rabbis other than Kirshner. Elizabeth's transgression results while catering a birthday party for some longtime summer visitors who request kosher food certified by a different rabbi. What does it mean that Elizabeth's openness to different authorities, seemingly a gesture of pluralism, fails within the novel, foreclosing future possibilities? And what kind of pluralism is involved in Elizabeth's action?

The crisis over Elizabeth's decision is framed as a fundamental dilemma of political subjectivity and the implications that follow from that political positioning. American or Kirshner, secular or religious—these are the implicit choices Elizabeth confronts. When she first considers the possibility of opening the store, Elizabeth consults her neighbor Andras, a successful businessman, who reminds her, "This is the United States of America. You can do whatever you damn well please" (271). Is it? Can she? While Hasidic enclaves in Brooklyn and upstate New York do not enjoy the sort of sovereignty Native American tribes do on reservation land, the choice to live apart and according to their own religious laws establishes religious authority as a sovereignty parallel to and superseding American political identification, if not law. Within the Kehilla—the rabbinically sanctioned community, including its communal space—liberal freedom gives way to communitarian affiliation, and individual choice is given up for rabbinical authority. Earlier in the novel, British-born Beatrix reminds her co-national Elizabeth that the Fourth of July is not really her holiday, a comment that ambiguously suggests that nationality as much as religion prevents her from celebrating the ideals of personal freedom embedded in the Constitution. Returning to the clichéd line, "This is America, you can do anything," we arrive at the crux of the multicultural dilemma for political theory: Does American freedom grant you the right to be un-American? Andras's equation of America with personal freedom suggests not only unlimited possibility, but also compulsion—you *should* do what you please.

This is America

Andras's emphatic declaration of the American way is in fact a rare moment when the wider context of the nation and its values are mentioned. Otherwise, the novel presents the world of the Kirshners as tightly circumscribed and self-contained, bearing European or Jewish values but not necessarily "American" values. However, this is an effect of the narrative frame, especially in its focus on women's lives and domestic scenes. Rarely does the

novel leave Kaaterskill Falls to trace the lives of the men who return to the
city during the week as members of the public daily workforce. America is
far more present in the lives of Goodman's characters than is initially evident, but precisely because it is the site of drudgery and merely utilitarian, it
is cast off by the characters themselves on the return drive up the mountain.

However, Goodman also signals that the mountain retreat is itself
America. Indeed, Elizabeth's decision to open a store comes as a startling
if ironic epiphany, at the end of a morning spent looking at American Romantic landscape paintings at the Frederic Church house, Olana. Olana is
a remarkable architectural site, and so it is not surprising that it would occasion romantic epiphany. The museum was built by the renowned American landscape painter and student of Thomas Cole, Frederic Church,
whose paintings of the U.S. landscape, South America, and the Middle
East were famous during his lifetime in the mid-nineteenth century. Late
in his career, Church, like several prominent Hudson River Valley painters before him, traveled to the Middle East and was captivated by the architecture and design motifs of Arabic and Persian buildings. Upon his
return, he began building Olana, now one of the most significant artist's
residences in the United States. Olana was designed by Church himself
to reflect many of the virtues of design he experienced in the East, and the
lavish attention to woodwork and tile resulted in a near-dizzying display
of geometric and kufic-inspired themes running throughout the house.[5]
When Elizabeth first approaches the house, she is surprised to find Olana
not a rustic retreat but a "palace":

> Vast and delicate, its brick and roof tiles set in intricate geometric shapes.
> There are terraces and balconies, fluttering with striped awnings. The whole
> construction outlandish and Arabian, more fanciful than any of the Victo-
> rian spires Elizabeth had seen in the mountains. When they park the car
> and come inside the house, they pass through rooms of treasures; jeweled
> stained glass and Persian carpets the color of dusty rubies. Inlaid tables, and
> marquetry floors, and tapestry cushions, are all intricately patterned. (80)

Elizabeth's fascination with the house has been shared for over a century—
an Arabian architectural jewel set in upstate New York. Scholars working
in areas as diverse as American history, art, religion, and literature have
documented the appropriation of Jerusalem as an allegory for America,

and the Hudson River Valley School painters in particular represented American landscape using biblical motifs of covenant and destiny, while those who traveled to the Middle East framed that historical landscape in terms conducive to American identification. Church's Olana, however, was something of a different order, literalizing the trope of the East and materializing it on the American landscape itself.

The peculiar motif of interiority suggested by the ship in the bottle is certainly amplified and redoubled by Olana and its presence in the novel, and it has something of the quality of a Russian doll as well. Consider the house's exotic and eastern profile on a quintessentially American landscape as well as the appropriation of eastern imagery for Romantic expression. Common enough is the placement of eastern imagery *within* American Romantic poetry, art, and literature, but with Olana, it is the image itself that houses the art—literally, insofar as the house is now the premier museum of Hudson River Valley paintings. The "Moorish" art and architecture for which the house is famous tells its own story about the place of eastern motifs in Church's romanticism. Moorish art and architecture dominated the medieval Iberian peninsula. Also called "Mudejar" or "Mozarabic," the style is characteristic of the historic pluralism that persisted in Spain under Christian rule, when Muslim craftsmen were employed in the construction of Christian architecture or in the conversion of Muslim architecture for Christian use. The "Moorish" style is in fact common throughout the Middle East, and in some places and periods it includes Islamic-styled art produced by Christian craftsmen. Historians call the culture that gave rise to architecture and design originating from Spain as *"convivencia,"* a term that nicely telegraphs the lived aspect of pluralism.[6] Guilds, craftsmen, merchants, religious and political authorities, not to mention worshipers lived in close quarters in Cordoba, Granada, Damascus, and Fez and had no choice but to rely on one another. However, the pluralism embedded in this sort of work is emptied of its specific cultural imbrications when transposed to Olana, as Church himself designed the floral and geometric motifs with a romantic and not specifically a cultural or religious aim. I pause on Church to point out how the romantic art movement in the United States, represented here by Olana, interpolates particular historical and geographic markers for the depiction of a transcendent ideal. In short, what Olana represents in *Kaaterskill Falls* is the American credo: *E Pluribus Unum:* out of many, one.

Elizabeth is primed for romantic encounter. Gazing into Thomas Cole's painting of Kaaterskill Falls, Elizabeth initially thinks it "much more dramatic on canvas" than in real life, but then the painting prompts her memories of her own experience at the falls and decides that "the un-abashed romantic colors are right" (82). Elizabeth, it seems, is the ideal viewer of Romantic art, allowing herself to be transported beyond reality, beyond memory, to an ideal truth transcendent of common experience. She concludes, generously, that Cole's "integrity ... seems to mark the truth in all the other [paintings]" (82). Earlier in the novel we learn that Eliza-beth romanticizes the secular over the religious, but here the truth is yet more ironic: Elizabeth is in fact a Romantic herself. Her romance will not take the form of paganism, like Ozick's Isaac Kornfeld, nor even will she pursue the creative arts, as do the secularists in Ozick's fiction. Rather, she will transform the banal into a calling. In a brilliant moment of ironic anti-climax, Elizabeth become supercharged by her experience of art:

> She has to make something; she has so much energy, she feels strong. Fear-less. . . . Elizabeth looks intently at the painting, that brilliant piece of the world, and gazing at the color and the light of it she feels the desire, as in-tense as prayer. I want—she thinks, and then it comes to her simply, with all the force of her pragmatic soul—I want to open a store. (83)

These lines, which conclude the first section of the novel, stretch the very boundaries of Romantic possibility—finding the transcendent in the mun-dane or transforming the mundane into something transcendent. After all, in what turns out to be a masterful bit of structural anticipation, Goodman has already instructed the reader as to just how banal, how *not* transcendent a ko-sher market is. The novel begins with description of Elizabeth's husband Isaac purchasing challah at the kosher bakery before driving up to Kaaterskill Falls:

> Friday afternoon, Edelman's Bakery in Washington Heights is like the stock exchange—paper numbers strewn across the floor, everybody shouting orders. . . . The air conditioner is feeble, and the bakery is mobbed with sweating customers: the women, in their long skirts and long sleeves, all cov-ered up, even in the heat. The men, just off from work, their faces flushed under their black hats. The bakery floor, and even the walls, are scuffed and dirty, the glass cases empty except for a few babkas on curled wax paper. Edelman's is rich only in the fragrance of its bread. (3)

Bookending section one of the novel with the mundane store—through hectic description or flattening anticlimax—frames how Elizabeth's choices are constrained within the logic of the communal and the domestic. Hers cannot be a quest for individuality, artistic excellence, or even dialectical consciousness. We may even be inclined to regard the idea to open a store as quixotic or falsely romantic and self-deludingly aggrandizing—but for the sincerity of Elizabeth's epiphany. Then there is the question of perspective: if, for many of Goodman's readers and perhaps even Goodman herself, Hasidic women's spaces are limiting, Elizabeth rarely strains against those limits; that her epiphany involves replicating rather than escaping her role as a provider of kosher food and practicality is one of many clues that liberal individualism will not be her liberating destiny. Not that the gendered implications of her options and choices do not matter. Indeed, they are precisely the matter, insofar as—ship in a bottle—novelty, insight, or transcendence occurs through constraint and limitation. Call it "the Kosher Sublime."[7]

Real Jews Are Not Religious

Goodman's novel has been widely celebrated for taking Jewish religious observance seriously, but just as notable, if often overlooked, is the fact that there are few instances of unambivalent religious zeal in *Kaaterskill Falls*. Elizabeth's preparation for Sabbath is typically feverish, her attendance at shul is distracting, and twice while listening to a rabbi's midrash, she feels depressed and oppressed by either the muddle or the rigidity of the speaker's thinking. That said, this novel is not about crises of belief. In contrast, say, to Ozick's "Bloodshed," in which the "secularist" Bleilip confronts the devout rebbe and is united with him only in his capacity for self-doubt, Goodman does not suggest a single spectrum of belief on which all characters plot. Even Elizabeth's secular acquaintances Cecil and Beatrix she perceives not as less religious but as adhering to different rules. And, where Ozick has her rebbe distinguish secular Bleilip as "you" versus the rebbe's religious "us," there is no doubt in Goodman's novel that Jews of differing sects and degrees of observance are nonetheless Jews. In short, whatever the problems that attend varieties of religiosity, they are not problems of Jewish *identity*.

In Ozick's story, kinship served as a hyperbolic symbol of essential Jewishness, where, as with family blood ties, being born into the group means being always and essentially a part of it. However, in Goodman's novel, the trope of kinship does not force but rather precludes the anxiety of identity while pressing a deeper set of questions about the viability of Jewishness in the United States. As already mentioned, the German-born Kirshner rabbi has two sons, both of whom fall short of his lofty and complicated expectations for being Jewish. Though both were raised in the same home, Isaiah follows his father's path as a strictly observant Kirshner, while Jeremy inherits his parent's philosophical bent, but without Jewish observance. After the Rav dies, there is no question who will inherit leadership of the clan, but the question of who holds the moral endorsement of their dead father is partly addressed in his will. To Isaiah, he leaves his house and headquarters. To Jeremy, he leaves all his books, including his treasured library of Jewish learning, but also books on art, philosophy, and literature. Though property seems at first to cleave along the lines of Hebraism and Hellenism (the functional house and legalistic role of leadership versus the broad collection of sacred and secular texts), it turns out to be a deferral of judgment after all. Rather than bequeathing an inheritance, the Rav leaves behind a quandary and a deferral of judgment. Each brother was wounded in his own way by his father's disapproval while he was alive, and in death the inheritance marks each as somehow incomplete.

In fact, the cleavage of art and learning, sometimes marked as secular and sacred in the novel, runs deep throughout the community, and indeed it turns out to be a problem for every Jew in the novel and perhaps even for Jewishness itself. Besides the Rav's family, Nina and Andras are a bleakly mismatched couple, she yearning for but rarely finding full satisfaction in religiosity, he tending toward existentialism but with a dread of mortality. The couple afflict their teenage daughter Renee, alternatively demanding pious rectitude and granting soulless release. And, as mentioned above, Elizabeth's own passion for Romantic art does not so much conflict with her religious practice as it clarifies its banality, in contrast to husband Isaac's singleminded absorption in meticulous religious observance. Competing values animating the different households may be analyzable in terms of gender, but looming over that dynamic is the pressure of history, specifically the Holocaust. In the Rav's own

home, we learn that it was his wife Sarah who nurtured the spontaneity and breadth of Jeremy's classical learning throughout his youth until
her death. Though she receives only a brief sketch in the novel, we learn
that Sarah was in fact an ideally integrated woman, at once devoted to
piety with meticulous precision *and* attentive to, even absorbed by, art,
philosophy, and literature. Her goal in raising Jeremy was that he would
"succeed his father, and yet succeed to the position with an extraordinary range of skills" (32). However, we learn too that Sarah's breadth of
learning and interests was once shared by the Rav, before the Holocaust
and the family's flight from Germany: "[Sarah] had lived to see [Jeremy]
ordained as a rabbi, but she died before he received his doctorate. She
had wanted him to achieve both, as his father had so many years before.
She had wanted him to become the rabbi and the scholar that his father
was, or might have been if not for the war" (33). The last line makes the
point, but it is not the most significant one. Here we learn that the war
and subsequent flight to the United States disrupted the continuity and
perhaps harmony of Jewish learning and classical education. The Rav,
for his own part, frequently muses on what is missing in his congregants;
simple, uneducated people with no joy or passion outside of observance,
they have "one thing but not the other." That it is Sarah, the mother, who
promotes this classical education, reorients the inquiry toward gender,
but what does it mean that she wanted Jeremy to be what her husband
once was, "or might have been"?

The phrasing here suggests that the trauma of war and displacement
does not manifest as loss but as separation, or a cleaving that runs right
through families and even through individuals. What once was whole
and integrated is now split and opposed: the one thing or the other, never
both. Mother Sarah is a melancholic presence in Jeremy's life, not because her death is a traumatizing loss in and of itself, but because her
loss suspended the effort of recuperating what was lost to history, thus
consolidating the historical sundering in a single absence. The ambiguous phrase describing the Rav, "the scholar that his father was, or might
have been," leaves it unclear whether or not the Rav was ever a whole and
integrated scholar or if even he had fallen short of the mark, nor is it clear
by the phrasing who shares this perspective—Sarah, the Rav himself, or
the judgmental narrator. The question is significant because at several
points the Rav muses on the failure of his congregants to integrate piety

with worldliness, raising the question as to whether it is in fact a failure of leadership on his part or the sundering produced by history. The fictional Kirshners, like other Hasidic sects in the United States, create a wall around the group—at once imaginary and material—with the ostensible aim of preserving a way of life otherwise lost in the modern world. Jonathan Boyarin has described the anachronism of Hasidim, an amalgam of pre- and postmodern practices, for its resistance to the dominant logic of history and progress, while, beyond atavism, nonetheless participating in the modern world—where else and how else to work and live in urban New York (160–78)?[8] We might add to Boyarin's assessment that the Kirshner community is, in addition to postmodern, also melancholic, preserving not something whole and fulfilled against the ravaging advances of modernity but the very experience of incompleteness itself. If it is the case that Rav Kirshner's followers have "the one thing but not the other" and that the Rav himself never had both "things" due to the intervention of the war, then the boundary of the kehilla marks the community as a melancholic space, identified not with prewar plentitude but postwar loss and irretrievable recovery.

That there should be separation in the first place is one of the striking legacies of the post-Enlightenment changes wrought upon Judaism, first in Europe in the nineteenth century and especially in the United States in the twentieth. Judaism as an identity category is notoriously difficult to pin down. Jews have regarded themselves and have been regarded by others variously as a race, a nation, an ethnicity within a nation, a culture, a civilization, and a religion. Wendy Brown traces this conflation to the French consolidation of the nation under the banner of the *Declaration of the Rights of Man and of the Citizen.*[9] French nationalism struggled to make sense of a number of religious affiliations, regional and provincial loyalties, and guild associations. The invention of the secular state served to consolidate the nation, as it was underwritten by the presumption of a universal, rational "man," who, in the public sphere, could meet and engage with all others in intellectual and moral equality. Other identity affiliations, be they embodied or practiced, were relegated to the private sphere. The spread of Enlightenment "tolerance" for Jews across western Europe "converted" Jews from a people apart to nothing more than a religion, forming modern "Judaism," and subsequent post-emancipation sectarian derivations (Reform, Modern Orthodox, Conservative, Reconstructionist, and so on).

Brown's hypothesis explains the change in Judaism as one from corporate identity to individual identity, as the right to be Jewish was at once granted but constrained to the individual Jew, while Jewish institutions and offices were either eliminated or subordinated to the state. The Jewish "problem" vexing the *Declaration of the Rights of Man and of the Citizen* concerned the Jewish problematization of citizenship itself. Being communally Jewish meant adhering to practices and obeying authorities that were unconducive to statist public virtues and sustaining institutions that competed with the state's regulation of law and order.

Brown continually reminds her readers that her hypothesis applies to Jews in West European Enlightenment states, but Laura Levitt pursues a similar train of thought with respect to East European Jews in the twentieth century.[10] Though East European Jews did not experience the same "Haskallah" or Europe-derived reform of Jewish practice, the sweep of socialism and the concomitant wane in Jewish observance in some quarters led to a self-conscious Jewishness that was not based in traditional Jewish practice. At the same time, observant communities, who, unlike their French and German counterparts remained unemancipated and unfree to integrate in the public sphere as even second-class citizens, persisted as wholly Jewish-identified Jews. Levitt explains that when these East European Jews—socialists in the late nineteenth and early twentieth centuries and Hasidim during and after World War II—emigrated to the United States, they encountered a construct of religion and secularity similar to the West European mode and at odds with the social norms from which they had been uprooted. In the United States, Judaism was a religion, not a social practice, and certainly not a *socialist* practice. Levitt explains that through the mid-twentieth century, the second and third generations of the American Jewish descendants of East European immigrants struggled to "convert" what was a public practice and social sensibility into a private religion. But "religion" is not an easy fit for Jews, and insofar as "secular" was presumed to be the opposite of "religious," Jewish secularists strained against the limits of that term as well.[11] However, as Levitt observes, because "Jewish" is not fundamentally a religion in the post-Enlightenment sense of the word, Jewish secularists ought not be under pressure to justify their claims to culture and tradition.

Indeed, secular Jewish political culture—socialism for many Jews in the United States and Europe in the late nineteenth through the mid-twentieth centuries, neo-Yiddishkeit progressivism in the present day—may be most efficacious if the communal Jewishness has a public and not merely a private life. As Michael Warner explains, writing about the efficacy of queer counterpublics:

> The bourgeois public sphere consists of private persons whose identity is formed in the privacy of the conjugal domestic family and who enter into rational-critical debate around matters common to all by bracketing their embodiment and status. Counterpublics..., on the other hand, are scenes of association and identity that transform the private lives they mediate. These public contexts necessarily entail and bring into being realms of subjectivity outside the conjugal domestic family. Their protocols of discourse and debate remain open to affective and expressive dimensions of language. And their members make their embodiment and status at least partly relevant in a public way by their very participation. (57–58)[12]

Counterpublics can open up new horizons of association and relationality—and, presumably, new politics and ethics—precisely because the sustaining beliefs and practices of their constituents live in the light of day in public and are not merely sequestered in private life. Moreover, in counterpublics, public cultural practice does not (or does not only) represent private lives in public, it also establishes pathways of culture from the public back into the private. In Jewish progressivism, for example, public political activism by Jews has led to a reconstruction of fundamental liturgy, from Ne'ila prayer to the Passover Haggadah to the current movement by some rabbis to rethink *kashrut* through the Slow Foods movement.

Which brings us to the rather delicate problem at the center of Goodman's novel. If Jews have been and once again are able to manifest as a sort of counterpublic with a Jewish sensibility permeating the wider public sphere in general, then the problem for the Jews in Goodman's novel is not an unaccepting and intolerant America but religious Judaism itself. Levitt may be right that the American virtue of the liberal public sphere forces Judaism to reshape tradition and observance as "religion," but in *Kaaterskill Falls,* the onus for change and the responsibility for failing to change is on the Kirshner sect itself.

The New, New Pluralism

Warner's description of a counterpublic is useful for understanding the peculiar appeal of a store for Elizabeth and for making sense of the store as a threat to and within the Kirshner community. Elizabeth's romance of secularism is harmless enough, but secular pragmatism turns out to be another story. If the romance of the secular, felt powerfully at Olana, occupies the place of religious fervor for Elizabeth, the pragmatic reality of actually running her store and sustaining it as a site, not of her own fantasy realized but as a service outlet in the public sphere for a diversity of Jews, has implications that reach back into her private life. It is precisely the collapse of the public into the private that makes the store dangerous, threatening the fabric of Kirshner separatism. Elizabeth's argument with Isaac over the ethics of her pluralism is keenly in tune with not one but two prevailing theories of pluralism. At the outset of her argument, Elizabeth makes a fairly conventional pluralist claim. When Isaac asks, "How can you sell food that you would not eat?" Elizabeth responds, "Is it so terrible to recognize that there are other rabbinical authorities?" (202). Building on her question, she asserts, "Just because you follow the Rav—you don't expect all the others to join you. Other communities have strict standards too. They exist; why pretend otherwise?" and then, "Do my parents in Manchester eat treife [unkosher] meat just because they don't eat food sanctioned by your Rav?" (202). Isaac has no answer for her, primarily because she has tied him in a knot, interweaving a conventional discourse of "recognition" with a question about absolute standards. Herein lies the conundrum of conventional liberal pluralism, typically disparaged as cultural relativism. Granting recognition to the values of different cultures seems to entail the end of absolute truth, but absent "truth," how can one assert any value whatsoever, including the value of pluralist recognition?

Subtly absent from the exchange is Elizabeth's own subject position. Casting her argument at "you" (Isaac) and "your Rav" does not mean that Elizabeth is no longer committed to the clan. Rather, her absence from her own argument demonstrates the one-dimensionality of conventional pluralism, which prioritizes liberal recognition of difference in the public sphere: "you" must recognize "them." Elizabeth challenges Isaac to recognize the independent worth of the value-choices of other sects, but by leaving herself out of the argument, she brackets the dynamism of her role as a conduit of exchange between and among these different value orders. Put another way, she casts her argument in conventional secular terms, but the conflation of the sacred and the secular, including the sacralization of recognition itself, demands a more supple and critical pluralist account of sectarian difference.

Because she is a complicated individual—appealingly like us!—with a dynamic feedback loop between public and private experiences, she embodies a pluralism even more complicated than the one she articulates to Isaac. Goodman narrates the exchange briskly and without narrative comment but subsequently allows a more complicated and elaborate interior contemplation for Elizabeth:

> Admittedly, hers is an ad hominem argument, but it encapsulates what she has come to believe. Elizabeth looks at the question differently now that she has a business. She has taken one opportunity and she can't help taking others. There are other families up for the summer, not just Kirshners. All those other families up for the summer with equal need, equal potential to be customers. She can serve them as well. (202)

Elizabeth considers the important challenge that she is motivated by profit but defends herself by holding out for a more broad yet undefined "success" (202–3). Whatever "success" means, it is something other than exceptional piety or religious correctness. Rather, having created a counterpublic with her store, Elizabeth herself has become a public person, with public responsibilities and opportunities. Without weighing in as to whether she is right or wrong to sell differently certified food, we may say that Elizabeth has significantly altered the relationship binding the kehilla, other Jews, and the non-Jewish world, initiating flows of influence and exchange that are not so easily walled off by religion or contained in separate spheres.

Put another way, Elizabeth upsets not only her community's values but also the preexisting pluralist stasis, inaugurating a deeper and more ramified ethos of pluralization. Describing the difference between the one and the other, William Connolly explains:

> A conventional pluralist celebrates diversity within settled contexts of conflict and collective action....But what about the larger contexts within which the pattern of diversity is set? How plural or monistic are they? To

what extent does a cultural presumption of the normal individual or the preexisting subject precede and confine conventional pluralism? What conceptions of identity (and difference) are taken for granted in pluralist celebrations of "diversity"? (*Ethos* xiii)

In the case of the Kirshners, and perhaps with quasi-sovereign religious communities in general, multiculturalism means asymmetrical relations between insider and outsider. Cecil and Beatrix, Elizabeth's secular friends, can do what they want and garner Elizabeth's admiration precisely because they are liberals and act accordingly, while Elizabeth, for her part, is absorbed by her community. Beatrix's liberalism casts Elizabeth as a finally like-minded creature of interesting but freely chosen religious practice, while for Elizabeth Beatrix may as well come from another world. Because the "contexts of conflict" are "settled" or even do not exist, the different beliefs take on the status of "cultures": observant culture, liberal culture, and, on the fringes of the novel, Anglo-Protestant capitalist culture. Ironically, under an ethos of public multiculturalism, as "cultures" each group's practices attain a sacred status insofar as each is treated with a tender respect. Beatrix and Elizabeth may be fascinated by each other, but neither attempts to appropriate or influence the practices of the other. Jonathan Boyarin's argument advancing a specifically Judaic *nomos,* cited in chapter 2, illuminates the condition of life within the *kehilla* in Goodman's novel as attaining something like a recognizable sacred status under federal law. Boyarin stops short of applying this concept to culture in general, but his legal argument captures the elevation of the importance of cultural difference in the United States since the 1970s: cultural difference came to seem like religious difference in corporate, institutional, and state practices. To be clear, I am referring to the *status* accorded to "culture" under programs of multiculturalism, or what Connolly calls "conventional pluralism," and not to the inner workings of culture. Precisely because cultures are deemed worthy of "recognition" in the public sphere and because, according to Charles Taylor and Will Kymlicka, among others, that recognition is crucial to sustaining the dignity of its adherents in society, multiculturalism treats culture as more than a series of secular choices and rather like religion itself, crucial to the well-being of any given adherent.

However, culture's sacred status within professions of multiculturalism is in constant tension with the concomitant liberal consensus that cultures are freely chosen and may be thus put on, taken off, traded, bought, and sold. In fact, "culture" loses that very status at precisely the moment it begins to circulate as an object of value, either as a material commodity or a commodity with social value. Put another way, "culture" is secular when it circulates, and Elizabeth's role as both a conduit for orthodoxy and a purveyor of kashrut places her on the borders of "culture's" passage from sacred to secular. Elizabeth's selling Kirshner-sanctioned food to Kirshners sustains the status quo, but choosing to set aside her own claims on kashrut in order to sell across cultures in the name of an unspecified altruism and for the sake of an undefined "success" constructs her as a curious individual hewing neither to liberal cultural standards nor to the communitarian ethos of her clan. In just these terms, the contexts of conflict are far from settled. It is not the contact of diverse cultures that occasions problems within pluralism but the way different cultural groups regard each other: "*We* have truth, and we tolerate *your* adherence to something false." The sentiment is easy enough to shrug off when cast from the outside, but when groups are opened to one another so that the truth claims of others are called into question as the very basis of their encounter, it is more than tense: it may be perceived as a threat to the very basis of the group. It would be one thing for Elizabeth to sell only Kirshner-sanctioned food to non-Kirshners; this practice implicitly calls into question the validity of other Jews' standards of kashrut without calling the Kirshner standard to question. It is another matter for her, a Kirshner, to sell non-Kirshner food, thereby casting doubt on the singular authority of the Kirshner sanction.

The question may be asked: Is this not a bit petty? Is this not the narcissism of small differences at work? Is there not a way to recuperate the differences between these fine distinctions into a yet more rich and robust ethos of pluralism? In his recent work on pluralism, Connolly describes the conditions and attitudes necessary for a full-fledged "multi-dimensional" pluralism, but it reads less as a recipe for success than as a diagnosis of pluralism's failure in *Kaaterskill Falls*.[13] Connolly explains that for pluralism to be successful in a dynamic society, "three interceded ingredients are critical: multidimensional pluralization, positive cultivation of the element of dissonance or mystery within faith, and a secondary practice of relational modesty added to devotional rituals" (61). The third in the list of pluralist practices is occasioned by the close quarters of Kaaterskill Falls, where Jews of different sects attend a common synagogue and send their children to a common day camp. However, the cultivation of mystery within faith that occasions crises for several of the characters, from Elizabeth's searching romanticism to Andras's existential dread to Jeremy's attempt to find an equivalent to Judaism in secular academia. In either case, characters may be open to "mystery" but garner doubt instead.

Certainly there is little "relational modesty" among the various Jews in *Kaaterskill Falls*. Though they all get along well enough and certainly tolerate one another, tolerance is the charitable impulse of arrogant self-regard and not modesty. We may recall Connolly's delightful phrase, "creedal ventilation," which appropriately if optimistically captures the summertime lifestyle of the Jews of Kaaterskill, where doors and windows stay open throughout the day, children run across one another's lawns, and adults sip ice tea on the porch. According to Connolly, beliefs are aired out—ventilated—not only when different faith groups are exposed to one another's beliefs but also when challenges emerge from within a faith group. Connolly gives the example of coming out as gay within a faith community and the subsequent theological struggle such an event engenders, a process that forces creed to confront world, but before we even get to this challenging scenario, in *Kaaterskill Falls* we are stuck with the seemingly simple but finally intolerable challenge of a plurality of kashrut standards.

The World, the Bottle, and the Jug

The pluralist challenge in Goodman's novel is not, after all, the individual tolerance for or even recognition of the worth of other cultures or faith groups but rather the acceptability of any liberal-centered project of recognition in a tightly controlled communal environment. The irony of the problem is highlighted by the fact that Elizabeth is apparently that very rare instance among the Kirshners of an observant Jew who has the one thing *and* the other, both learning and worldliness or, in conventional terms, the sacred and secular. In fact, parsing it this way borrows from the Rav's terminology of melancholy and loss and seems to miss the mark with Elizabeth. The Rav longs for the integration of sacred and secular, but precisely by dividing the two into categories this way, he—like his sons—will always be in one category or the other: "Such a simple people. They are afraid of the mind, and to read. They keep one thing, the religious, alive. It is the most important, but they have lost the other. They have forgotten poetry. There is not one of them who is what we used to call an Educated Man" (106). Is the poetry separate from liturgy? Is the liturgical also the poetic—or is it the reverse, as in the case of Elizabeth's Romanticism? The Rav's great failing is that while he values the ventilation of sectarian belief with worldly knowledge, he is unable to find a way to nurture that ventilation in his community. It is telling that the narrative allows the elder Rav's thoughts to emerge only when he is being transported in an ambulance, en route between the *kehilla* and a public hospital. Upon his death, the division of his kingdom between his two sons—books to his secular son Jeremy, religious rule to the pious Isaac—further separates the spheres rather than integrates them. As expected, the succeeding Rav, his son Isaiah, takes just the opposite stand—against worldliness, he explicitly condemns not only the secularism of the world at large but the differing pieties of other Hasidic Jewish communities too. While for the Rav, the war and emigration sunder the possibility of being a whole, fully cultivated Jew from the possibility of religious observation and devotion, we see in Elizabeth precisely that joining.

Goodman underlines the issue with Elizabeth's sense that her Judaism is not an object of observance but a fundamental component of *who she is*. This initially may strike us as an ideal joining of coterminous points of religious and personal identity—the individual defined by her community, the community embodied in an individual. However, Kirshner religiosity is anti-individual; or, better, religion and individuality can only cohere within the sanctified space of the Kehilla—the certified dominion of Kirshner authority. Here, the erasure of the subject/object distinction is at once the boon and the bane of Elizabeth's facility with the multisectarian and secular world of Kaaterskill and New York at large. Totally at ease with religion, she is likewise at ease to view the nonreligious world, with no fear of the erosion of faith. It's not faith. There's no mystery. And there too is the bane. Because her religious life is instinct rather than mystery, she conflates her self with Judaism, allows the two to appear coeval. In this way, she may in fact embody the lost ideal of Judaism described by Levitt, when European Jews had not yet transformed their social, cultural, and political way of life into an American-style religion.

Elizabeth's "ship in a bottle" analogy finally indicates the stunted relationship between the *kehilla* and the outside world: in it but not of it, able to look on while remaining untouched, curious to those on the outside but intact and undisturbed on the inside. The image calls to mind Ralph Ellison's famous analogy of "the world and the jug," deployed in a rejoinder to Irving Howe's now-notorious critique of Ellison's cosmopolitanism. Howe criticized Ellison for not writing with an interiorized sense of African American life, to which Ellison responded by accusing Howe of "writing in blackface," for speaking on behalf of a caricature of African American experience.[14] Ellison rejected Howe's crude and reductive pluralism, projecting as it did "black experience" and "white experience" (notably, not "Jewish experience") with a more nuanced cosmopolitanism. Ellison claimed that Howe would have him and other black writers stymied by segregation, destined to know and write about only the black experience. In contrast, Ellison describes his experience of segregation during his southern childhood as like living life in a clear jug, through which he was separate from but wholly aware of the world around. In this way, despite the experience of segregation he claimed the freedom to draw from the whole of the American and European literary traditions as it suited him. Goodman complicates the metaphor, however: Elizabeth's pluralism—the equivalent of cosmopolitanism in Ellison—results in her isolation, in the community but no longer totally of it.

By the end, Elizabeth's solution to her problem is symptomatic of how the community polices her desire. After her shaming loss of the store when the new Rav revokes its kosher status, she comforts herself (and thus exposes her anxiety) with piety: "She will bind herself with the commandments. She will not fold herself in a tallis, but like [Isaac] she will fold herself in prayer.... And there is beauty in this. Such observance is ordinary to her mind, but there is something beautiful in the constant conscious and unconscious work, the labor of it, ornamenting each day with prayer, dedicating each month, and season, and every act, to God" (254, 311). It is a good line, but it betrays the disciplinary struggle within. The first word, "And," suggests an evaluation of devotion that is not devotion itself—a point of critical removal or the reservation of a personal space apart. The vague contrast of "ordinary" with "something beautiful" suggests an unfulfilled desire for the sublime. The sublime experience is an integrating one in this novel—the centering of the self through an experience with the transcendent. Thinking on the beauty of the Kaaterskill Falls—the waterfall itself—one character reflects, "I remember looking up at the falls, and everything rushing and white and beautiful. You looked up there and you felt that you could do anything. That absolutely nothing could ever stop you. Do you know what I mean?" (323). Elizabeth does indeed, having had the Romantic inspiration to open her store in the first place while viewing the Cole painting of the falls. That you *could* do anything does not mean that you *should*, however, and precisely because religious "culture" instructs and guides personal behavior, plural possibilities are an oxymoron. Rather, pluralism for Elizabeth, as it is for Ozick's characters, is a catalogue of all the things she can never be.

The novel ends with a discussion of the most apt translation for the Havdalah closing prayer, which Isaac conventionally hears as "Blessed be he who separates the holy from the profane." Elizabeth moderates with "the sacred from the secular," a milder but equally conventional formula. The last word goes to a heretofore minor character, the conservative rabbi Sobel, who offers his translation: "the transcendent moment from the workaday world." (324). The discussion itself is a model of pluralist dialogue expressed with an ethics of care. But there is no denying that Sobel's formula, despite its parallelism, locates the transcendent—what Elizabeth ardently longs for—outside the received formulas of a community where the separation of sacred and secular is commanded rather than chosen.

Kaaterskill Falls enriches our understanding of the limitations and possibilities of 1970s-era pluralism due to its anachronism—both its retrospection and its overlay of Victorian-era themes and virtues onto a modern plot. To paraphrase a recurring motif, the novel is set in but is not of the 1970s. With its focus on pluralism in American Jewish life, Goodman's novel unhinges debates about the ethics of pluralism from coterminous debates about ethnicity, assimilation, and identity politics: within its orbit, those debates are moot; everyone is Jewish. *Portnoy's Complaint,* though caustic satire, does not advance readers into a better understanding of intersubjective and intercultural recognition but rather leaves the old terms and practices intact, if sullied and exhausted. Ozick, for her part, likewise leaves prevailing social frameworks of group difference intact, reserving only for Judaism a claim for moral truth. By linking the three novels in this first section, I intend to show at least one lesson of the 1970s: rather than define itself within the given social frameworks of identity, Jewish American writers would have to—and did—liberate literature from them.

Lore Segal's novel, *Her First American,* the subject of chapter 4, evades the grip of historically determined identities and the fraught politics of recognition through literal elisions of the political, championing an ethics of human empathy and leaving merely a blank space for politics. International human rights falls into that blank space and thus out of the novel, despite its centrality to the novel's plot, but in chapter 5, on Tony Kushner's play *Homebody/Kabul,* I explore how Kushner transcribes politics directly across a field of ethics, yielding a compelling account of human recognition. In the 1960s and 1970s, Jewish writers critiqued and attempted to revise the developing consensus on civil rights, though as a consequence of that dissent Jewish literature fell out of categories of multiculturalism and, more importantly, out of the subsequent conversations on the politics and ethics of race, rights, and recognition. At present, Jewish writers are addressing a global discourse of rights and recognition: international human rights and the commodification of cultural difference. This literature, some of it discussed in the following chapters, is an urgent meditation on these topics, an urgent address to a discourse again in need of critical interruption.

Part II

Recognition, Rights, and Responsibility

4

Recognition and Effacement in Lore Segal's *Her First American*

Protocol

Near the beginning of Lore Segal's *Her First American,* Carter Bayoux, a middle-aged, depressive African American journalist and erstwhile diplomat sends the novel's heroine, Ilka Weissnix, a telegram announcing his basic life philosophy: "PROTOCOL IS THE ART OF NOT RE-PEAT NOT LIVING BY NATURAL HUMAN FEELING" (41).[1] The telegram illustrates Carter's sincere cynicism, the oxymoronic attitude attending political processes of give and take, whether local or national, in D.C. or the UN, during the novel's present time of the 1950s or our own moment. Carter would know. Covering the United Nations for the fictional newspaper *The Harlem Herald* in the 1950s, Carter is a witness to and an occasional participant in the most hotly contested debates at the UN Commission on Human Rights, including the NAACP's petition to the UN to investigate rights abuses in Mississippi and Alabama, the polarizing debates on Israel's occupation of the Palestinian territories, the mediation of the Suez Canal crisis of 1956, and African decolonization throughout the decade. Protocol may guide the give and take in order to curtail the otherwise seething hostility, racism, and political hegemony that attends these affairs, but protocol also has its obvious costs, as Carter's odd formulation reveals: "PROTOCOL IS THE ART OF NOT RE- PEAT NOT LIVING...." The repetition signals how protocol requires "not living" as the price for participating in bare-knuckle politics, while a different sort of lifelessness is protocol's grim reward—Carter's elec- tion to the league of the few, the cosmopolitan black men who circulate in elite intellectual circles, cut off from the wider reality of black life in the United States. Carter's urbanity and his deployment of protocol in nearly all situations smoothes his passage through a rough environment, where it otherwise may be hard to be an intellectual black man who is not drawn into either the compromises of middle-class domestic life or the rough battles for civil rights and social recognition in the United States. Carter's protocol amounts to an anti-politics, and despite his rage over racism and his drunken meditations on white hegemony, his refusal to engage *with* political others, *as* a man of politics, traps him in an economy of feeling and beyond the economies of political power. Likewise, *Her First Ameri- can* is an urbane novel, traveling an equally smooth path through tempes- tuous times and places. Though it invokes topics of slavery, segregation, the Holocaust, Israel, and American anti-Semitism, it bears neither anger, nor resentment, nor guilt, somehow side-stepping what we've come to ex- pect as the "natural human feeling" of Jewish American literature. In this way the novel too is set in a raw political moment in American Jewish life: During the decades when Jewish Americans were beginning to settle on a vocabulary for talking about the Holocaust and when liberalism was being tested against other forms of political recognition, Segal's characters suffer for lack of political rights and social recognition, yet evade all ave- nues for pursuing either remedy.

A recurring motif of *Her First American* is "interruption." The novel's closing lines note a gathering of black cultural nationalists eulogizing Car- ter, pausing just briefly when "Ilka interrupted" with her own humanizing homage. This tableau, with the Jewish voice interrupting without neces- sarily altering the discourse, may characterize the novel as a whole and, as I have been arguing, describes the work of several of the texts examined in this book. This book is about literature that intervenes in discourses of race and rights and exposes their basic premises and implications. In the 1970s and again in the 1980s, as social identities are reified and social policies legislated and as a new regime of race and rights displaces the old, new orders of cynicism, exploitation, and social hierarchy emerge in social policy and discourse. In the second half of this book, I examine literature's interruption of that emerging consensus.

Though *Her First American* obviously narrates the mutual attention and suspicion between African Americans and American Jews after the Second World War, the novel's insights extend to the very heart of the political and philosophical paradoxes inhering in concepts of "rights" and "recognition." Though often operating in tandem, these two concepts suggest very different ways of securing public status and social freedom: ethical and political. Rights—civil or human—are simultaneously inherent and universal as well as acquired and local; both the basis for ethics and, insofar as rights violations are common and ubiquitous, evidence of the failure of ethics. Recognition is equally frustrating, seeming to bypass the political implications of "rights" by opening up language for the mutual affirmation of humanity, yet social programs for recognition, including affirmative action or multicultural education, are necessarily political. Over the second half of the twentieth century, American Jews and Jewish institutions worked within and in response to these paradoxes, successfully securing both rights and recognition through normative, liberal, and state-based claims. Other domestic minority groups and postcolonial nationalists around the world have critiqued these regimes of rights and recognition, and as culture has become increasingly a global commodity and nations have become resources of human capital, the paradoxes of rights and recognition have drawn renewed, vigorous attention from theorists and practitioners. In the second half of this book I examine literature that disrupts, deepens, or (again) satirizes both the political and cultural conundrums of rights and recognition and the cultural and theoretical response.

Her First American depicts a series of events in which parallel efforts by Jewish and African American rights activists began to cross: The formation of the UN Human Rights Commission, the establishment of the state of Israel, and the Nuremberg Trials brought worldwide attention to the breadth and depth of Jewish suffering and the mechanisms for legal justice and future normalization of and protection for Jews around the world. In the United States, corporate and university quotas for Jews disappeared, and Jewish social and political ascension for Jews proceeded. At the same time, African Americans, who found American Jews to be largely allied in their quest for rights and recognition, saw many of their petitions to the UN Human Rights Commission stymied, while African decolonization agitated and occasionally polarized the position of African Americans. Rights and recognition may have been mechanisms for universal human protection, but they advanced Jewish and African American interests quite differently. This social chiasmus is in fact the crux of Segal's novel, and though her work does not posit a deeper philosophical conception—and hence a way out—of the paradoxes of rights and recognition, it interrupts the narrative crossing of African Americans and Jewish Americans in the 1950s long enough to consider their conjoining and mutuality.

Her First American consistently looks abroad, to Europe's recent crimes, international diplomacy, and the daily debate about rights and recognition at the UN. In doing so, the novel alludes to the developing global consciousness of human rights, third-world autonomy, and international political recognition in the 1950s. However, rarely does the novel link these concerns to the domestic scene. For instance, there is virtually no mention of the American South and its seething white supremacist reaction to a nascent civil rights movement, which was occurring during the novel's present time. As the novel spans the mid-1950s through the early 1960s, it overlaps the development of the modern civil rights movement, from its origins in protests for equality and faith in political process to the mainstreaming of militancy and separatism. Put another way, the novel begins during the peak of black and Jewish cooperation on liberal issues of rights and ends with the rise of black nationalism, a subject of consternation for liberal Jews and the beginning of the end of the fabled black-Jewish alliance. As such, it moves through and comments on the efficacy of political thinking underlying these social developments but insists on prioritizing an ethics of recognition and care superseding the political.

The elision of social inequalities and political responses in this novel about an African American and a Jewish émigré opens up a space for the romance between Carter and Ilka, but that space finally collapses underneath the pressures of the novel's social and political context. At the beginning of the novel, Carter's protocol and Ilka's immigrant naiveté permit a flourishing though unpromising relationship, but the end finds Ilka nearly as hard-boiled as Carter and Carter dying from the pressure of holding history at bay. I do not posit that Segal affirms some thesis or mode of either political or ethical recognition; instead I investigate what costs are incurred for the characters, and for literature itself, for *not* passing the story of a life through the normative political designations of social identity. Segal's elision of Jewish and African American history is a way of holding off the most conventional sorts of plot points and character traits—the midcentury Angry Black Man, the universalizable Jewish Survivor—and the elision amounts to an effacement of the social relevance of race. By "effacement" I suggest a swerve away from both a politics and an ethics of social identification, where the face of the other is both the metonym for ethical recognition and the synecdoche for social race. Segal's novel effaces a politics of race that would otherwise require her characters to contend with the differing social histories and contemporary pressures of "black" and "Jew" and likewise forgoes a more trenchant ethics of recognition that would have raced characters find meaning in commonly plotted historical experiences of dispossession, disenfranchisement, or social alienation.

When race is effaced, what kind of relationship, what kind of story remains? It turns out that it is the story of effacement itself, or the temporary interruption of a gathering social moment that culminates in the late 1960s, when race became *the* salient way of registering social selves. Indeed, the closing words of the novel are "Ilka interrupted," underscoring the novel's own awareness of its limited ability to hold off the inevitable rise of nationalist scripts that would subsequently plot so much ethnic American literature (287). Lacking a common language, not to mention a common optics of race, Carter and Ilka proceed as if one were not necessary, as if the simple capacity of care, compassion, and mercy were sufficient. The novel succeeds insofar as it marks all that it cannot contain, but its bleak engagement of the political with the ethical leaves much work undone. The next two chapters, on Kushner and Shteyngart, will examine what an ethical engagement with the political looks like, for better—Kushner's dramatization—or worse—Shteyngart's satirical novel—but here we examine how Segal's attempt to sustain a characterization independent of the political necessarily leaves a blank space in her writing.

Though the novel's surprising reticence to confront its social context head-on will be the sustained topic of this chapter, we begin here by observing Carter's rationale: being an intellectual, light-skinned, educated African American seething with anger over American racism while also seizing the opportunities his education and charisma afford him requires cloaking his true self to the world and growing callous to racial slights and overt insults. Contrasting worlds with and without protocol, Carter's telegram to Ilka continues:

BUMP INTO A LONDONER AND HE BEGS YOUR PARDON SO YOU BEG HIS PARDON STOP LONDON RUNS ON PROTO-COL BUT A NEW YORKER BUMPS INTO YOU AND KNOCKS YOU DOWN AND TELLS YOU TO WATCH WHERE YOURE GOING SO YOU KNOCK HIM DOWN AND HE KILLS YOU AND YOU KILL HIM BACK STOP NEW YORK RUNS ON NATURAL HUMAN FEELING STOP. (41)

Close readers of Segal may note some ironic space between the writer and Carter, as Ilka and Segal herself spent some difficult years in England after escaping Austria via the 1939 *Kindertransport,* documented in her riveting memoir *Other People's Houses.*[2] But for Carter, London's stiff upper lip suits him fine. His "protocol" is a version of disengaged engagement, where political actors wear civil masks to hide their brutal anger. In Carter's scenario, "protocol" has an ambivalently ameliorative effect, staunching rage but casting a shell over one's being. Carter's scenario calls to mind two similar scenarios that go far in explaining the double binds of "protocol" and lead us to the core question of this chapter: Can there be a form of recognition outside of the sphere of the political?

Carter's New York Manichean allegory recalls the opening of *Invisible Man* by Carter's contemporary, Ralph Ellison, where the price paid for living at a distance from the political givens of identity categories is invisibility.[3] In the early pages of *Invisible Man,* Ellison's narrator describes a scenario nearly identical to Carter's paradigm of a world without protocol. The narrator bumps shoulders with a stranger on the street and becomes so enraged that he brutally assaults the man. At the moment he pulls out his knife to finish the man off, he realizes, "the man had not *seen* me, actually;...he, as far as he knew, was in the midst of a walking nightmare!" (4). Ellison's scenario maps onto but inverts Carter's. Invisible Man remains unseen not because he wears the mask of protocol but because he has wrestled free from all of the pat political designations heaped on him over the course of his life. He is no longer the Booker T. Washington figure of his youthful valedictorian days, nor the native informant to a hegemonic communist party, and he has escaped the clutches of the black nationalist, Ras the Destroyer. But for all that freedom *from* identification, he remains unseen and unrecognizable to others around him and lacks a public outlet for his rage. The genius of the novel, of course, is that the reader recognizes the character, if not with the political designation "black man," then with the more universal if subtle "lower frequencies" of common humanity (Ellison 581).

The play of recognizability between character and novel for Ellison illustrates a truth about recognition itself: recognition is, among other things, a narrative project, garnered by texts that declaim their humanity in terms that the reader is apt to already honor or value—and probably already shares. Ellison's narrator escapes the plot of other racial stories, and his successful narration of that escape *produces* him as a recognizable subject for the reader. In our current moment, the best exemplar of writing to claim recognition may be Barack Obama's autobiography, *Dreams of My Father,* which rather brilliantly hails familiar typologies of the assimilative immigrant and the angry black man, reconciling the two in Obama's political vocation, which involves dialectical integration with American social structures and progressive revision of those structures.[4]

Ellison's version of a recognizable life may be more appealing for its evasion of political traps, but his "lower frequencies" lack the generative rhetorical capacity of a more politicized tale. Obama's ability to synthesize known types and resignify them is part of the reason he ended up in the White House, while Ellison's character's evasion of pat foundations of identity leaves him literally in the basement. A person cannot live a public life on the lower frequencies, and a political identity appears to be necessary for advancing personal experiences and affective commitments into public progressive action. In contrast, Obama's dialectical fusion of immigrant and American-urban tales illuminated the term *African American* in a revisionary way that suggested political "change" during the 2008 election, but this claim on the semantic field of black identity does not exempt the president or anyone else from further revisionary and racist claims. No matter how you define a black political identity, it still remains a political and politicizable identity. Returning to Carter, then, protocol is a politics of disengagement, where political names and political action are evaded, and the only recognition is a mutual avoidance of conflict before each agent goes his or her own way. The semantic field of race remains the same, and Carter still remains subject to it, with no political claim with which to revise it and no narrative from within which to contest it.

Carter sends his telegram at the end of a long, awkward evening with Ilka, whom he barely knows. A young Viennese Jewish woman who has escaped from Europe, Ilka is as naive as Carter is worldly and does not even realize that Carter is, according to the American racial idioms, a "Negro." Thus, when they attend a wedding party and Carter suffers what he considers a racial insult by the groom, she cannot really fathom his outrage, and as he subsequently unloads his anger over American racism, she begins to understand that he might be telling her he is a black man. Carter, it turns out, had previously slept with the bride, who is white, and he is outraged when the groom (also white) tells him that he knows "about your sleeping with her...and it's all *right*" (35). After Carter storms out of the party with Ilka reluctantly in tow, he tells her what the groom was *really* saying: "He was saying, 'I am a white liberal and you're a black son of a bitch'" (40). Carter's pronouncement teaches Ilka how to see him—"he is definitely a Negro, thought Ilka with relief"—and what she sees endows his words with meaning, a dialectic of recognition where optics and discourse are conjoined to produce Carter's politically recognizable self at precisely the moment he would abdicate it (40). The groom's fault, Carter insists, is that he failed to observe protocol, which in this instance means he failed to suppress the most obvious and significant personal facts between himself and Carter.

Between Carter's protocol and Ellison's invisibility, we are left with a conundrum at the heart of projects of political recognition, one that still affects us to this day. If, when observing you, I take note of your race, gender, or visible sign of religion, do I treat you as more or less of a human than if I take note of you as a singular individual? Does taking note of your individuality mean precisely that—that I catalogue your race, gender, religion, and so on? Or is the reverse true—ought I see you independent of the signs of social identity? There seems to be a double bind, a corollary to Dubois's famed double-consciousness, where calling attention to race or seeing above, beyond, or through race means negating, hyperbolizing, or otherwise straining the social categories of public life. During the last three decades, we have developed a sensitive grammar for identities, so that identity is the politically salient, salutary, yet still contested mode of political recognition. If I expect you to see my "race," it means I expect you to see me in the here and now, but it also means I expect you to know my history. And racial, ethnic, religious, gender, or sexual affiliation may be the way of claiming a seat at a significantly tilted roundtable of political wrangling. No politicized identity, no seat at the table.

Since the institutionalization of multiculturalism and the advances made by feminism, the politics of recognition involve seeing the vectors of identity in the other and requires taking the public claims of the group seriously. In good part, the politics of recognition *is* a politics because it requires give and take—giving up some measure of individuality for the gains made through and on behalf of a group, while the group asks the ruling regime for public rights, benefits, and protections. For feminists, cultural nationalists, or gay activists (to name a but a few examples), asserting the primacy of identity helps change the rules of public life, making discrimination based on such identities increasingly untenable. For democratic advancement of civil rights and human rights, the question is persistently troubling. As one French liberal put it, upon extending rights to Jews at the end of the eighteenth century, "We must refuse everything to the Jews as a nation and accord everything to Jews as individuals."[5] With the spread of liberal rights, everyone counts, but also everyone is reduced to their mere countability, their barest individuality. The commensurate politics to this liberal individualism occurs at the voting booth every two or four years or in the expression of opinions to pollsters, processes that allow one to feel counted. But what of the count of the uncounted, as Jacques Rancière puts it, those aspects of experience, social location, or conditions of social abjection that are outside of polity?[6] For black Americans in the 1950s, blackness itself was the basis of discrimination, processes that rendered millions of people "uncounted," outside the sphere of political recognition, a situation that drastically changed in the 1960s with the re-signification of blackness as "Afro-American" and with the rhetoric of cultural nationalism. At the opening of *Her First American* in the mid-1950s, Carter has already spent decades in close proximity to political power working for the federal government and then at the UN, but always with the knowledge that his racialization remains outside of the sphere of the consensus-building norms of the State Department and the UN. Carter's protocol begins to make sense, as a mode of remaining proximate to and countable within normative political power and as a way of precluding a more radical reaction to racism that would remain unrecognized according to liberal norms.

The novel's work of effacement is more complicated than it seems, well, on the face of it. Indeed, the cover of the 2004 paperback edition features a photograph of a man with his back to the reader, whose graying, close-cropped hair and tan-toned skin ambiguously hint at a nonwhite identity, but with the face averted, how can we know? Better, the cover photo's effacement prompts a desire to see the face, perhaps followed by a self-critique of the dubious assumption that seeing the face would clarify the subject's race. But the subject of effacement becomes more ironic still when we learn that Segal's Carter is based on a real person, Horace Cayton, and that several passages from the novel intersect with and revise Cayton's 1965 autobiography *Long Old Road,* which is itself a narrative *de*facement of the social salience of race.[7]

If Cayton's name does not ring a bell, it once would have: Horace Cayton was a prominent sociologist; coauthor with St. Clair Drake of the significant two-volume study of race and labor in Chicago, *Black Metropolis;* longtime friend of Richard Wright; and for decades a columnist for the *Pittsburgh Courier.*[8] How Cayton's name and work have dropped out of academic notice is beyond the scope of this chapter, but that it did drop out is significant. Turning to Cayton's autobiography, we find yet another troubling set of ellipses, lapses of memory, and narrative gaps beyond what Segal depicts, and Cayton was even more troubled by the problems of self-representation and self-disclosure than Carter. About Cayton, Segal has said that he was a brilliant talker but not a gifted writer; while this may account for the limited range of tone across his life story, it does not explain how or why Cayton's life story lacks a sense of direction, purpose, or teleology.[9] In fact, *Long Old Road* ends with Cayton mildly hopeful but lacking any unified statement on either the meaning of his life story or his anxiety-producing passage between cosmopolitan and cultural-nationalist social circles. To conclude an autobiography in 1965 and *not* arrive at a thesis on race and the individual in America—in contrast to contemporaneous theses by Ellison, Baldwin, and Wright and the public self-disclosure of Malcolm X—meant going into discursive exile, outside the settled territory of (differing) modes of racial identification.[10] Segal's novel does not reinscribe Cayton into an archetype of black masculinity but gives a clearer context and ethical rational for Cayton's refusal of archetypes. Several scenes from *Her First American* seem lifted right out of Cayton's autobiography, though according to both Cayton and Segal, the two were writing and sharing their work simultaneously. As Cayton struggles with sustaining an "I" that is not sociologically reducible, Segal honors that struggle, if not its outcome.

If escaping the reductive tendencies of racialization now seems the worthy goal of literature—rescuing the "raw I" from the overwhelming pressure of a "we," as Roth's Coleman Silk puts it in *The Human Stain*—during the novel's present time of the 1950s there was very little room for an "I" to exist socially outside of the domains of racialization.[11] As Hannah Arendt argues in *The Origins of Totalitarianism,* if you are not a member of a race, class, or nation, no one will stand up for your rights. Arendt explains that it is "not the loss of specific rights, then, but the loss of community willing and able to guarantee any rights whatsoever [that] has been the calamity which has befallen ever-increasing numbers of people. Man it turns out can lose all so-called Rights of Man without losing his essential quality as man, his human dignity. Only the loss of polity itself expels him from humanity" (39).[12]

Arendt's point is clear enough in the case of the Jews, Gypsies, and gays and lesbians in Germany, who, when stripped of all political standing, had no political body to appeal to, no one who would recognize their rights. Arendt herself struggled to transpose her reading of European refugee dilemmas to the United States, and I refrain from suggesting that either Ilka or Carter are ever on the verge of the scenarios Arendt describes. Arendt's attempt to account for the status of African Americans is instructive precisely because she gets it wrong. She believed that "if a Negro in a white community is considered a Negro and nothing else, he loses along with his right to equality that freedom of action which is specifically human; all his deeds are now explained as 'necessary' consequences of some 'Negro' qualities; he has become some specimen of an animal species, called man. Much the same happens to those who have lost all distinctive political qualities and have become human beings and nothing else" (43). Arendt's logic depends on understanding "Negro" as a nonpolitical category—a dubious assumption—while she fails to appreciate the possibility of black Americans making other kinds of efficacious claims on political citizenship. Well after the passage of the Civil Rights Act of 1964, black Americans often found the privileges of citizenship, namely civil rights, wedded to a premise of liberalism, when clearly real privilege was rooted in class and racial affiliation—whiteness itself. Black cultural nationalists in the 1960s succeeded in re-signifying blackness so that "black" became a political sign and not a sign of abjection, at the same time denaturalizing whiteness by calling attention to its symbolic place in the semantic field of race.

Among the many who look to Arendt today, Jacques Rancière is especially helpful for transforming Arendt's diagnosis of political recognizability into a thesis for radical democracy. Rancière explains that the remedy for political abjection is the re-signification of the very terminology of the abject: "Political activity...makes visible what had no business being seen, and makes a discourse where once there was only place for noise; it makes understood as discourse what was once only heard as noise" (*Disagreement* 30).[13] So though "Negro" may have been synonymous with rightslessness in the 1950s, black nationalists re-signified blackness through pan-African consciousness in the 1960s, making "Afro-American" a recognizable political signifier. Black people became legible as a people and audible as protesters within a broader, rights-granting polity. However, *Her First American* rejects the black archetypes that invigorate protest as well as the *bildungsroman* frame of *Invisible Man* that would allow an escape from race's overdetermining narrative forms. The novel exposes race as a political field without asserting a political identity, as Arendt and Rancière would recommend. In fact, the novel quite literally elides political identification. In several key moments in the novel, when characters are hailed as political actors or when racial re-signification has the potential to enact new forms of democratic recognizability, the character or the narrative itself inserts ellipses, marking the space of the political while denying politics an effective role in the novel.

Ellipses

For all of Carter's glib protocol, he is clearly depressed, insomniac, and addicted to whisky and sleeping pills. Ilka's struggle to find the right response is at the crux of their relationship, for it becomes the occasion both for her extraordinary care for him and for her growing sense of self—a self she finally needs to save from him. The novel does not reveal directly why Carter is depressed, and this may be its central plot-based ellipsis. On the other hand, if Carter's condition had a cause, then Ilka could devote herself to the cure, which would in turn preclude her maturation and ultimate independence from him. Their relationship thus suggests a political analogue in the fates of blacks and Jews in American society in the 1950s and 1960s, namely social stasis versus social progress. Prophesying the Jewish flight to the suburbs, Carter tells Ilka that even she will seek shelter from falling property values when blacks move into her neighborhood: "'You will be the last to move,' said Carter, 'but you will move'" (93). This lugubrious prediction is both sociological and personal. Carter is telling her she will succumb to the social imperatives of whiteness and that, in time, she, like so many white women before her, will leave him.

Carter's depression and alcoholism frequently result in interrupted dates with Ilka, but the first interruption is prompted by racism. The interruption occurs in the opening pages, when Ilka and Carter first meet for a sandwich in a Nevada pub. Sensing hostility from the other patrons over his temerity in dining with a white woman, Carter sends Ilka up the road, following only after it will appear to others that they are no longer together. Though the two meet up later, the meal never materializes, this time because Ilka needs to return to the station to catch her train. The whole episode is limned by a discussion Carter is having with the bartender when Ilka walks into the pub. The bartender is telling Carter about a man he knows who was injured on the job and received a "lump sum" as compensation (12). Being mangled on the job is worth a "lump sum," the barkeep concludes, so Carter begins toying with him, proposing a federal program wherein all citizens willingly submit to a good government mangling in exchange for a lump sum (12). The riff on the charged themes of reparation and social disadvantage at the very beginning orients the reader to Carter's ironical point of view: playing the trickster, he can draw out the edgy themes of social injustice, all the while allowing his interlocutor to remain in a safe space of his own ignorance, a mobilization of protocol that staunches the ramifications each man's political subjectivity has for the other. However, nothing like this occurs again in the novel, because Carter's usual white society is far too selfconsciously enlightened to be led down this road. In fact, the discussion of reparation and the portrait of white male resentment belong much more to the time of the novel's writing—the late 1960s—then to the narrative's present time. It's as if at the outset Segal nods to her reader to acknowledge the quotidian persistence of racism in the 1950s only to relegate it to the background of Carter's and Ilka's relationship.

Nonetheless, all subsequent interruptions are traceable to racial tension. In this first instance Carter walked a precarious line, balancing his free conscience with the imperative to survive in an unchangeable racist public. Though he abandons his meal with Ilka, he nonetheless clarifies his intention: "I would have liked to make love to you.... When a man hasn't managed to buy a woman dinner, it is not conducive" (21). If romance is forestalled by dinner interrupted, and dinner displaced by white supremacy—a fact Carter knows and Ilka does not—Carter and Ilka proceed in their relationship by negotiating a politics of interruption, wherein the facts of racial designations continually appear and re-form around them.

Segal takes the raw material of this exchange—interracial sex, ellipses, and interruption—and recasts it for a subsequent episode that further reveals the role racial identification does and does not play in the novel's developing account of recognition, the perceived insult at the wedding party and Carter's subsequent explanation of it to Ilka. At the very moment he would seem to decipher the codes of naming—"I'll tell you what he was saying"—and control the names themselves—"white liberal" and "black son of a bitch"—he entirely misses the moment of naming occurring in front of him, Ilka's conferral, "He *is* a Negro." Before she can even visually recognize blackness, Ilka is learning a particular and rarefied black narrative, the tale of the black intellectual. She is becoming increasingly fluent in the black semantic field at the very moment that she is baffled by who and what Carter is. Whether or not Carter is able to imagine that Ilka cannot read the visible signs of race, a more germane problem pertains, namely, how can Carter declare his blackness? In this instance, he tells a story of discrimination wherein his blackness is the overextended identity eclipsing his full self. Ilka deciphers this story to mean that he is the subject of his story—the subject of a story with the unstated title "to be a Negro," but that does not solve the problem of where the authentic self lies: within or beyond social and historical race.

The novel is set at a time when American geography mattered on the world stage. Racial oppression in Mississippi, Arkansas, and Alabama was routinely a topic of concern raised by critics of America at the UN

Commission on Human Rights.[14] To counter criticism, the State Department sent black diplomats and liaisons to the UN and overseas to tell a different story. At the same time, African delegates to the UN, working successfully for decolonization in Africa, observed that they were ultimately more free than black Americans. Though these complicated international vectors may not have registered strongly for uninterested Americans, they regularly made front-page headlines in the nation's two major black newspapers, *The Pittsburgh Courier* and *The Amsterdam News*. Cayton covered the UN for the *Courier,* while Carter held the same beat for *The Amsterdam News'* fictional counterpart, *The Harlem Herald*.[15] Carter's work at the UN as an occasional pinch-hit diplomat places him at the center of several unfolding events significant for the developing international regime of human rights and rights to national self-determination. Many political leaders and intellectuals made overt connections among disparate geographies based on common or symbolically associated histories. As *The Amsterdam News* put it in a 1956 headline, "[Martin Luther] King [Jr.] Says More Interest in Hungarians Than in Al[abama] Negros."[16] And Israel's response to African independence, most notably its skirmish with Egypt over control of the Suez Canal in 1956, placed that country—and American Jewish affiliation—in a precarious position, somewhere between fledgling independence story and colonial holdover. These events create a context for Carter and Ilka's relationship, but strangely, despite the seemingly obvious and compelling mutual interest, they have no place in it.

Ilka's lack of interest in foreign affairs is conspicuously marked by ellipses, thus jettisoning key moments of history and diplomacy from the novel. Though these elisions are frustrating, they neither interrupt the plot nor seem false to Ilka, due to Segal's concentration on characterization and relationship and her swerve away from prevailing master tropes of Jewish American literature, including "identity," "home," and "religion." Put another way, though she is a Jew living in New York and a Holocaust survivor to boot, Ilka has very little in common with Roth's, Ozick's, or Goodman's characters. Thus, when an international crisis is brewing at the UN and Carter brings Ilka along to witness his reporting-cum-diplomacy, Ilka hardly pays attention. The episode begins with Ilka reading a newspaper headline: "'SOVIETS IN BERLIN REFUSE...' said the black headline and underneath it said 'U.S. DENIES...' Ilka raised her face to the face of the man hanging on the same subway strap and said, 'Will it be war?'" (114).

The ellipses here prevent history from actually entering the novel at this point, and they also wall off politics from any standard of value. Without a referent, the headline is cynical politics without content, as both global superpowers are cast as denying some point of interest rather than affirming some claim of right. A man tries to explain the article to Ilka, but she fails to understand. What with the ellipses, the diplomat-speak, and Ilka's growing apathy, we never do find out what international crisis is all about.

At the UN with Carter, Ilka listens to a group of men—some combination of diplomats or reporters, it is never clear—discussing maneuvers by and among African nations, the Chinese, and Israel. Is this the Suez crisis of 1956? A negotiation for Northern African decolonization, also taking place in 1956–57? A debate on human rights sanctions, either against the Soviet Union (advanced by the United States) or against the United States (advanced by the Soviets)? Any of these is quite likely, and all three topics were regularly featured and debated in *The Amsterdam News* and *The Pittsburgh Courier* during the 1950s. And clearly, any of these issues would seem to have more than passing professional interest to Carter, while the subject of human rights, emerging as it does from international responses to the Holocaust, would be right up Ilka's alley. However, "it was at this juncture," the moment for problems to be identified and solutions proffered, "when Ilka faced the immediate danger of learning the facts in this matter, that her spirit removed itself" (118). The passive construction suggests that Ilka cannot help her lack of interest, that she is allergic to international affairs.

For his part, Carter's approach to the diplomatic crises is a rupture of protocol and a seeming breakout into the politics of solidarity. Carter adjourns the diplomatic meeting enthusiastically, declaring, "We've got them by the balls! It's when *you* grab hold of your black power, and not a moment sooner, that we black Americans will be free!" (119). To whom is Carter speaking? Is "black power" specific to African Americans, or is it a source of consciousness suitable for claiming and granting recognition? Who is *"you"*—is he speaking to himself, to the African diplomats in the room? Leaving a blank spot in the text curtails the efficacy of political subjectivity at the very moment of its enunciation.

Turning to Horace Cayton, we find Carter's line appearing as Cayton's maxim at least twice in his newspaper columns and again in *Long Old Road.* In a column on the politics of race in the U.S. State department, he inserts this non sequitur: "Africans will get their freedom when they are strong enough to take it, not before. Freedom has never come on a silver platter. It has to be fought for and won."[17] In another column, on the Suez Canal crisis of 1956, he ventriloquizes the thought: "I asked a famous world's statesman what he really thought. He answered that all of the criteria discussed were important but that was not really the crux of the problem. 'In the final analysis' he said, 'a country is ready for self-rule when it can take it.' This is apparently what Egypt did."[18] The urbane tone drops altogether when he continues, "This act of defying the Western imperialist countries thrilled every colonial country in the world. It destroyed even further the prestige of white European nations whose power, strength and right to rule have been more and more open to question. Win, lose or draw, Egypt's act has destroyed to an extent the hold of Europe and England and their right to rule and determine the fate of Middle East and African peoples. It applied the coup de grace to European control of North Africa."[19] There is a clear note of celebration here, and the high tone of "coup de grace" suggests a sentimental thrill over the African victory.[20]

The admiration for black power in this passage becomes more complicated and ambivalent in *Long Old Road,* where black power is the subject of a debate and not a maxim. Cayton describes meetings with delegates from Tanganyika who believe that their fight for decolonization and independence will necessarily assist Cayton and other African Americans who seek civil rights in the United States.[21] Different from Segal's depiction of Carter's unalloyed affiliation through the conjoining term "black power," Cayton professes a much more reserved affiliation: "'I'm interested in the ambitions of Africans,' I said, 'but it's a sentimental thing. I sympathize with all dark people who have been mistreated by the white man. But how is the freedom of Africans going to help the American Negro?'" (363). It may be difficult to apprehend the intellectual and affective struggle at work in Cayton's seemingly tepid affirmation. Indeed, this semi-nationalism is just the sort of "brotherhood" mocked in Shteyngart's *Absurdistan,* and in nearly the same tone. Cayton's sophistication is in not rushing naively into a false identification with Africans, including his denigration of identification itself as "sentimental." The delegate rejoins that Africans "will break the international color line, a line that runs from Cape Town to your Mississippi" (363). Cayton, however, remains skeptical, sliding between nationalism and cosmopolitanism right up to the end of the memoir. Preparing to leave New York for San Francisco, he declares to "Lore" that he will live as black man and not a cosmopolitan:

> "Will you live as a Negro? Or will you live in between two worlds as you do here?"
>   "I don't know. Until Negroes have total equality, I'll be with them. What I'd like best, as this stage, would be to live as an individual—just a plain American without a special cause. But that's impossible, I guess." (399)

Lore frames the question of how to live with a subtle incoherence. To live "as a Negro" suggests a choice, but living "between two worlds" indicates how the choice is constrained between two polar identities. There is no "outside" to race, and Cayton's own "just a plain American" only begs the question as to what that could mean given the vexed landscape of race in America described in the preceding 398 pages. The autobiography thus ends in the dark on race, recalling the end of Ellison's *Invisible Man*. Cayton finally declares, "I had no identity, but I could no longer risk destroying myself trying to provide one for every other Negro. I must go through some sort of personal catharsis; perhaps in the writing of the book, I might at last find myself" (400–401). By ending in the dark, seeking refuge from the welter of the racial struggle, Cayton conflates the struggle for justice with the struggle for identity, and though this conflation is not sorted out or made sensible in the autobiography, Segal gives it an intelligible sequence in her novel.

Read in the context of Cayton's quandary, Carter's evocation of black power is optimistically pan-African, though his enthusiasm does not pan out. In the space of half a page, Carter and Ilka travel to Washington, D.C., so that Carter can enact his plan, but then they are back on the train to New York with no word as to the outcome. D.C., perhaps like politics in general, remains outside the frame of narration, but on the return trip, Carter is in a foul mood and appears to provoke a racial slight by smoking in the non-smoking car, garnering a disapproving white woman's "tut tut" and then treating the offended reaction as evidence of racism (119). The downward slope from "black power" to the phallic cigarette suggests that we read Carter's frustration in part as a crisis of masculinity, where white men retain the power to approve his sexuality, and that international politics itself summons but then betrays black power.

In *Long Old Road,* Cayton transmits his own aggrieved masculinity and resonates with Eldridge Cleaver, when he explains his frustration with living in New York. Describing one of his first conversations with Lore, Cayton tells her that New York is "big and brutal, gaudy and rich. In a way I love it, but it frightens me.... New York is my bitch. A cruel, lovely bitch I can't enjoy or leave alone" (377), and he follows up immediately, explaining, "New York isn't America; it's like a different country, an alien country. In many ways it's a Jewish country," whereupon Lore tells him that she is Jewish (377–78). The exchange does not seem like the promising basis for a relationship, unless the two are mutually committed to the iconoclasm of all racial, ethnic, and geographical identities. Cayton may be, and he does not blink about Lore's revelation, asking rather glibly, "Then you must have been through the Hitler mess?" (378). She responds with an equivalent toughness: "I don't think about it much. It doesn't bother me. I don't think it really affected me" (378). Between his characterization of New York as both a "bitch" and a "Jewish city," and Lore's unwillingness to discuss Europe and "the Hitler mess," pan-ethnic consciousness is subsumed by personal, paranoiac, or post-traumatic denials. New York is cosmopolitan but un-American, and it is a site of psychic pain and masochistic denial.

In Segal's novel, New York is likewise exceptional and disconnected from the rest of the country, save for one chapter when the American South makes its lone appearance. Like the prior instance, Carter is ready to drop protocol and claim a black affiliation with his southern interlocutors, but he is once again thwarted. Carter's intellectual evaluations of race in America bounce off his interlocutor, who wears the stony mask of protocol. The moment occurs when Carter brings Ilka along to interview a famous southern gospel singer Ulalia Dixon, up from Alabama to tour in New York. Carter has prepared lengthy, heuristic questions, channeling Richard Wright and Frantz Fanon. Segal has Carter proffer Cayton's diagnostic "fear-hate-fear" complex, "the vicious circle that turns fear of the white man into hate of the white man into fear of retribution into more hate" (Segal 95; Cayton, *Long* 264–65). But Ulalia resists Carter's sociology and his leading questions, parrying his race talk with monosyllabic answers (mostly "no") or citations of New Testament verse. Her obsequious manager attempts to ease the interview by adding homey stories, which she then shrugs off. The awkward tension is only relieved when Ilka, characteristically clueless, asks, "Alabama—is that Southern?": "Each of the three Negro faces underwent an alteration.... Ulalia looked suddenly not absent and turned her face in Ilka's direction; the manager stopped trying to look sly and in a different, normal voice said, 'Man, is Alabama Sou-*thern!*'" (95). The question may be soliciting geographical information, but it garners insider knowledge instead, and though the manager's reply is not given, his "normal" voice, including the drawn out way he emphasizes "Sou-*thern*" breaks down the odd posturing. The interruption temporarily realigns Ulalia and Carter, as he chimes in, "Southerner they don't make 'em" (95). By calling attention to herself, Ilka inadvertently accomplishes what Carter could not, namely aligning the three in the room as black Americans sharing a common knowledge and point of view. Ilka's own subjectivity is harder to pin down, though to all in the room, her accent and the question itself surely signal that she is something other than "white." Perhaps it is precisely this ambiguity of identity and therefore Ilka's very lack of political subjectivity in this situation that permits the other three to step out of their adopted roles. However, Segal swerves away from any possibility of a productive realignment after Ilka's interruption, always subordinating the political as an adjunct of and by no means an allegory for the personal. Thus, when the two men briefly leave the room to fix Carter's tape recorder, Ulalia heaves a sigh, hoists her skirt, and unhitches her girdle, imploring Ilka to keep watch on the door. When the men return, the women are as proper as ever—even if Ilka is hiding the girdle behind a sofa cushion—and the text suggests they are both hiding behind the inscrutable mask that was heretofore worn only by Ulalia.

"Carter Must Have a Real Name": Effacing, Defacing Race

Despite Ilka's elliptical view of Carter, he may be, as Stanley Crouch claims, among the most complex and full black men to appear in American literature since *Invisible Man,* a position affirmed by the literary critic Philip Cavanaugh, who acknowledges Carter's irreducibility to pat black types and insists that "Carter must have a real name" (Crouch xi, Cavanaugh 489).[22] Cavanaugh's assertion is a credit to the verisimilitude of Segal's narration, but his emphasis on the real and on disclosure takes us to the heart of the problems of self-representation, where the elliptical nature of representation only suggests a more real subject beneath the opaque or elliptical account. For instance, when Ilka cannot discern Carter's place in his own story at the wedding party, she stumbles into a dilemma of auto-biography, where accounts of the self are both driven and diverted by the logic of race. Paul de Man observed that "the autobiographical moment happens as an alignment between the two subjects involved in the process of reading," or in Carter's case, when Ilka aligns the speaking Carter with the subject of his story, "a Negro" (de Man "Autobiography as Deface-ment" 922, Segal 39).[23] Ilka's conferral of recognition does not come from some point of mastery—at one point she even mistakenly thinks he might be telling her he is Jewish—but through an assimilation into the American vernacular of race, as Carter narrates a series of subtle slights.

Nor does Carter command the terms of his own story, as de Man ex-plains: "The interest in autobiography, then, is not that it reveals reliable self-knowledge—it does not—but that it demonstrates in a striking way the impossibility of closure and of totalization (that is the impossibility of coming into being) of all textual systems made up of tropological substitu-tions" (922). The first half of de Man's sentence clarifies how Carter is not so much telling the story as enacting it—and so tells the story of dinner interrupted, while again forestalling dinner with Ilka—while the second part suggests why the story of racial encounters can never be teleological. The end of the story that would confer meaning on the racial encounter is forever deferred, and the story is always open to further inscription: Carter tells his story by telling another story. The proliferation of storytelling is evidence not merely of the impossibility of closure when giving an account of a life but also of the substitutive quality of narrations of selfhood within the racial imaginary: you are always either one thing or another, a raced self or an enlightened individual, and the activity of giving an account of that self amounts to substituting the one self for the other.[24] Notably, there is no "authentic" self, as Carter makes clear: trying to account for it always ends up producing its substitute, where the narrated version of the self oc-cupies the place of what can never be there.

In autobiography, we may either pass the story of a life through a set of inadequate and reductive signifiers or demonstrate the failure of story-telling itself. In the first instance, we become beholden to a set of arche-types, plot points, and social virtues that overwrite our self; in the second instance, we stand outside of language but remain no less constituted by it as we measure our authenticity in terms of our incapability with social scripts. In either case, as de Man puts it, "Autobiography veils a deface-ment of the mind of which it is itself the cause" (930). De Man's term *defacement* bookends his essay, in both the title and the final line cited here, but throughout de Man talks about language, figuration, and disfigura-tion. His insistent framing of representative language as being like a face, however, signals how our face is the part of our exterior selves we can only see through some form of mediation—a mirror, say, or the gaze of the other—and how the face, like storytelling itself, is defaced through representation. Moreover, it is the compulsion to tell our story, to identify ourselves, to place ourselves within a framework we neither choose nor even endorse, that "defaces" us.

In de Man's terms, Cayton's *Long Old Road* continually depicts the de-facement of the author's mind, as the subject telling the story is undone by the story told. Consequently, like Invisible Man but without any of that character's hopefulness, Cayton literally loses all sense of who he is. He describes one rock-bottom day when he is out of money, desperate for a drink, and painfully aware of how his depression and alcoholism have dislodged him from his former elite station. He spends a humiliating day at a blood bank selling his plasma and then heads off to a restaurant look-ing for a drink. What follows would be farcical if it were not also the unraveling of his self. To keep up appearances, he orders food, despite his lack of appetite and growing nausea. Fearing further loss of dignity, he continues to play the gentleman diner until his stomach rebels and he wretches forth his meal. He just barely manages to purchase a bottle of whisky and to return to his basement apartment, where he falls into a stupor, at the end of which he recalls a prior unraveling, including an at-tack of amnesia suffered years earlier in Pittsburgh. During that episode, he recalls, "[I] realized with horror that I didn't know who I was. I could feel my body trembling and I fought down my panic....a feeling of shame at not knowing who I was swept over me, followed by an equally intense stab of fear" (343).

The story of his amnesia is an odd kernel at the core of Cayton's fram-ing story. It is tempting to say that in the framing story he loses control of his body—selling his blood, losing his meal—and in the second story he loses his mind. While still amnesiac, Cayton runs from his room in a panic and begins to calm down only when he finds his wallet containing his identification in his pocket. From there he reconstructs his recent past, first discovering upon inquiry that he is in Pittsburgh and eventually locating help and support. It is not uncommon in autobiographical writing to present the loss of self as the nadir from which the writing self originates and upon which he or she looks back. However, in Cayton's telling of it, recounting dispossession and humiliation only leads to more of the same. There is no redemptive current arising from the abyss, only more darkness.

If the autobiographer aspires to be the self that is narrated and if this results in the mind's own defacement, we find in Cayton's account an ideal performance of the problem. Telling his story yields not coherence but madness, and at the heart of his story is the loss of self. For instance, Segal's narration of Carter's outrage over the insult at the wedding party appears in *Long Old Road* but with a less stable account of how and why Cayton feels insulted. Cayton explains to Lore that when he slept with the bride, Carol, she asked him just before they made love, "Are you doing this to me only because I'm white?" (382). The thrust of the question is hard to place—doing this *to* me may mean the same as *with* or *for* me, though it's not clear, nor is it clear if Carol's question is directed at Cayton—"do you simply want to sleep with a white girl?"—or herself—"are you being agreeable to sex because I, a white person, command the scene?" (382). At the party, Carol's husband Harry assures Cayton that he knows "about everything" and he's "glad to meet" Cayton, and the ridiculous geniality gets "under [Cayton's] skin," another catachrestic metaphor signaling at once how Harry's attempt to look beyond race is itself a statement of race privilege and how Cayton's desire to look past race is always thwarted by the other's presumption of racial context (383).

Cayton complains to Lore that he's "tired of forever giving reassurances about color. Telling white people it's all right for them to react to Negroes as if they were human," insisting that he will henceforth date only "foreign" women, including Lore (384). Cayton's "as if" betrays contingency and not certitude about the status of being human. Responding to an unwanted recognition, Cayton also exposes how recognition can "get under the skin," infecting him with its own logic, making him incoherent at the very moment he marshals his self-defense. In contrast to Cayton's "defacement of the mind," Segal's *effacing* of Carter's story through oblique glances, ellipses, and deferrals of closure appears to be her attempt to recuperate Cayton from the self-destructive imperative of autobiography. Granting him the hard shell of protocol, Segal shields him from the appropriations of social recognition.

Black Face, White Noise

If the life story of being black is hard to pin down, both Cayton and Segal suggest that being Jewish may also slip the grip of narrative command. In *Long Old Road,* when Lore enters Cayton's social scene, the dialectic of black and white is disrupted, and again we must recall that "Jewish" in the 1950s did not function as the anti-essentialist, in-between state that deconstructed the binaries of race—the basis for Roth's path-breaking satire in *Portnoy's Complaint* and Shteyngart's postmodern critique of capitalist exploitation of global racism in *Absurdistan*. Instead, "Jew" could be seen as an interloper between black and white, especially for African Americans who had developed a significant stake in the political resistance against white supremacy. Cayton introduces the problem that "Jew" poses between black and white seemingly out of the blue, though the lack of context seems of a piece with the relegation of Jews outside of American political space. Speaking of his friends Brunetta and Sidney, who are black and Jewish, respectively, Cayton begins:

> "We were always taught," Brunetta might say, apropos of nothing, "that Jews were not white people."
> "What are they, then?" Sidney would demand furiously.
> "I don't know," she would reply, then add with charming illogic, "We used to say, for example, that there were some white people and Jews at a gathering. I don't know what Jews are, but they aren't white, no matter how anxious you are to think so." (385)

The vague opacity ascribed to "Jew" here is wonderful all by itself but would eclipse the more subtle opacity of how Cayton relays the material. If Brunetta's remarks really did originate "apropos of nothing," then Cayton hints that defining the Jews' race was an anxious existential imperative, casting no light on any particular Jew or Jewish context and thus illuminating no political understanding of Jews' relation to other American ethnicities and races. The "Jewish question" has no history, no context, and consequently no answer. Apropos of nothing, the Jew becomes the dark continent up whose river Cayton reluctantly ventures.

But it seems hard to imagine these remarks originating out of nowhere, especially in the presence of Jews and at least one white person, in addition to Cayton and Brunetta. And the question is further complicated by Lore's foreign background, in contrast to Sidney's American Jewish ethnicity. Elsewhere Cayton considers filial recognition between black Africans and African Americans, but here the Jew is deterritorialized and dehistoricized, neither American nor European but something else. If we recall Ralph Ellison around the same time favorably situating Jews between black and white in his famous rebuke to Irving Howe, going so far as to quote from the Talmud to underscore Howe's Jewish affiliation, here we have something more stark and troubling: "I don't know what Jews are."[25] The Jew is different beyond the semantics of recognition.

A generous reading of Cayton would grant that he is attempting to get beyond the immediate and at times debilitating limitations of liberalism and even paternalism that were already being pinned on Jews by black critics of the famed black-Jewish alliance in the late 1950s. Seen this way, Cayton's account recognizes that Jews are free from the metonymies of both black and white. However the Jew is constituted, he or she is not a part of *that* dilemma. At the same time, singling out the Jews in this way is fundamentally essentializing. As Segal will demonstrate in her novel, Ilka hardly feels in touch with American Jewish life and is nearly as bewildered by her cousin Fishgoppel as she is by everyone else she meets. What is finally spoken here is that the Jew is not in a triangulation, is not "neither black nor white yet both" (Sollors) nor a "whiteness of a different color" (Jacobson), is neither some "big nose version of wasp" (Roth) nor on a spectrum moving from black to white (Brodkin).[26] Instead, the Jew is some other thing, wholly outside of and not in the least constituted by the black/white economy.

If there is any question as to Jews' role as political agents in reorganizing an American racial polity in Cayton's memoir, Segal places her Jews outside the advancing social history of racial realignment. Segal recasts Cayton's friends Sidney and Brunetta as Carter's friends Sidney and Ebony, and the two couples retreat to a borrowed farmhouse in Connecticut, where they join another white family and even a Richard Wright stand-in named

Percival Jones. Collectively, the group supports racial equality and the harmonious cooperation of black, white, and Jew, but they regularly fall into a pantomime of hegemonic racial roles. Sarah, the niece of the owner of the house, continually leaves her crying daughter with "aunt" Ebony, while Ebony appears to court the domestic role with passive aggression. Segal depicts little Annie as generally intolerable, little more than a screaming voice, a greedy mouth, and a diaper in need of changing, thereby setting up a structural rather than affective relationship: the little white girl is there to be served, not loved.

Ignorant to the dynamics, Ilka consistently misunderstands her own role in the scene. When the housemates walk over to a nearby lake, they draw many curious stares, though Ilka is unsure if that is due to their mixed composition or Ebony's attention-getting silver swimsuit. Ebony, mammy-like, takes the young white girl Annie by the hand and leads her to the water to wash her hair, and then she dips her head to allow Annie to wash her own. The scene is one of several pantomimes where Ebony—a hostile woman, keen to note all racial slights—plays the servile "auntie" to young Annie and her parents. While Ilka watches, surely understanding very little, the enigmatic German Victor, father of Annie, whispers in Ilka's ear, "Jews not permitted here" (210). Later, upon accusing Victor of anti-Semitism, Ilka learns that he is in fact Jewish, and the tranquil moment at the lake flips entirely for Ilka. Where before in her race-blindness she saw a scene of tranquility and affection and believed herself barred from happiness as a Jew, she discovers a scene of passive-aggressive race hostility, the repetition compulsion of centuries of racial domination, and is ironically advised to avoid getting caught in between (219). Underscoring the novel's difference from Cayton's framing of the question, Segal demonstrates the Jew's unrecognizability as rooted in variegation and not essential being. European like her and similarly a refugee—"I told you, I'm from Berlin!"—Victor's Jewishness is neither essence nor surface, though it may be said to lie in his ironization of social identification (219).

The revelation by Ilka's coreligionist occurs at the end of an apocalyptic passage, when the spirit of cooperation and the milk of human kindness are finally exhausted and the summertime conviviality of black, white, and Jew comes to a crashing end. The summer began with a charade of democracy, with Carter presiding over a mock forum for the "little polis" to verify that all are settled with the arrangements (173). Carter asks simply,

"Does anybody want anything that they do not have, or want not to have anything they do have?" and the modesty of the question, including the appeal to individual desire, dooms the project from the start (174). More than a group of individuals, the "little polis" is an interracial group committed to communism, socialism, or, in Ilka's case, futile colorblindness. They seek to transcend racial inequality but are unable to escape the deeply embedded histories and cultural narratives that structure that inequality in the first place. Though they jokingly call the shared Connecticut house "the big house" and regularly "beat the boy"—that is, tell humorous or humiliating stories about overcoming or succumbing to racial injustice—they develop no language for recognizing the emotional, psychological, and narrative differences that structure what are otherwise their common positions. Equality of *having* and *wanting* may be a socialist ideal, but the veneer of equality blocks a more trenchant inequality: the *histories* we have, the *futures* we want. Seen this way, Ebony's racial pantomime and Carter's mock "polis" are less unconscious performances than a calculated setup, a drawn-out bit of agitprop theater.

The apocalypse occurs when housemate Sarah—the white mother of baby Annie and the niece of the woman who actually owns the house—complains that she has not received Ebony's support for her attempt at interracial adoption, has had all her attempts at friendship rebuffed, and has not been able to choose her role in the community. "You play at democracy," Sarah charges unironically, "and deny me my vote" (219). Carter's reaction clarifies that this upending of roles, including the condemnation of democracy, was precisely the outcome he had been courting all along. Later that evening, Ilka declares the whole episode "not fair." "Damn unfair!" Carter replies, "and he laughed and he laughed" (220).

Carter's pronouncement is not exactly a refusal of the political as a demonstration of all that the normative political mode cannot encompass. Not only does the prevailing democracy deny the vote, it assumes that the vote is all there is, when in fact a person's interest in preserving what they have and garnering what they want originates in a complex welter of acknowledged and unacknowledged identifications. Segal's writing matches the insight. On her first day at the house, Ilka observes "an undeterminable number of persons like black paper cutouts. They would not stay put and would not stay attached to the names Carter kept telling Ilka" (168–69). The problem is not that the people are all alike but all different: black, white, Jewish; male, female; artist, writer, intellectual; American, Communist, expatriate, refugee. Generally committed to democratic progress but each existing as a teleology unto him- or herself, the people form no democratic polity that will produce a common political identity. Segal's image of paper cutouts further effaces political selfhood, but Carter's democratic theater reveals something more: "And this was the first time, since she had known him, that Carter's face did not please Ilka...the arrogant look of one impenetrable to anything [anyone] might have it in her power to say" (219). If the inability to put people in their place is bewildering to Ilka, Carter's warping of democracy is literally defacing, as he embodies the false promise of a politics he has evaded all along.

Ultimately, Carter's life is tragic because he is so canny about the complexity of American racial history, on the one hand, and so clear-sighted on the insufficiency of normative politics, on the other. The tragedy is that Carter fails to come up with any alternative. He is neither an Ellisonian improvisational individual speaking at the "lower frequencies" nor a committed revolutionary à la Richard Wright, and the time had not yet arrived for a highly educated, light-skinned, charismatic, urbane black man to take his place in postracial America.

At the end of *Her First American,* Ilka searches for a way to characterize her relationship with the sometimes charming, sometimes depressive Carter. She recalls William Blake's lines, "Mercy has a human heart, Pity a human face," and concludes, "I have thought that Carter and I were merciful to each other" (285). It is a curious moment if you consider that Segal could simply have had her character declare herself merciful, without Blake or even with only half the Blake line (or the full four-part structure of Blake's poem, for that matter). The pairing of the two syntagms—mercy/heart, pity/face—with the clear choice of the former is especially interesting for all that "face" and its abnegation might mean at this point. Choosing heart over face draws attention away from skin color and toward something more inexpressible, the heart being a metaphor of one's very humanity, beneath the surface-level encounter with the body. Likewise, mercy's mutuality trumps the one-way hierarchical regard of pity. And by the mid-1960s, the time of the novel's closing, "pity" expresses all that is wrong between blacks and Jews, summed up in the portrait of condescension and opportunism found in *Portnoy's Complaint.*

Often in discussions of ethics, especially the ethics of responsibility, the face is a synecdoche for the other's singularity, consciousness, or humanity, but here "face" signals nothing so much as one's political being. We pity a face because in a given context its age, skin color, or gender signals some social disadvantage that we ourselves do not suffer. In *Her First American* faces disclose psychological refraction, political cooptation, and linguistic disfiguration, and the right response is to look away.

At the end of *Her First American,* Carter's life story is eulogized and radicalized by a new generation of black intellectuals hostile to Ilka's cosmopolitan impositions. In the final pages one of Carter's students delivers a talk on the psychological burdens of bearing a slaveowner's name, Segal's own clever turn on how the "real name" does not deliver the story, even if names and naming may be the origin for future storytelling. Though the student's talk is undeveloped, the topic is enough to register the cultural movement for Afro-centric identification popular in the late 1960s and to hail one prevailing theory of political identification, namely that cultural nationalism was necessary for African Americans to reorient their understanding of themselves as not just objects but subjects of American and world history. The point was not simply to strike a new strategy but to find an original identity. Peeling back the name, like the contemporary probe for genetic evidence of African origins led by Henry Louis Gates Jr., insists that identities are real, intrinsic, and ultimately revelatory and that the search for one's true identity is something like a human right.[27] Ilka's response to the students' racial nationalism is simple—"Weissnix...meant 'Notwhite,'" a dry rejoinder that affirms nothing other than the capacity to be human *outside* of identity (287).

Her First American closes with a suspended contest between political recognition and an ethics of effacement, and though there is no resolution to the conflict, history tells us which side triumphs. Ilka holds on to her "tragic, cosmopolite lover," but the students reinscribe Carter as "recognizable...a black man among blacks, a man among men" (286). Against the stabilizing categories, "man" and "black," Ilka's "Notwhite" evades political recognizability, first because "Notwhite" declares racial categories inadequate, and second because she ventriloquizes Carter speaking not about himself or about blackness but about Jewishness. In this moment of racial affirmation and cultural nationalism, Ilka has inserted a cosmopolitan counterpoint, but though the students give her a patient moment to say her piece, no response is necessary, for neither Ilka nor Carter claim a political counterweight for Jewish subjectivity, and Ilka certainly is not advancing political liberalism after all her time as a political agnostic. Rather, she is simply giving voice to the man she knew, while the students are wholly reconstructing him, not for memory but for nationalist historiography. In contrast to Arendt's lugubrious forecast of the inefficacy of black identity and in accord with Rancière, black political subjectivity, as advanced by Eldridge Cleaver, Malcolm X, and Stokely Carmichael, was very much the source of political agency; in Roth's and Shteyngart's novels, black nationalist politics and culture take over the space once occupied by Jewish social activism. If both writers are derisively satirical of black experience and black popular culture, they are even more scathing, albeit indirectly, on the no-place of Jewish culture in contemporary politics. Segal, however, concedes both the march of history and the vanishing point of Jewish abnegation from political subjectivity in the 1960s.

There is an acute sadness in Segal's representation of the "outside" of politics. Recalling Arendt, political subjectivity is supposed to rescue man from the sphere of bare life, but in Segal's telling, the sphere of the political bears a dangerous, life-absorbing gravity, drawing in and warping not only the story of a life, as in the students' retrospective incorporation of Carter, but the living Carter too. Perhaps it is Ilka and not Carter who more clearly intuits what Ellison's Invisible Man knows, that living outside of all given forms of political being yields a kind of invisibility. Carter will have a rewarding afterlife through cultural reinscription, while Ilka's effacement of polity also means she will drop out of Carter's story. Neither "black" nor a "man," there is no place for her in the "recognizable" if retrospective story. Where Roth and Ozick draw their characters as filled with rage as a counterweight to a new regime of racial recognition and ethnic nationalism and where Shteyngart subsumes the very idea of culture to the machinations of global capitalism, Segal's claim for Jewishness, named as an interruption, barely leaves an echo.

5

Responsibility Unveiled

Tony Kushner's Homebody/Kabul

Written in the late 1990s, Tony Kushner's play *Homebody/Kabul* has been called "uncanny" and "eerily prescient" for anticipating and address-ing the violence between the United States and Afghanistan leading up to and sustained after 9/11.[1] Kushner explains that he had been thinking about Kabul and the relationship between Afghanistan and the United States since the 1980s.[2] As for the prescience of the play, Kushner remarked that if a playwright could anticipate terrorism and reprisal, the real ques-tion should be, why was Washington and the U.S. press looking the other way?[3] What *was* the nation attending to when the 9/11 hijackers were plot-ting destruction? Ahh, 1998...Bill Clinton, Monica Lewinsky, the blue dress. The widespread mock surveillance marking that event seems like a parodist's prologue to the post-9/11 climate of surveillance: Linda Tripp recording phone calls, Monica Lewinsky saving forensic evidence in her closet, the rumor of Abu Ghraib–style photos of the president's genitals. If Kushner is viewed as "eerily prescient," eerier still is the redeployment of the Clinton-Lewinsky costume box: the blue dress became the burkha, extralegal wiretapping and other forms of surveillance were mobilized to catch foreign rather than domestic "evil-doers," and rumors of lurid photos gave way to stacks of naked bodies at Abu Ghraib.[4] They became us.

Nathan Zuckerman's defense of Bill Clinton in Roth's 2000 novel *The Human Stain*—"They ought to hang a banner outside the white house…that says 'A HUMAN BEING LIVES HERE'"—is an attempt to humanize and universalize the seemingly strange and perverse (3). That novel's representation of monstrosity without monsters helpfully forecast global politics after 9/11. Though these distinctions, human and inhuman, were not part of public rhetoric in 1998, they certainly comprised the subsequent framing of global politics after 9/11. Along with the widely circulating dichotomies of "freedom-lovers/freedom-haters" and "with us/against us," where "freedom" and "us" are the presumed stable terms of virtue, defining enemies as negations, we find the rhetorical dichotomy of "human/inhuman." Subsequent U.S. intervention involved politically aligning with those in Iraq and Afghanistan whose values reportedly most matched our own and waging war on their behalf against agents of terror, totalitarian dictators, and "fundamentalists." Remarkably, if temporarily, the poster-person for the humanity we sought to liberate was the Muslim—especially Afghani—woman, who, beneath the burkha and despite her having been denied an education by the state and, often, her family, despite her grinding poverty, despite her lifelong experience with invasion, war, ethnocide, and regardless of her professions of fidelity to Islam, was in fact, like "us."

This chapter, focusing on Tony Kushner's play *Homebody/Kabul* but containing a significant detour into popular depictions of the veiled Afghan woman, is about the politics and ethics of recognition and responsibility, especially as it pertains to the Western engagement with Afghanistan. Here I advance the book's claim that Jewish writers continue to excavate the normative bases for contemporary thinking on national identity, universal human rights, and concomitant accounts of universal human being. Though geographically more cosmopolitan than Roth's *Portnoy's Complaint,* where Portnoy's psychology provides the provincial frame through which he sees the United States and Israel, the play and the novel circulate a common exposure of the social and theoretical structures that sustain inequality, domestic or global. *Homebody/Kabul*'s characters are not conscious agents manipulating a corrupt system, as Roth's Portnoy is, but privileged Western consumers who are dimly aware that Western zones of safety are sustained through opportunistic and exploitative relations with the developing world. However, unlike *Portnoy* and every other literary text under review here, *Homebody/Kabul* is not about Jewish characters, let alone Jewish history, geography, or identity. Kushner does not juxtapose Jewish cosmopolitanism with histories of nationalism and civil rights, as Segal does, for instance. On the contrary, Kushner's characters experience their Western privilege as something like oblivion and are far too caught up in personal problems to think clearly about the global arrangements of rights. Even the title character, the Homebody, who indeed feels guilt over third-world suffering, loathes what she considers her own self-serving affection. The play's social and ethical dramas, then, are wrapped around personal and domestic dramas; his cosmopolitan characters are in fact provincial after all, and it is through Islam that cultural and group affiliation impinge on Western liberalism.

Rather than locate a Jewish subtext or find warrant for Jewish analysis in the playwright's Jewish background or his other Jewish writing, this chapter traces the family resemblance in Kushner's attention to the same political and ethical concerns found in the other texts discussed in this book. The play is Jewish by proxy, where proximity, more than identity, allows for something to be itself and to be in relation to an other, which, I hope, is an adequate formula for at least placing the play in contingent relation to the other works covered in this book. In chapter 1, proximity permitted a pairing of Roth and Cleaver, a model borrowed from Reinhard's neighboring of Lacan and Levinas (a pattern inspired by Lacan's "Kant avec Sade"), and this chapter extends the implications of proximate relations hinted at late in chapter 1. Kushner is read against another proximate text in the next chapter, Gary Shteyngart's *Absurdistan*. And indeed, proximity, as I discuss below, is the basis for reconstructing a theory of recognition heretofore only satirized or otherwise elided by other Jewish writers.

Linking recognition and responsibility is the play's challenge, as formulated early on by the eponymous Homebody: "What else is love but recognition? Love's nothing to do with happiness. Power has to do with happiness. Love has only to do with home" (28). The "to do" here may be vague, a placeholder for a well-wrought theory, but this statement at the beginning of the play lays out the challenge: to illuminate how love, recognition, and home submit to and evince a politics and ethics of recognition and responsibility. When the Homebody links love, home, and recognition, she also links the personal and the political. There are "consequences to *everything,*" she maintains, and most Americans, from pacifists to warmongers, can see how caring for your family at home may mean attending to global dilemmas abroad (27). To be sure, it is doubtful that most people in the United States are interested in Afghanistan on its own terms—or in Islam, for that matter. Afghanistan stands as a unique example of a country seemingly alien and immune to the salvational powers of this democracy and capitalism, lacking readily exploitable natural resources or market share and hosting cultural and religious allegiances that are far from liberal. Nonetheless, among the goals of the 2001 invasion of Afghanistan was the establishment of a nominal democracy, under the premise that elected government and an "ownership society" are the birthright of all people.[5] It goes without saying that in the West, the burkha is widely regarded as illiberal for its occlusion of individuality as well as its subordinating effects. Less philosophical is the affective aspect of the burkha: it scares us and makes its wearer seem profoundly alien to us. However, undergirding the push for liberalism is the faith that beneath the veil is a consumer, someone who can buy and sell, just like we in the West do.

This sort of recognition underwrites the spread of global capitalism and liberal democracy: capitalism leads to free democracies, and free democracies are constituted by free markets. The neoconservative conviction that no group of people is immune from the sway of democracy trumpets the spread of global capitalist enterprises, because it is presumed that capitalism itself is democratizing, liberalizing, and culture-changing.[6] At work in liberal recognition is the premise that when you strip away the accretions of culture and ideology, you find a freedom-loving, reason-possessing, and democratically inclined individual. Nasty "fundamentalism," religious fascism, and woman-restricting patriarchal social practices turn out to be corruptions or cooptations of the liberal virtues necessarily present in all faiths and all human aspirations for an approximation of the good life.

In this chapter, I argue that *Homebody/Kabul* is about a different sort of recognition and that the play may teach us how to think about our post-9/11 global cultural encounters, against the grain of liberalism. Kushner's play stages both the need for and the ethical and political difficulty of recognition while remaining independent of the philosophical underpinnings or political implications of both liberalism and multiculturalism. In *Homebody/Kabul,* knowing one's own self, let alone the other, is derailed by our psychological complexity, our ideological interpellation, and our reliance on flawed and simplified narratives to comprehend our place in the world around us. As the Homebody puts it, "The touch which does not understand is the touch which corrupts" (28). Yet even if recognition is not achievable between individuals, Kushner represents the struggle to find or construct a discursive world wherein recognition may occur—a language that says "you are a person that may be recognized"—as a challenge for which we might risk our lives.

Recognition, still? Given the substantive critiques, complications, or outright deconstructions of recognition from the fields of philosophy, feminist and gender studies, psychoanalysis, and political theory, recognition poses an elusive, even illusory challenge. To see another as like yourself, human in the way you are human, vulnerable in the way you are vulnerable, capable in the way you are capable, requires a clearer moral vision and a more singular account of the human subject than most critical fields would allow. More to the point, recognition always occurs within a politically determined field of vision, and there is no guarantee that a liberal humanist recognition is not simply a narcissistic projection of the imago onto the other or that a multicultural recognition that grants difference is not in fact an implicitly othering and subordinating strategy. On the other hand, as Segal's *Her First American* demonstrates, merely granting the given terminology of identity politics may be an anti-ethical reduction of the self within an occluding linguistic register. Multiculturalism would require us simply to grant the name that the other ascribes to itself, but Kushner begins by destabilizing this very foundation of self-authorization, in this epigraph to the play from the *New York Times:*

> In Washington, Pentagon officials said that a U.S. warplane missed a Taliban military target at Kabul airport and that a 2,000 pound bomb the plane was carrying apparently struck a residential neighborhood.
>
> At the scene of the hit, one man sat in his wheelchair, weeping next to a pile of rubble where his house once stood. Other residents wandered about in a daze.
>
> "We lost everything, our house and property," one woman said. "We are so afraid of the attacks we have forgotten our own names and can't even understand what we say to each other."

> —*New York Times,* October 13, 2001

Most fundamentally, the trauma of war splits the subject right down the middle, dividing self from subjectivity, and would seem to preclude both the Hegelian scene of recognition and the postcolonial imperative to let the subaltern speak. The breakdown of language here, the inability to remember one's own name, would seem to make recognition moot.

Interestingly, if we take the woman seriously, we grant that she cannot speak to her neighbors, but she speaks with terrific clarity to the *New York Times* and, by extension, to Western readers. Bombs and rubble starkly illustrate the hierarchical global arrangement of the United States and Afghanistan, a political setup wherein a whole series of self/other ties emerge between Western readers and this Kabuli woman: moral culpability, political objectification, and ethical responsibility. Still, the Kabuli woman quoted in the *New York Times* tells us from the outset that what we can best understand about her is that we cannot understand her. The trauma of war explodes intersubjective communication.

The Kabuli woman's address to the *New York Times* reporter illustrates what Judith Butler identifies as the responsibility for recognizing the precariousness of life. Cautiously attempting a thesis on the nature of this responsibility, Butler explains:

> It is about a mode of response that follows upon having been addressed, a comportment toward the Other only after the Other has made a demand upon me, accused me of failing, or asked me to assume responsibility. This is an exchange that cannot be assimilated into the schema in which the subject is over here as a topic to be reflexively interrogated, and the Other is over there, as a theme to be purveyed. The structure of address is important for understanding how moral authority is introduced and sustained if we accept not just that we address others when we speak, but that in some way we come to exist, as it were, in the moment of being addressed, and something about our existence proves precarious when that address fails. (*Precarious* 130)[7]

The scene of encounter is structurally Hegelian, but recognition's mode is discursive and not ocular. Moreover, the attempt at recognition takes the form of an address, doomed to Derridean failure. Turning Levinasian ethics upside down, it is not the success of the address—the appeal of the "face" in Levinas—but its failure that engenders ethical responsibility. Failure would seem to be inevitable, eventually, and when the address is preceded by dropped bombs, failure is the fundamental condition of the address.

Compared with earlier, loquaciously confident iterations of trauma theory by Shoshana Felman and Cathy Caruth, Butler's "some way" and "something" at the end of this passage should be taken as a welcome theoretical modesty.[8] Butler approaches the ethics of recognition and responsibility tentatively, aware that the inadequacy of language, the false promise of autonomous self-possession, and the inequalities that structure categories of self and other imperil any account of responsibility. Nonetheless, a project of recognition and responsibility begins with an openness to the call of the other and proceeds in being responsible for the failure of address. Though Butler closes without clarifying of what this responsibility consists, her reticence on the point is to be taken as a hesitancy to commit the mistakes of recognition's typical consequences, some modern version of the white man's burden, say.

As predicted by the epigraph, unstable language, dispossession, and structural inequality disorient *Homebody/Kabul* from the very beginning. The play's characters either lack sufficient self-possession or cannot make themselves understood across multiple languages, including French, English, Dari, Pashtu, and German. The play's title character, an upper-class London woman known only as "the Homebody," speaks English but with such hyperarticulate precision that she often seems more a foreigner than the very center of Western civilization. She holds the stage for a compelling forty-minute solo "conversation" with the audience and then disappears after traveling to Kabul—either a murder victim or, improbable as it seems to her family, a new convert to Islam, in hiding. The play presents both options—death or the abandonment of cultural propriety—as equally unfathomable. Appearing with a strange sort of symmetry is Mahala, a Kabuli woman whose background is never entirely clear; she is either the first wife of the Homebody's new Kabuli husband—and thus extraneous and in need of refuge—or a fraud preying on the Homebody's family. Mahala begs the Homebody's daughter Priscilla to take her back with her family to London, as Priscilla and her father Milton eventually do. How to save a woman who has apparently fled from a comfortable life in the West? How to rescue the unknowable other? At the heart of either question is the crux where individual volition meets cultural respect: it is arrogant to try to save the Homebody from her own chosen fate, even if that means joining an illiberal culture and submitting to a patriarchal tradition. In contrast, Mahala demands liberal refuge, insisting that the Homebody's family bring her back to London with them. What kind of cultural reconstruction does this require? Can she persist as a Kabuli Muslim in liberal London, or will she be transformed into some sort of cosmopolitan? Tragic, like Segal's Carter, or transcendent?

This chapter proceeds by examining the two-way road of recognition and the cul-de-sac of response common in global multiculturalism before settling in with a close analysis of Kushner's play. The detour is necessary, I believe, because Kushner's approach to the problems of recognition and responsibility is so novel as to be nearly unrecognizable. The play initially tracks but then swerves from popularized accounts of recognition and responsibility, and in its conclusion it comes up with an ethics of care and hospitality that is demandingly original. That is at least one way to account for the play's relative obscurity, despite Kushner's renown and the play's topicality. After all, *Homebody/Kabul* received nothing like the popular acclaim attending his earlier *Angels in America*. That play gave us a happy vision of something we had long ago conceived of and consented to: cultural pluralism. *Homebody/Kabul,* however, operates within an outline of globalization we only dimly understand and illuminates it in ways we are hardly prepared to see.

Looking, Seeing

At one point in the play, the shady Quango (a British man working for a quasi-NGO, hence the nickname) expresses his admiration for Afghanis, asking, "Have you noticed their remarkable jade-colored eyes?" (101). Milton responds that he hasn't left his room since arriving in Kabul, but we can assume he has seen them, all right. We all have: a girl's face, warm olive skin framed by dark brown hair and a russet-hued shawl, jade-green eyes staring out with apparent frank intelligence and defiance. The familiar image belongs to of Sharbat Gula, and it appeared on the cover of *National Geographic* in June 1985.[9] The cover was published during the height of the Soviet Union's battle with the Afghani mujahedeen, as Reagan's "freedom fighters" battled communism in the name of Islam with assistance from the CIA. In 1985, *National Geographic* sent a reporter and photographer into northwest Afghanistan and the refugee camps in Pakistan to document the displacement of Afghanis as a result of the war. The famed photo, taken by Steve McCurry during the chaos of the assignment, emerged with no caption and no biography, though it quickly became the icon of the article and then an icon of *National Geographic* itself. The editors did not know the girl's name, nor did they anticipate the tremendous value of her image once it was published. The precarious relationship between the story and the image is itself instructive: the story was over five thousand words long, a comprehensive, researched, on-the-ground account of the lives of refugees and internal exiles forced to flee or fight in the war. The image, initially a single snapshot of the crisis, came to stand for nothing other than the magazine itself.

The 1985 story was reprised in April 2002 when *National Geographic* reentered Pakistan after the fall of the Taliban, in search of the famous face of the anonymous girl, who, if still alive, would now be a grown woman. In the seventeen intervening years, the image circulated as an object of economic, erotic, and ethical value—in the latter case, standing as an appealing visage of third-world poverty and struggle. What would happen when and if the image was sutured back to the life narrative of the actual subject of the photo? The adult Sharbat Gula was in fact located, and "A Life Revealed," the story *National Geographic* tells about her, suggests a logic of recognition and response that will sharpen our understanding of the dilemmas facing Kushner's characters. As the reporters for *National Geographic* tell the story, Sharbat Gula was exotically different but shared the universal traits of motherhood; living a life with its own particular and culturally coded value, yet in need of western intervention. The language of *National Geographic,* including the use of terms like "lost" and "found," suggests mutuality—she has been longing for our return, just as we have been searching for her. *National Geographic*'s point of view overcomes Sharbat Gula, characteristic of the magazine's cooptation of third-world otherness. For instance, though "A Life Revealed" begins with the pseudo-shamanistic invocation, "Names have power, so let us speak hers," the *National Geographic* website nonetheless still offers her image for sale with the photographer's name inscribed at the bottom—*twice* (in block and in signature), with no mention of Gula.[10] The elision of her name, despite its professed power, is startlingly symmetrical with the Kabuli woman who told the *New York Times,* "We have forgotten our own names," suggesting that commodification and bombing have at least one common result.

When we look at Gula—when looking becomes longing, imagining, purchasing, and searching—the gaze is the specular leading edge of a project of intervention. Longing for her, we identify with her; identifying, we desire some form of intervention into her life. Of course, we are powerless as individuals. No one of us can give her or her family a better life, but the state—which grants us our "good life"—can and so (as a response to those eyes) must. Relying on the state to intervene on our behalf, we may come to feel the strange condition of our human rights: we "have" them, but they are effectively retained for us by the state. And paradoxically, so long as we have them, we don't really need them. It is the man-outside-of-citizenship—either the noncitizen resident, or the person stripped of citizenship, de jure or de facto—who is the subject of rights, but paradoxically, this is the one who cannot use or invoke these rights, as we learned from Arendt in chapter 4. We think of the captives in Guantanamo Bay, but also of José Padilla and anyone who can be stripped of citizenship and tried as a nonstate "enemy combatant." In a somewhat cheeky formulation, Jacques Rancière, responding to Arendt, suggests that the rights of man are unusable upon individual application and so are "returned to sender"—back to the state, the rights-granting institution—to be held in reserve as the rationale for "humanitarian intervention" ("Who is the Subject?" 308).[11]

The political corollary to "humanitarian intervention" is the promotion of democracy in theocratic or totalitarian countries. The spread of democracy is particularly appealing to the West, according to Slavoj Žižek, because in democracy's spread, "the West seeks for its own lost origins, its own lost original experience of 'democratic invention'" (*Tarrying* 200).[12] The promotion of democracy in Afghanistan and Iraq, for instance, naturalizes democracy as the most basic and virtuous type of state practice and depends on the corollary naturalization of liberalism, such that all people the world over, regardless of religious profession or cultural difference, are, at the core, proto-liberal, proto-citizens of the democratic state. Looking to the East, whether in eastern Europe, Asia, or the Middle East, we see versions of our original democratic selves.

This reflexive gaze east is neatly captured in *National Geographic*'s search for Sharbat Gula, where a photo that would symbolize the Afghan refugee story ends up as a metonymy of the storyteller, so that by the time the magazine sends reporters out to look for her in 2002, the venture can only mean more explicit coverage of the magazine itself. The title, "A Life Revealed," speaks immediately to the disclosure of the facts of Gula's life while implicitly linking her story to the magazine's venture—revealed by *National Geographic* as a service to its audience, for surely her circumstances can only be deemed mysterious by readers taught to see her as an opaque object in the first place. The verb "revealed" is a play on words, syncing with the photo of the adult Gula in full burkha, holding in her cloaked arm a copy of the original magazine issue. The image is a bit dizzying, for the adult Gula holds the original cover as if it were a prop, though insofar as the image and the person of Sharbat Gula are now commodity objects, the live version is just as much the prop for the magazine cover.

In "A Life Revealed," Sharbat Gula repeatedly expresses her irritation at being photographed unveiled, especially in front of men outside of her family, but the editors insist on the necessity of confirming her identity.[13] In fact, she confirms the original photo is of her because she has a sharp memory of being angry at being photographed in the first place. Her memory and her look back at *National Geographic* are negated, however. Instead, for confirmation *National Geographic* contracted John Daugman, a British researcher also contracted by the FBI to develop means of identifying and intercepting suspects on the international terrorist watch list.[14] The scanning is supposed to reveal signature patterns in the iris more detailed than a fingerprint, but unlike fingerprinting, the scanning is ostensibly a simple affair that occurs without the subject being aware of it. Employing Daugman and his technology to confirm Sharbat Gula's identity seems like an allegory of object fixation that is the very opposite of Hegelian recognition, where the gaze between two subjects is mutual.

To borrow from Elizabeth Povinelli, the technological "objectivity" of *National Geographic* demonstrates the "cunning of recognition": "Recognition is at once a formal meconnaissance [misrecognition] of a subaltern group's *being* and of its *being worthy* of national recognition and, at the same time, a formal moment of being inspected, examined, and investigated" (39). *National Geographic*'s article is premised on this plank of being/being worthy, and the editors go so far as to compel Gula to reveal her story and her physical self by suggesting that Western sympathy will generate material and financial support for her and others like her.[15] The question must be asked: if the eye scan had revealed someone other than the girl from the original photo, by what terms would she *not* be worthy of attention and remuneration?

The magazine's emphasis on Gula's eyes as the basis of her identity posits the eyes as ocular jewels, a kind of buried treasure, lost, but not forever, destined to be found. What any of this has to do with Gula herself remains unclear, but as one Pakistani ophthalmologist, summoned to give preliminary authentication of Gula, tells the *National Geographic* crew, "You have found the holy grail."[16] The metaphor obviously draws attention to the orientalist fantasy sublimated throughout the *National Geographic* story: buried in the rubble of Afghanistan, we will find some part of ourselves, something that we lost a long time ago and that, if found, redeems our military adventure. To push past the metaphor, then, the process of looking and finding and the narration of reclamation and redemption suggest how looking outward is structured by and ends up as an affirming look inward. This inward and atavistic metaphor is repeated at another level, when the invasion of Afghanistan was labeled a "crusade" by the Bush administration. On the other hand, appeals to "common humanity" by the likes of Laura Bush end up aggregating Afghani women as "passive, undifferentiated objects," self-evidently justifying western liberation and unveiling (Cohler 248).[17] Or, as Kushner's character Priscilla puts it when she rebukes this spirit, "Common humanity. It's crap, really" (59). The line condemns not the idea of the human per se but the rhetorical construction of "commonality" through universalizing projects.

Behind the quest for universality is fear, evident in a speech by Laura Bush, on November 17, 2002: "Civilized people throughout the world are speaking out in horror—not only because our hearts break for the women and children of Afghanistan, but also because in Afghanistan, we see the world the terrorists would like to impose on the rest of us" (341–42).[18] The very real terror, destruction, and death of 9/11 is unquestionable, but it does not follow that "the world of the terrorists" could somehow become our own. The ubiquity of "our way of life"—global capitalism and consumer culture—remains unthreatened, at least by terrorism. Laura Bush seems to be saying, given the glories of global capitalism, how could the terrorists not want a share? How could they possibly want to live in such a premodern way—illiteracy, disease, starvation, and, yes, the confinement of women: this "way of life," hardly unique to Taliban-controlled Afghanistan, is what horrifies us. Žižek puts it this way:

> The national Cause is ultimately nothing but the ways subjects of a given
> ethnic community organize their enjoyment through national myths. What

is therefore at stake in ethnic tensions is always the possession of the national Thing. We always impute to the "other" an excessive enjoyment: he wants to steal our enjoyment (by ruining our way of life) and/or he has access to some secret, perverse enjoyment. (*Tarrying,* 203)

If Žižek is right, it may explain why, to paraphrase the bumper sticker, living well was thought to be the best revenge against the enemy in the weeks after 9/11. Political leaders urged Americans to remain aggressive consumers, to show that "they" can't beat "us." Žižek concludes somewhat formulaically, that fear of the cultural other is nothing more than the haunting terror that at the heart of our very own enjoyment, there is really nothing there, and thus we project that terror onto an other. However, U.S. consumer culture is far from meaningless. On the contrary, U.S. consumption of ever cheaper and more cheaply made items from low-cost retailers significantly reduces global profit margins for manufacturers and in turn suppresses wages for workers, to say nothing of the consequential environmental destruction. The Homebody gets it right when she laments the West's relationship with Asian, African, and Latin American manufacturers: "You know, Third World junk.... which we, having waved our credit cards in its general direction, have made into junk" (17). In this way, in stark contrast to Laura Bush's fear, U.S. and Western consumer habits do far more to alter the culture and lives of people throughout the Middle East and Asia than those people could possibly do to alter the lives of people in the West.

Kushner's Homebody readily admits to her own role as a culpable Western consumer, and she fantasizes about personal and individual acts of reparation. Having already told the audience that "all touch corrupts," yet "all must be touched," she singles out the maimed hand of an Afghani hat merchant, whom she encounters while shopping in London, as the very emblem of the West's influence on the third world (11). In a fantastical reverie, the Homebody imagines the merchant disclosing a list of possible, mutually exclusive causes for his injury, including punishment for allegiance to the Soviet army in the 1980s, for support of the mujahedeen who fought them, for double-dealing with both, or for thievery in order to feed his starving family. By channeling the merchant, the Homebody appears to give herself over as a conduit for his testimony. However, she speaks too much, relaying not a singular story but an amalgam of Afghani civil and political incoherence, and so the merchant's particularity is eclipsed by what can only be the Homebody's redaction of her knowledge of recent history. Indeed, her version of the hat merchant's story comes off like an incoherent summary of *National Geographic*'s own reporting.

The Homebody's faux-testimony updates some familiar questions from postcolonial studies, from "Can the subaltern speak?" to "If we let the subaltern speak, can we stop feeling guilty for commodifying his culture and life?" The answer may be legible in the Homebody's posture of witness: paying attention while paying for her merchandise—the zeugma of payment establishes the Homebody in the commanding role, albeit as empathetic witness. As her fantasy continues, she further arrogates control precisely as she presumes her own submission. She imagines that she and the merchant are transported to Kabul, where they make love: "We kiss, his breath is very bitter, he places his hand inside me, it seems to me his whole hand inside me, and it seems to me a whole hand" (26). In her erotic fantasy, the Homebody heals the merchant's wounds, aligning her desire with his healing. Instead of the fear that the other wishes to "steal our enjoyment," or even the negative question, "Why do they hate us?" the Homebody's fantasy illustrates the liberal presumption that introjection functions as reparation. The fantasy comes to an end when the Homebody, back in reality, looks to see the merchant's hand not healed but joined with her credit card, a prosthetic that itself unites the couple in a mutual if unbalanced relationship of commodification. Her conclusion, "that which was once Afghan . . . we, having waved our credit cards in its general direction, have made into junk," is a bitter assessment that applies equally to her story and *National Geographic*'s merchandising of Gula's image. Healing the body, or healing with the body, is preceded and contained by already established relations of consumer and consumed.

What's a reader to do? Whether the Homebody with her outdated guidebooks, a subscriber to *National Geographic,* or even this reader of the text of Kushner's play, we arrive at the same place, aware of the staggering inequities between citizens of developed and undeveloped nations and likely aware of the extent to which Western comfort and consumption depends on third-world economic deprivation. The "white man's burden" has a long history, and among its functions for those who profess liberal convictions is to change the subject of attention from them to us.

Worrying about the costs of intervention becomes a form of self-regard, at the point where narcissism meets self-loathing. Either we are so powerful and so good that we must replicate our self-image around the world, as Michael Ignatieff and David Brooks have argued, or we must withhold the corrupting touch, as Wendy Brown and others have countered.[19] The Homebody dramatizes both positions, summing up the dilemma with a mocking self-reflection: "[Here] stands the homebody, safe in her kitchen, on her culpable shore, suffering uselessly watching others perishing in the sea, wringing her plump little maternal hands, oh, oh. Never *joining* the drowning.... The ocean is deep and cold and erasing. But how dreadful, really unpardonable, to remain dry" (28). The self-mockery of "oh, oh" illustrates the political short-circuit of self-critique; turning the gaze back on herself, the Homebody makes it all about her.[20]

Self-regard is turned inside out in the brutally abrupt description in the second scene of the Homebody's mutilated corpse and the announcement of her missing body. Only moments before, the Homebody had appeared on stage, articulate to a fault, and now she is suddenly the object of disarticulating medical jargon, the object of a coroner's report. The empirical certitude of the report is undermined by the missing body, and the Homebody's daughter Priscilla begins to probe reality's fissure. Though Milton insists, "SHE IS DEAD! *Reuters* has reported it!" the disappearance allows a more complex if apparently irrational account of her life to emerge (41). That the search for the Homebody begins with the *failure* of empiricism suggests how the play reverses the prioritization *National Geographic* gives to stories of empire and surveillance. Both stories are about missing women who are identified through scientific scrutiny, but while *National Geographic* links empire's ascension to successful surveillance and specifically U.S. intervention in Afghanistan with the redemption of Gula's life, *Homebody/Kabul* supplants this teleology with an open-ended investigation into the very ethics of recognition. Simply put, a death without a body makes little sense to Priscilla, but no alternative—including the emerging story that the Homebody has married a local Muslim and gone into hiding—makes any more sense. The problem for Priscilla is not surveillance or finding the body but interpretation, understanding her mother's story. And she unwittingly inherits the terms of interpretation from her mother, as she has to reinterpret the destabilized values of love, recognition, and home.

The Loss of Loss

Right after the coroner leaves the hotel, Priscilla comments on his anatomical description of her mother, ironizing his empiricism: "And if they have ripped her open, at least I'll finally get to see her fucking secrets" (42). That her secrets are never revealed and only hinted at to the audience in her monologue suggests the durability of human difference. Against the liberal presumption that beneath the veils of culture and social identities we are all in fact rooted in a common reason and motivated by a commonly held self-interest, the Homebody's mysteries, including her apparent abnegation, are never resolved, indicating difference without end. The shift from optical clarity to epistemic occlusion—that is, from seeing the body to encountering the secret—is a shift away from conventional forms of recognition that ultimately prioritize the knowability of the other, whether liberal philosophy or cultural anthropology. Instead, through Priscilla, Kushner suggests something we might call traumatic recognition, or being witness to the radical difference engendered by trauma.

To simplify, in *Homebody/Kabul* recognition comes down to better and worse forms of being a witness to the life of another. The Homebody's attempt at recognizing the hat merchant is a failure because of her reliance on a literal optics—seeing his hand—and on the solipsism of heroic intervention. Successful recognition instead requires a self-critical but not self-regarding subjectivity and may mobilize the metaphor of optical looking, but it cannot rely on the ocular veracity of the gaze. Priscilla's trope on sight acknowledges the violence that comes with literal looking, and though she does not anticipate it at this moment, the play forecasts how recognition requires a passive letting-be: letting secrets be secrets, or letting human difference be acknowledged even where it is not comfortably understood. In this way, Priscilla faces what Cathy Caruth calls "the unavoidable imperative" of "the one who must tell *what it means not to see*"—not to see or to be a witness to the death of her mother and thereby give up on her mother as an object of empirical knowledge (Caruth 105). In trauma theory, sight is the trope for presence while blindness is akin to falling asleep on watch—missing the critical moment of a life and having to live with the consequences of that absence. But what if the "missed experience" could also be the basis of an ethics of recognition, where recognition is not based on seeing, understanding, or identifying with the other, nor even on the other's capacity to connote self-consciousness. Instead, *Homebody/Kabul* suggests that the missed experience of trauma or the incapacity of recognition may be the basis for incomprehensible otherness, dis-identification, and self-alienation.

Upon her arrival in Kabul, Priscilla necessarily assimilates to her mother's quest for strangeness when she dons the burkha and ventures into the streets of Kabul. Structurally, Priscilla replays her mother's dangerous travel, imperiling her own self by recklessly walking out into the street alone, with cigarettes and a CD player. At the same time, as Priscilla's own story emerges through Milton's telling—told in betrayal to Quango—Priscilla likewise assumes the role of the mysterious abandoning mother. While she is offstage, we learn that the year before, she had attempted suicide and consequently aborted her fetus. As a trauma, the loss of her mother is a belated event and more than a "missed experience," as her mother abandons her repeatedly throughout her childhood and teen years. The Homebody admits in the first scene that she "withheld her touch" from her daughter, and Priscilla herself remarks, "I should be in the hotel room, grieving but... I've done that. Years of that" (60). This final loss, her disappearance, is given limitless rather than singular meaning. Doubting that her mother has actually been killed and thus facing the even more estranging possibility that she has chosen to live as a pious Muslim in Kabul, Priscilla remarks, "So now... she's scattered all over Kabul. The whole city. It's her" (60).

For Priscilla and Milton, there is no accounting for why the Homebody left liberal London for Kabul and Islam. Lacking the Homebody's theory of culture—all touch corrupts, all must be corrupted—culture itself becomes the unstable object of inquiry. Milton states the problem in terms practically drawn from liberal feminism: "And she... *married* a Muslim? Which, allow me to point out, she might just as easily have done in London, and a nice Western sort of Muslim too, not one of these... barbarians. So that she can spend of the rest of her life... draped in parachute sheeting stirring cracked wheat and cardamom over a propane fire?" (93).[21] Milton's scenario, offered as an incredulous critique of Priscilla's belief that her mother lives, introduces the problem of global bicameral ethics, where Westerners deem certain practices and lives intolerable for themselves but acceptable for others. If it is undesirable for the Homebody, why shouldn't it be undesirable for Mahala, or any Kabuli woman who wants out? The hinge between the Homebody's and Mahala's fates is stronger still, as several Kabulis, including Mahala, insist that the Homebody has in fact married Mahala's husband, thereby displacing Mahala. This scenario creates a vexatious ethics: Priscilla has the choice of believing either that her mother is dead or that she has relinquished Western culture; choosing "life" then means giving up on her mother's claim to Western liberalism. At the same time, that very choice would obligate Priscilla to help Mahala, the woman whom her mother putatively replaces. Priscilla is asked to believe in this fiction, but it is hardly the wish-fulfilling dream that her mother still lives. Rather, it would mean that the Homebody has willingly chosen to give up her claim to her family, property, and country—in short, her culture.

The Homebody's abnegation dislodges "the West" and all its syntagms from its privileged station as the universal object of desire. Consequently, Priscilla must consider just what is lost, and the play suggests that "loss" may not even be the right concept at this point; whatever her response, it needs to extend beyond her intimate and personal relationship with her mother. Indeed, the personal loss seems subordinate to the larger question of why her mother would give up on her social station. Based in the very heart of the West and afforded time, money, and personal freedom, she would seem free to explore and perform acts of the contrition she feels she owes the world. Instead, she gives it up. Is it possible to believe that the Homebody relinquished free choice and feminism for submission and patriarchy? Luxury for poverty? Our "way of life" for a culture that is figured as nothing more than the West's negation? Mourning's redemptive circuits would redeem loss by installing the lost object meaningfully into the symbolic order, but relinquishing freedom means relinquishing that very symbolic order as such. Read as self-sacrifice, the Homebody's journey to Kabul is a solipsistic failure, for it puts the "self" at the center of the story of the other. But as a radical relinquishing of self-possession, as releasing and thereby denaturalizing the forms that bind self to culture, culture to territory, the Homebody's journey points the way toward a different sort of ethics, an acknowledgment of the precariousness of the other.

Priscilla's role as a daughter of Western culture transforms in step with her increasing willingness to believe that her mother is in fact alive and converting to Islam. For her first trip out into the streets of Kabul, Priscilla throws on her burkha but recklessly carries contraband outlawed under the Taliban, suggesting her sense of Western privilege and protection. Priscilla is nearly beaten by a Talibani official, but Khwaja shows up to take the beating in her stead and to offer his service as a public, for-hire "uncle," a necessary escort for a single woman in Kabul. The fictive reassignment of kinship, along with the dread seriousness of the burkha, marks the beginning of Priscilla's journey toward her mother. Notably, she is not copying her mother, for she gains her "uncle" before hearing the story of the Homebody's new family. But after hearing it and meeting Mahala, Priscilla finds herself likewise displaced from her family. When burkha-draped Priscilla enters her hotel room in the second act, Milton's scream of "Wrong room, wrong room!" maintains a fiction of inviolable Western space within Kabul, while the metonymic burkha converts Priscilla into the alien other (61). Subsequently, Milton and Quango become increasingly hostile, bullying, and rapacious toward Priscilla—in short, acting with the patriarchal oppressiveness imputed to the Taliban. And Priscilla's burkha indeed becomes a protective cover with which to shield her body. Though it may be difficult to imagine, much less believe, that the Homebody has converted to Islam to live in Kabul, Priscilla's experience suggests what such a life would look like. She is bullied by her father, who also trades her secrets to Quango in exchange for opium before finally banishing her for the dishonor of abortion. Priscilla walks in Kabul neither with an insider's faith nor a Westerner's presumptions. Beyond "loss," Priscilla is exiled from the economy of symbols with which she might mourn her mother and thereby regain a place in the symbolic order propping up Western cultural constructs of women's freedom.

Kushner presents the breakdown of the symbolic order for Priscilla not as a crisis but as a gathering self-consciousness, mediated through an encounter of recognition with the displaced and dispossessed women of Afghanistan. What is more, the scene of recognition confronts the solipsism of looking and permits ethical engagement. The moment occurs when Priscilla is searching for her mother in the desolate women's hospital and sees something at once strange and familiar:

I saw horrible things today. . . . Horrible. But it was *me* there, seeing it, *me*. I thought, what kind of person watches herself seeing such things? Conceited, yeah? But I watched. I did, conceited, so what, doesn't matter. Them, these women, suffering. And me, there in the room with them, proximate.

I…marveled at that. I marveled at myself. Ooh, Priscilla! Priscilla Ceiling
in Kabul! Embarrassing. Never really done that before. Marveled. All day,
I've felt like laughing. Inappropriate. (65)

The scene at first suggests a Hegelian moment of recognition, though the
defensive tone along with the admission of "conceit" is something else.
The charged difference between "seeing" and "watching" in this passage suggests a self-awareness beyond passive looking, while the urge to
laugh is a return to her own body, a reincorporation of her self at this moment that precludes facile identification with the women she sees. She
acknowledges but then dismisses the fact that her self-awareness is "conceited" and regards herself more accurately as "inappropriate," an interesting term in this instance for the way it signals the loss of self-possession,
and in tension with "conceited," a term derived from *conceive* meaning
roughly "self-born." *Inappropriate* literally means lacking proper possession or ownership of one's self, an understandable condition given Priscilla's situation. However, the inappropriateness is checked by the critical
awareness of what is appropriate in the first place, and how the self is out of
sync with that appropriateness. That is, between *seeing*—the passive gawk-
ing at the horror—and *watching*—the critical reflection on her own role in
the scene—Priscilla finds herself dislodged from a conventionally Western perspective regarding third-world suffering. She is aware of the suffering of others but does not identify with it, at least not transparently; she
shares her mother's view of herself as "inappropriate" but is without her
mother's self-loathing and her urge to erase herself. The Homebody's first
response is a self-loathing performance—"Oh, oh, ringing her plump little maternal hands"—and then the self-annihilation of traveling to Kabul.
Priscilla shares her mother's self-critique—"Ooh, Priscilla!"—but not the
totality of her "conceit"—"so what, doesn't matter"—focusing her attention instead on "them."

The key term in the passage cited above is "proximate," defined by
the *Oxford English Dictionary* as "coming immediately before or after in a
chain of causation, agency, reasoning, or other relation." "Before or after":
marked as neither cause nor effect—and hence, without imperialist
implications—Priscilla is nonetheless in a contiguous relation with the
women she sees. In relation to them how? Because she is a Westerner
and on some global level bound up in their suffering; because she is there,

seeing them, unable to turn away yet seemingly unable to do anything for them; because she is a woman, and in Kabul the burkha signals her vulnerability to patriarchal violence; because her mother is said to have suffered the same fate as these women for violating laws of decency; because—as she will shortly learn, when she returns to her hotel—her father is trading her secrets to Quango for a bowl of opium and will turn her out of the house for failure to produce a grandchild.

Judith Butler analyzes the role of "proximity" in relation to ethics in her reading of Emmanuel Levinas's essay "Peace and Proximity."[22] Butler explains Levinas's difficult philosophy where proximity to the other subordinates self-regard to responsibility. And because the face of the other, akin to discourse itself in Levinas's thought, precedes and produces our selves, we are caught up in and bound to the ethical care of the other, even as it places our own selves in precarious vulnerability. This circuit of ethics is not exactly recognition but the outline of recognition's failure. As Butler puts it, "For Levinas, then, the human is not represented by the face. Rather, the human is indirectly affirmed in that very disjunction that makes representation impossible, and this disjunction is conveyed in the impossible representation. For representation to convey the human, then, representation must not only fail, but it must *show* its failure" (*Precarious* 144). In this instance, Priscilla witnesses the vulnerability of the women, and only later will she intuit her own responsibility to them.

Feeling responsible is one thing, but responding is another, to paraphrase the Homebody's original conundrum. Kushner recasts the question of responsibility, however; what was previously a hierarchy between the Homebody and the hat merchant becomes an equivalence between Priscilla and Mahala. More than proximate, Priscilla is assigned culpability for Mahala, because, as the story goes, her mother has displaced her. But through a symbolically evocative gesture, Mahala marks Priscilla as a fellow exile by squeezing her arm in insistent supplication, leaving a bruise that recalls the "mark of Cain." Cain's name resonates as the very essence of the foreigner in the Homebody's opening monologue, and we recall that Cain's mark is not a sign of damnation but of sanction: god exiles Cain but bestows upon him his own mark, as sort of super-visa allowing Cain to wander and resettle unharmed.[23] Inverting and ironizing the biblical roles, however, in Kushner's play Mahala begs for salvation—and a visa—from Priscilla. The moment also ironizes the political as such, for Mahala is making a claim on Priscilla's Western status at the very moment she loses proprietary claim on it. Still, this irony gets it right. Priscilla's "humanitarian" intervention mobilizes the apparatus of politics without naturalizing the political as the site of "the human." That it is the exile Mahala who does the marking, installed in god's role, indicates the imperative of responsibility and the absence of the transcendent to redeem responsibility's implications. To paraphrase Priscilla, no one will save her or Mahala other than themselves (115).

From Loss to Sacrifice

We need only contemplate the American occupation of Iraq and Afghanistan to grasp how the ethics of responsibility become complicated by the politics of intervention: well-meaning Americans of various beliefs may feel that it is time for the U.S. military to end its occupations in either country. But how to do so? Does leaving make the countries better or worse? Who is to say, and on what terms? All scenarios lead to chaos and murder, and the debate is over which accomplishes the least of these. Knowing what we do—the moral necessity to end the occupation and the political consequences of withdrawal—we remain paralyzed in debate. With a parting shot of wisdom, the Homebody crystallizes this dilemma in a single phrase, "Might and Do":

> We all romp about, grieving, wondering, but with rare exception we mostly remain suspended in the Rhetorical Colloidal Forever that agglutinates between Might and Do....What has this century taught the civilized if not contempt for those who merely contemplate; the lockup and the lethal injection for those who Do. (24)

Endless hand-wringing about, say, human rights abuses across the globe is contemptuous; action, condemnable. Knowing this, too often we remain paralyzed between the two. Indeed, "Might and Do" capture the antagonistic op-ed debates about the politics of humanitarian intervention and human rights in general. Academics and think-tankers debate action in Darfur, Baghdad, or Haiti, with contemplation leading not to action but to more contemplation—talk about action being its own kind of activity. Of course, action itself plays out as imperialism, and imperialism takes as its rationale "human rights intervention."

The Homebody offers up her own example of misguided action when she describes her fantasy of healing the hat merchant's maimed hand, but the merchant's silence, passivity, and status as object betray the Homebody's act of reparation as a fulfillment of her own erotic longing. Still, rather than dismissing reparation outright, the play pursues it as a possibility. The basic elements of erotic reparation persist in Priscilla's salvation of Mahala, though with a decidedly more complicated comprehension of the intersubjectivity of the event. Priscilla trades sex with Quango for Mahala's safe passage. The moment itself is disturbing and seems to be evidence of the *failure* of ethics and a representation of politics at its most brutal. Quango strikes his deal with Priscilla by arguing that since she has in the past attempted suicide, she should not be squeamish about trading her body. Quango treats her as one who is already dead but does not offer to redeem that death through the trade. He is not making a Faustian deal—giving her more life in return—but a logical proposition, claiming her good-as-dead body.

Though Kushner here represents the political as the very corrupting aspect of human relations, there may be no space outside of the political, no mode of engagement that escapes the political. The task, then, is to represent an alternative model of the political that is not only not corrupting but that better matches our inner and intersubjective states of being in the world. Being an insider but dislodged into the status of an outsider to the political category "the West" affords Priscilla just this position. Priscilla does not think of herself as Kabuli, as her mother is presumed to, nor does she falsely identify with Mahala. Rather, along with Mahala and the other vulnerable women in Kabul, she is among "the part of those who have no part," as Jacques Rancière puts it. Rancière's phrasing, paradoxical on the face of it, captures the political in-between of those who are in a political space—a community, a state, or an occupied territory—but have no named role in it, not even as political opponents. Less than "the oppressed," they are those who remain unrecognized by all other valid political designations and so lack even a name by which to resist oppression.[24] The phrase captures the political affiliation between Priscilla and Mahala, and their "part" is a placeholder until the politically unrecognized find a voice and speak the political name that allows the human subject and the political subject, both inhering in any individual, to cooperate.

What does the "part" of "no part" look like? What part of us lies outside the political, and how can we interface that human part with the political sphere and still maintain our humanity? Rancière would have us rename ourselves within political discourse in order to gain political recognition and thus go about securing our right to have rights. Kushner takes a different turn here, however, back to citizenship. But in contrast to the publicly validating claim "We will be citizens" that closes *Angels in America,* Priscilla's political claim on her citizenship imagines citizenship not as redemptive but as technical: Priscilla's EU citizenship means she can assist Mahala, even sponsor her for residency.[25] She mobilizes her political subjectivity but is not now constituted by it, and she is able to draw on her political and ethno-racial claims in order to help Mahala, precisely when they have most directly failed her (she has traded sex for Mahala's permissory note with the acting representative of the British government, after all).

The practical efficacy of citizenship is subordinated to the ethical problem of recognition, and Kushner elides the mechanics of emigration while highlighting Priscilla's agonizing choice to save Mahala. Even after Priscilla consents to trade sex with Quango for the permissory papers for Mahala, she later denies to Khwaja that she has them. It is as if she is caught in the "Rhetorical Colloidal Forever" of "Might and Do," only in her case Priscilla has committed the action but is halted by its contemplation. She replies to Khwaja that "no one will save [Mahala]. She'll just … die. She's just one of the people who dies, and no one minds" (115). Priscilla herself has already been installed in that role, dead to her father and then to Quango. And her proximity to the women she saw earlier at the hospital confirms that she does care, precisely because she is "proximate." Still, having taken action, she has not yet taken ownership of it. Priscilla pivots toward acceptance when Khwaja recites a Gnostic poem for her: "Deep within, someone waits for us in a garden. She is an angel, perhaps she is Allah. She is our soul. Or she is our death" (118). The figure in the garden is both the fate that we cannot avoid and the self that we are. The poem's Gnostic equivalence of god, the soul, and death (presumably of our material self) predicts a form of self-recognition conditional for assuming responsibility for another. Notably, this dialectic maps onto but significantly alters the Hegelian formula for recognition, where self-consciousness is conferred by another. Here it is not the gaze of the other but the other's appeal for help, the cry to take responsibility, that precedes the poem. Priscilla's experience teaches her how to read the poem, and the poem teaches her how to act. The poem's separation of self and soul and the anticipated merging of the two in the garden recall Priscilla's division of "watching" and "seeing," only now Gnostic self-conception and self-possession (the opposite of "inappropriate") come together.

The poem and its occasion capture the dialectical interplay of individuality and responsibility at work throughout the play, and the poem suggests how to read the intertextual resonance of Milton's name. Upon his introduction in the second scene, the suggestive irony of Milton's name hearkens the poet of *Paradise Lost,* but the play wholly confounds the Manichean discourse of good and evil, or even the discourse of "evil-doers" vs. "freedom-lovers" resounding at the time of the play's opening in November 2001. Khwaja's garden and the gardens at the end of the play are hardly the paradise of Milton, conjuring a Gnostic rather than a Christian vision, and there is no face of evil other than the void of the other, which stares back. Crucially, in *Homebody/Kabul,* that void is shown to be ideologically constructed, and Priscilla looks past its boundaries to find her own uncanny mirror image. In Khwaja's garden poem, the material self gives way to the waiting angel, or Allah; in the context of Mahala's circumstance, the passage suggests that the broad material and political ramifications of rescuing Mahala are best preceded and comprehended with a search inward, to the core of a spiritual and more deeply knowing self. At the same time, it is this vision of the garden that prompts Priscilla to admit that she has the passage papers for Mahala. Furthermore, the knowledge of and in the garden leads not only to the freeing of the self but also to a commitment to another, Mahala. Gnostic individualism is yoked to an ethical being-for-the-other, while the garden is deterritorialized, a paradisiacal site of being-for-the-other.

In *Homebody/Kabul,* being-for-the other is less an ethic than a vexation of ethics. What does it mean, after all, that Priscilla gets thrown off track and ends up rescuing Mahala instead of searching for her mother? Indeed, ethics and responsibility seem opposed here, as Priscilla's responsibility for Mahala requires giving up on her mother. Writing on the sacrifice of Isaac in Genesis, Jacques Derrida explains that sacrifice represents precisely the conflict between responsibility and ethics. Ethics, Derrida explains, are always communal and widely shared and imply substitution: what is good for one is good for all, and ethical duties between, say, a parent and child pertain to all parents and children (*Gift* 60–61).[26] In contrast, as represented in Genesis, Abraham's responsibility to God is singular, secretive, nontransferrable, and untranslatable. Moreover, Abraham's responsibility does not simply cancel out or overwrite his duty to his son, it depends upon it; the sacrifice only counts if it is a violation of Abraham's ethical duty. Summing up the impasse between responsibility and ethics, Derrida concludes, "Abraham must assume absolute responsibility for sacrificing his son by sacrificing ethics, but in order for there to be a sacrifice, the ethical must retain all its value; the love for his son must remain intact, and the order of human duty must continue to insist on its rights" (*Gift* 66). In these terms, Priscilla must give up on her mother and give in to the incredible story of her survival, even though accepting that story betrays Priscilla's connections to her family and country.

Derrida goes on to observe the myriad ways we are called to responsibility every day when we witness the poverty, suffering, or inhuman treatment of the poor, foreign, or oppressed, and the way we refuse the singularity of sacrifice—*what, you mean I should personally give something up to help another?*—in favor of public ethics—*better we all agree to pass a good law to help those poor people* (*Gift* 85–86). Priscilla's initial response to Mahala is the opposite—"she'll just…die"—but it is no less a widely shared public attitude and likewise an attempt to refuse responsibility. Mahala is no transcendent figure, no absolute other, and so instead of the singularity of responsibility in Genesis, *Homebody/Kabul* requires the mutuality of recognition. Mahala marks Priscilla, recalling God's sign granting safe passage, but Priscilla gives it right back. Recognizing that they are both marked for death and that only she can save their lives—and that "save" can only be contingent and temporary, requiring mutuality—Priscilla accedes to her responsibility. Her parting line to Khwaja, "I can't be blamed when it all goes wrong," comedically suggests that responsibility will indeed come crashing into the realm of the publicly acceptable—all the political and ethical rules governing public behavior (118).

The Sacrifice of Sacrifice

One way of reading the ending of the play—limited, I will argue—is that Kushner provides a relatively simple solution to the utterly complex problems of recognition and responsibility. Consider the elision of the mechanisms of immigration, the problematic of exile, and the difficulty of assimilation, all of which must accompany our understanding of Mahala's resettlement in London. Yet none of these factors are depicted. In the final scene, Mahala lives in London with Milton, in the Homebody's home. She seems all too easily to evince a spectacle of cosmopolitanism that is politically problematic, not to mention rare. After all, she may well be just the sort of Muslim whom Milton sarcastically sketches as an apt mate for his wife the Homebody—liberal, tolerant, and at ease in the West. What does it mean for a political reading of the play that the Muslim woman Kushner presents to us is neither impoverished nor alienatingly devout—not in the end Sharbat Gula, but someone more like Irshad Manji, the celebrated activist for Islamic reform? Carrying on in this way, given the obvious didacticism of the play, from the Homebody's history lesson on Afghanistan to Priscilla's demystification of the burkha, if Kushner is aiming to teach us "tolerance" for Islam in the west, there is little about Mahala that needs tolerating. She gardens, she reads from the Homebody's library, she speaks English, and she knows her way around a modern kitchen. Perhaps we like her too well: She's more familiar to us in some ways than the Homebody herself.

However, it is on just this point, Mahala's occupation of the Homebody's position, that I advance a different sort of reading of the end, by returning to Žižek's notion of enjoyment, and the concept of "rights of desire" discussed in the first chapter. The play's elisions at the end draw our attention away from the life-and-death aspects of migration and, surprisingly, to the *quality* of life. Mahala is more than saved: she *enjoys* her life. Those things that we initially associate with Western upper-class culture, including the garden and the library, are appropriated for the pleasure of this Kabuli Muslim. And though the Homebody's books are "strange" to Mahala, she is up to the challenge: she is a librarian, fluent in the international language of the Dewey Decimal System, a code for placing books independent of national origins (140). More to the point, Mahala already "possesses" the English canon: she has Milton. But at the end of the play, Milton is conspicuously absent. His final gesture in the penultimate scene is to attempt to bribe the mullahs for Mahala's freedom, an act that might belie his claims of cowardice but is already foreordained by the Homebody as a kind of corruption: "That which was once Afghan...we, having waved our credit cards in its general direction, have turned into junk." Obviously not "junk," Mahala finally credits

Priscilla, and not Milton, with saving her.[27] In what sense, then, does she "have" Milton? His name alone suggests that she is now linked with a fundamental part of Western values, and the circulation of paradise lost and regained is appropriated for her story, albeit ironically.

The ironic implications of Mahala being ensconced in Milton's home are underscored when we recall a similar (and likely influential for Kushner) scenario in Mary Shelley's *Frankenstein*. As Gayatri Spivak notes, Victor Frankenstein's creature absorbs the western canon and is thus instructed in the protocols of being human, while observing the Turkish immigrant Safie's lessons in English culture:

> Education in (universal secular) humanity takes place through the monster's eavesdropping on the instruction of... Safie, the Christianized "Arabian" to whom a "residence in Turkey was abhorrent" (*F,* p. 121). In depicting Safie, Shelley uses some commonplaces of eighteenth-century liberalism that are shared by many today.... Having tasted the emancipation of woman, Safie could not go home. The confusion between "Turk" and "Arab" has its counterpart in present-day confusion about Turkey and Iran as "Middle Eastern" but not "Arab." (257)[28]

And the confusion between Arab and Afghani, one might add. Kushner's ironic update is to have "universal humanity," in the form of the library, subsumed by the still-Muslim woman, who is surely instructed by but casts judgment upon the "strange" fruits of Western Civ. The lofty aspiration of universal humanity is rejected, while the canon persists as a propaedeutic of relationality and intersubjectivity. Like Safie, Mahala enjoys the freedom of the Western woman. But also like a contemporary proto-cultural relativist (or "monstrous" multiculturalist), she judges the culture around her at a remove.

Milton is also the hinge linking Mahala's appropriation of the Homebody's "strange" books to her cultivation of the Homebody's garden, which is not so much a paradise regained as a home restored. Notably, "home" and not "Homebody" is restored—the idea of a proper place of dwelling persists, but without the corollary concept of proprietary claims on home. Mahala perceives the Homebody's garden as "neglected," but this judgment likely signals her misunderstanding or misrecognition of the tradition of English gardening, which tends to be more informal, wild, and romantic. Seen this way, the Homebody's garden is a site of melancholy, a space for Romantic contemplation that persists despite the exhaustion of Romanticism in the Homebody's milieu. Mahala has taken over the garden, though it is not clear whether this means assimilating to its Romantic form or creating a more formal, Islamic-style garden, including geometric patterns, flowing water, and fruit trees, arranged for the stimulation of the senses. Mahala tells Priscilla that "a garden shows us what may await us in Paradise," and this remark obviously echoes, yet relocates, Khwaja's poem announcing the Gnostic garden (140). Metaphorically, then, the garden is no longer "English" per se, as Mahala's comment suggests. It carries the mystical connotation of the poem but also the Islamic traditional virtue of keeping gardens as a living metaphor of heaven. But even that notion of the garden is unsettled by the play's final lines: "I have planted all my dead" (140). Meant as a metaphor, the lines direct our attention to the symbolic rather than the literal fact of the garden. The garden may show us what is to come—paradise—but for now it is a site of grief. Taken together, grief and "planting" suggest that the work of mourning is in the future, the work to come in another, better season.

If we recall from Žižek that fear of the ethnic other is a fear that she will somehow steal our enjoyment and thus threaten our possession of our "national way," we see that Kushner has positioned Mahala very much at the center of a stereotypical English way of life, oddly resonant with the Homebody's life. The Homebody herself hardly enjoyed her life, and her irony suggested melancholy detachment. That the play does not restore the Homebody but rather resurrects the Homebody's rightful *enjoyment* through the person of Mahala short-circuits rather than suggests a teleology of redemption. Mahala does not dedicate her life to the Homebody, nor does she redeem her in any way. Rather, she lives in substitution for the Homebody, enjoying her life. In this way, the loss of the Homebody is not a conventional sacrifice with a one-to-one ratio of return, or even the promise of something greater in return. Nothing is returned, in fact, and the only one who benefits is the one who is and remains other to the Homebody. This is all a rather belabored way of saying what is obvious but painful to acknowledge: Mahala is not the redemption of the Homebody but her substitution. As substitution, she is installed as the one who exists *instead of* the Homebody, to invoke Emmanuel Levinas, so she bears a relation of absolute responsibility for the Homebody.[29]

Though sacrifice entails responsibility, responsibility need not entail sacrifice. Indeed, the economy of substitution that Levinas describes is commanded not by a transcendent other—god—but by the pre-ontological condition of otherness that is the source of the self (Levinas's important difference from Derrida). Mahala's substitution for the Homebody does not mean that Mahala has to live the life of her precursor, or live for her, or in her name, though an ethical obligation pertains nonetheless. Rather, she is obliged to *enjoy* the Homebody's life. As Kenneth Reinhard explains:

> For both Lacan and Levinas, substitution does not imply an act of self-sacrifice within an economy of expiation and redemption, but rather the *sacrifice of sacrifice*. The moral economy of sacrifice entails giving up enjoyment for a place in the symbolic order (always advertised as a "higher" pleasure). The sacrifice of sacrifice, on the other hand, insists not on the enjoyment that attends responsibility, but rather on the responsibility for enjoyment, the obligation to maintain the *jouissance* that makes responsibility possible. (Reinhard 793)[30]

This responsibility does not amount to living out her life in terms of demands made by the Homebody but living in proximity to the Homebody's death:

> Rather than imaging the substitution of one-for-the-other as an equation in which the redemption of life from death reinstates the clear distinction between the two... substitution involves the calculus of a one-*with*-the-other, an asymmetrical transaction that insists on the infinite proximity of life to death. (Reinhard 789)[31]

Thought of in Reinhard's terms, planting the dead in the garden is hardly a burial for forgetting or even an exile of the loss into the symbolic order, as the work of mourning is. Rather, it is sustaining the proximity of life and death, including the death of the Homebody.

Proximity, whether as contiguity or the nearness of global capitalist "touch," results in a sense of relationality that is not causal but is a state of responsibility for the other. To be proximate to the dead, as Mahala is at the end, is to be responsible for their pleasure, which is obviously not the same as trying to please them. Rather, "enjoyment" of life means being fully human, open to the world, and aware of the life you do not live and for which you are responsible. This is the ethical insight at the end of Philip

Roth's *The Ghost Writer,* when holocaust refugee Amy Bellette asks Nathan Zuckerman what he had during the war. He is overthrown when his banal reply, "my childhood," is met with Amy's response that she had "somebody else's" (168).[32] To conceive of a life as lived in substitution for the other collapses the space between selves and bears the pressure associated with proximity. Zuckerman's response to the felt proximity is writing, vividly portraying all possibilities of a life (as in Roth's celebrated novel *The Counterlife*). Mahala's response is to plant her dead and in that way live with them. And finally, for the live audience of the play, who mere hours earlier had vibrated in resonance with the living Homebody and who with the final curtain realize that she is not coming back; the audience who has been proximate to the Homebody and is now proximate to Mahala; Kushner's audience is obliged in the end to acknowledge and sustain—through enjoyment—Mahala's substitution for the Homebody.

GLOBALIZATION'S COMPLAINT

Gary Shteyngart's Absurdistan *and the Culture of Culture*

Common Humanity. It's Crap, Really.

What does it mean for the concept of "culture" that Tony Kushner's *Homebody/Kabul* gives its audience an ethics without a programmatic politics? Spirituality without religion? Religion without territory? Deterritorialization without postmodern anxiety? The resolution of the play occurs as its characters traverse, transcend, or utterly shatter all normative frameworks of being and belonging. Nation, ethnicity, linguistic community, culture, religion—none are left intact to function as the site or source for a continued extension of the play's final acts of recognition and responsibility. The challenge of *Homebody/Kabul* is the question of replication: If Priscilla does the right thing, how can we act in a similar fashion? Or is the idea of a common humanity and therefore a common responsibility "crap," as Priscilla puts it early in the play?[1] Given just how, ahem, *familiar*-seeming we are likely to find the Homebody herself, has the play taught us to feel anything other than her ironic emptiness or her despairing guilt? To what do we turn? And to force the question yet further, let us consider Gary Shteyngart's 2006 novel *Absurdistan*.[2] Shteyngart gives his readers a politics that is always against ethics, religion drained of spirituality, territory that has too much religion, and the political unconscious of late capitalism writ very, very large on the body of its hyperconsumptive narrator and hero, Misha Vainberg. *Absurdistan* maps onto *Homebody/Kabul* distressingly well: all characters are consumed by the melancholic ennui symptomatic of global capitalist consumption, Western culture and geopolitics dominate the lives of the novel's Eastern characters, and its hero longs to emigrate, but to New York rather than *Homebody/Kabul*'s London. If we read *Portnoy's Complaint* as a satire on the politics of liberal civil rights, surely *Absurdistan* is effectively "Misha's Complaint"—a satire on the sort of cosmopolitanism and humanitarianism evinced in *Homebody/Kabul*.

What the two texts have in common in fact anticipates where and why they diverge. The play and the novel upset normative categories of belonging as resources for a positive ethics of human care and responsibility. Nation, religion, culture—none are the source of humanitarian ethics, nor are they justifications in and of themselves. In Shteyngart's novel, all ethical impulses are corrupt from the start, because all individuals, including the Candide-like narrator Misha, are so fully interpellated into ideological systems as to have no access to their own core humanity. But Kushner, while sharing Shteyngart's distrust of social systems and group formations as wellsprings for ethical relations, nonetheless allows for humanity, posited in dialectical human interactions such as interpretation, empathy, and recognition.

It may be difficult to recall that before our current, widespread distrust of identity, Jewish writers made it their business to meditate on the meaning of religion, culture, race, ethnicity, and nationality. Emma Lazarus, Abraham Cahan, Anzia Yezierska, Henry Roth...although all explored the end of certain forms of belonging, each also charted new modes of being Jewish and American. Concurrently, Jewish American philosophers and intellectuals critiqued but never doubted that something definably Jewish, and American, existed and that the categories of "nation," "culture," "religion," and "people" were the wellsprings of human values. Contemporary developments should not be entirely surprising in light of the previous chapters' demonstrations of how frequently contemporary Jewish American literature quarrels with the prevailing formulations of categorical belonging, from Roth and Ozick in the 1960s to Segal and Goodman in the 1980s and 1990s. But the quandary between Kushner and Shteyngart is how to locate or illuminate human ethics outside of discredited forms of often hierarchical belonging. And more sharply, given the vast scope of inequality, objectification, and exploitation that occurs between Western developed countries and underdeveloped countries in the Global South and Central Asia, is there any way of responding ethically that is not imprisoned in or otherwise burdened by affiliations with the very unequal and exploitative structures in the first place? The question animates postcolonial theory and globalist accounts of cosmopolitanism, but this chapter reflects more modestly on why, after the public consensus for multiculturalism in the 1980s and 1990s, we find two prominent authors writing so despairingly about culture.

One way of characterizing the dilemma posed by the two texts is to think of them both as written under the sign of poststructuralism, which we may initially generalize as the deep critique of the ubiquitous but invisible ideas inhabiting culture, religion, and, of course, philosophy. Jacques Derrida's great intervention was to observe how Western philosophy is centered on foundational concepts like presence, truth, or consciousness, none of which remain clear or stable in and of themselves after his searching rhetorical analyses. At the same time, especially in the United States, Derrida's most significant intervention touching on culture was his critique of Claude Lévi-Strauss, published as "Structure, Sign, and Play in the Discourse of the Human Sciences," in which he exposed anthropology's fallacies at the heart of its attempt to differentiate and thereby analyze cultures.[3] Commensurate with and in some ways in response to Derrida's critique of Lévi-Strauss, anthropologists Clifford Geertz and Peter Berger, among others, sought to categorize the way cultures rely on or produce the symbolization of common life experiences, and the upshot was that while the content of given cultures may seem significantly different, culture itself as a system of meaning-making was the same the world over.[4] Geertz and others continued by determining religion as another name for culture, declaring that the modern spread of secularity, combined with religion's secular function—primarily meaning-making, only secondarily eschatology—significantly leveled all schemes of cultural differentiation.

Geertz and company argued that the demystification of culture—the "disenchantment of the world," in Weber's famous terms—was coeval with the spread of secularity, but we may also consider that among Western artists and intellectuals, the deconstructionists and poststructuralist anthropologists in part fostered that secularization. After Geertz, Derrida, Foucault, and to a lesser extent Lacan, it became very hard to look for, write about, or perhaps even believe in capital-T transcendence or truth. The dissemination of these thinkers into broad academic and intellectual consciousness occurred in the 1980s, and it is evident in Kushner's theater beginning in the 1990s and of course in Shteyngart's deeply ironic work. What exactly is "it"? Without attempting a full study of influence, it seems clear enough that a significant distrust of grand narratives of nation and peoplehood (originating in postcolonial theory), a rejection of received notions of Truth and Transcendence (from Derrida's critique of logocentrism), and a wariness about reconstituting objective forms of identity such as nation, religion, and ethnicity (from Foucault) informs the work of many contemporary writers in general and is consonant with a Jewish method of critique in particular.

At the end of my previous book, I argued that many Jewish writers, critics, theorists, and intellectuals were comfortable with the poststructuralist and postmodern critiques of identity.[5] Jews have a long history with the ambivalence of several "Jewish questions," including the ethical value of diaspora, the ambiguity of identity, and the instability of concepts like race, ethnicity, and religion. It is fitting that one of the most powerful representations of contemporary Jewish identity is Philip Roth's 1993 novel *Operation Shylock,* a poly-vocal, postmodern narrative that deconstructs the religious, historical, racial, and ethical bases of modern Judaism.[6] Roth's novel channels the theoretical valorization of diaspora evident in the critical work by Jewish theorists Jonathan and Daniel Boyarin, which in turn is amplified in several critical projects, including Jonathan Freedman's *Klezmer America* and work by Benjamin Schreier, with both arguing against reified assumptions of Jewishness and Freedman in particular for an appreciation of the improvisatory, boundary-queering capacity of Jewishness in twentieth-century America.[7]

However, at the same time that poststructuralist theorists, philosophers, and anthropologists were arguing against the possibility of old-fashioned historicism, the coherence of cultural systems, or even the efficacy of symbolism itself, a generation of African American, Chicana/o, and Native American activists and scholars was involved in quite a different project.

Though their activist agendas and critical interventions often clashed, it is safe to say that a common project was the recuperation of underrepresented or repressed histories, the reimagining of cultures, and the establishment of literary canons and traditions. This is where Segal's *Her First American* ends, with a gathering of black cultural nationalists recasting the complicated, ever ambiguous legacy of Carter Bayoux into proto–black nationalism. Segal catches the spirit of the moment by casting the revisionists as Carter's "students," because university students were acutely aware of how canons of history and literature could write whole groups of people in or out of social reality. Segal's closing scene acknowledges the growing power of cultural-nationalist narratives and revisionist history but also observes the stark difference between an individual life and a cultural history, and Segal refuses to close the gap.

The activist construction of canons, curricula, and commensurate identities was theoretically incompatible with the agenda of the poststructuralists, and both groups were rising to prominence in the same places during the same period. Early African American Studies, Chicana/o and Latina/o Studies, and Ethnic Studies programs were established on the east and west coasts in the 1970s and early 1980s, around the same time that poststructuralist theory was also gaining ground. But if the two movements are theoretically contradictory, it is possible to see them as politically aligned. Writing about Derrida, Robert Young has connected the deconstruction of Western metaphysics with a concomitant postcolonial rebellion against Western global domination, while Homi Bhabha creatively folds Derrida into a sweeping agenda of postcolonial and ethnic studies.[8] Bhabha concludes that postmodernism and postcolonial thought are one and the same: the hybridity, cultural subversion, indeterminate agency, and breakdown of structure that characterize the former is the condition of the latter.

In fact, it is startling to consider how frequently the "Jewish question," or several Jewish questions, appear in postcolonial, postracial, and deconstructive writing. In addition to Derrida's own frequent and thorough deconstruction of Jewish historical identity in his autobiographical "Circumfession" and elsewhere and Jean Francoise Lyotard's argument that Jews are synonymous with modernity in *Heidegger and "the jews,"* Edward Said often pointed to Jewish mobility, while Paul Gilroy repeatedly noted Jewish diaspora as a model for thinking about transatlantic race studies.[9] Aamir Mufti's recent *Enlightenment in the Colony* finds European responses to Jews in the eighteenth and nineteenth centuries crucial for a postcolonial analytic of European responses to Indian nationalism, culture, and language, while Michael Rothberg's *Multidirectional Memory* finds the discursive overlap between discourses of European genocide and discourses of European colonialism.[10] Jonathan and Daniel Boyarin offer the most trenchant critique of the deployment of "Jew" as a sign of irreducible difference in contemporary theory, but, as I argued in the introduction, if Jews are not synonymous with exile, ambiguity, or modernity, the modern European and American Jewish experience allows a study in the deep complexity of identity, race, religion, and history.[11] This alone does not add up to a totalizing theoretical account of Jews or the reification of Jews into an analytic device, but it does suggest that Jewish critiques of politics, ethics, and culture rarely end with an assertion of an identity-based model, no matter how progressive.

Globalization's Complaint

One might think that after some decades of deconstruction and flat-out scandalization of ethnicity, culture, and Jewishness in general, there would be little left to attack. Responding to Jonathan Freedman's argument that Jewish American culture is always involved in breaking boundaries and cracking foundations, Riv-Ellen Prell recently conceded the point but asked, without foundations, what is there that is "Jewish"?[12] Prell's question may be directed at the reigning methodologies of Jewish critique, which find Jewishness evaporating upon inspection, but the question becomes a little more charged when considered in light of new Russian American Jewish literature, which updates immigrant and assimilationist paradigms with self-consciously global and postmodern experiences. Shteyngart's *Absurdistan* stands out in particular not for its novelty but for the degree to which it maps onto the literature of a prior generation. A globalized *Portnoy's Complaint, Absurdistan,* like its predecessor, moves its character in and out of various Jewish contexts as its narrator attempts to square his own enormous self-absorption with the filial command somehow to be loyal to his people, the Jews.

The novel begins by describing how Misha Vainberg came to America, suffered a botched circumcision, and ended up as a mouthpiece for corporate multiculturalism, a strange itinerary for a secular Russian whose Jewishness was originally outlawed under the Soviet Union. However, Misha explains that his father Boris sustained a commitment to Judaism throughout decades of political persecution and imprisonment, where Judaism was but one of his several suspect practices. For Boris, Judaism was less a religion than a sign of anti-Soviet protest, bundled with a faith in capitalist entrepreneurship and general hostility toward the law, signaling a quest for liberation, on the one hand, and source of frustration, on the other. When the Soviet Union falls, Boris becomes not a democrat but a gangster, and his suspect entrepreneurial spirit is sourced in his more deeply held commitment to his own ruthless individuality. The Judaism he forces upon his son Misha combines the resentment, criminality, and self-aggrandizement of his gangster capitalism. What was for Alexander Portnoy a "complaint"—a psychological complex traceable to his Jewish American demographic—becomes *ressentiment* for Misha: the painful source of his trouble and the constituting origin of his embrace of diversity. While Portnoy understood minority relations as opportunities for advancing personal prestige, Misha's register is empathetic. With power never in doubt, being a minority means being psychologically damaged and longing for the conflated father/fatherland to grant acceptance.

As a hedge against American assimilation, Boris arranges for Misha to undergo circumcision when he first arrives in America, the summer before beginning college. The procedure is performed by a group of drunken Hasids, and between the poor surgical form and the subsequent infection, Misha is left with what he regards as a "crushed purple insect," a bodily organ that bears witness to his loyalty to his father as well as his resentment toward Judaism. With his subsequent embrace of multiculturalism at college, Misha's loyalty is pulled in different directions. As readers of this book know by now, academic and corporate multiculturalism in the 1990s had very little interest in, let alone love for, Jewish history and culture, and Misha's superficial celebration of diversity in college suggests a commodity form of cultural belonging compared with his more deeply historical, psychological, and culturally impacted commitment to Judaism. But unlike academic debates about culture, Misha's conflicted commitments are not reconciled through better and deeper accounts of culture origins, for at the root of his multiculturalism and his Judaism, culture is simply a commodity form and a kind of political ownership.

The crux of the conflict—self-interest versus communal loyalty—occurs in the novel's final pages, when Misha, exiled to the hinterlands of the eponymous nation Absurdistan and longing to emigrate to New York, draws inspiration from one of his father's favorite maxims: Malcolm X's "BY ANY MEANS NECESSARY" (328). Misha comes across this line beneath a monument to his father erected by "the mountain Jews" of Absurdistan in honor of Boris Vainberg's fortitude, first as a Soviet Jewish prisoner and then, after the fall of communism, as an entrepreneurial gangster.

For Boris, the motto telegraphed an ethic of survival encompassing self, family, and ethnic community, prioritized in that order, which the novel demonstrates as the triumphant aftermath of the collapse of the Soviet Union. Boris's brutal belief that "you have to lie, cheat, and steal just to make it in this world" is in fact the truism of all the novel's Russians, Absurdis, and Americans (329). Everyone is on the make; no transcendent moral value, nor institution, nor governmental system is reliable; and only the most brutal survive. Boris's motto is not particularly Jewish, but the novel places it in a Jewish context, in the improbable village of the mountain Jews, thereby lending the ironic ethnic specificity to what is in fact a universally adaptable credo.

The motto instructs Misha to act with renewed cynicism and self-interest. A scion of Russia's 1,238th-wealthiest man, heir to his murdered father's millions, beset by most of the same psychosexual afflictions as Alexander Portnoy but lacking Portnoy's rage, Misha becomes everyone's dupe; he even fools himself with his deeply sentimental though poorly understood commitment to multicultural equality. At the novel's close, however, he abandons all his political and ethnic affiliations and makes one last-ditch attempt to circumvent the INS and enter New York. Misha's hard-hearted self-interest, his refusal of ethical responsibility, and Shteyngart's satire of multiculturalism would seem to rebuke Kushner's valedictory presentation of the same topics in *Homebody/Kabul*. Indeed, Shteyngart includes a moment of appeal comparable to Mahala's marking of Priscilla's arm in *Homebody/Kabul,* when a desperately poor war refugee offers to sell Misha her five-year-old daughter to do "whatever you want" (287). Lacking Priscilla's capacity for self-reflection, a horrified Misha punches the woman in the face. Though constantly beaten and verbally abused, Misha absorbs punishment and rarely responds, and his violence here is a rupture with his formerly passive, guilt-ridden self, a break from his facile faith in multiculturalism and a step toward his father's ethic of self-loyalty. As Misha tries to flee the scene, the woman's young daughter latches onto Misha's ankle with her teeth, and he drags her down the street as he runs before she finally falls away (288).

If there is a geopolitical allegory in this scene of shocking violence, it is a dark one. Though widely loathed and ridiculed, American-identified Misha is *large,* and his size combined with his wealth—the legacy of his dead father's criminal enterprise—insulate him from the blows he regularly receives. *Absurdistan*'s closing pages occur on September 10, strongly suggesting that all of the novel's consumer excess, political nihilism, and ethical darkness are about to be swallowed up into something far worse and far more globally consequential. *Absurdistan* leaves no part of culture, religion, or personal selfhood untouched by the corrupting hand of market commodification; in contrast to Kushner's play, there is simply no ethical self available to bear the responsibility Priscilla bears for Mahala. So Žižekian as to make the theorist obsolete, *Absurdistan*'s characters not only enjoy their symptoms, they also purchase their desire and can only have it in the act of consuming it. And all this takes place *prior* to the rearrangement of the globe into democrats and evil-doers by George W. Bush.

Though none of the ethics of *Homebody/Kabul* can be located in or recuperated from *Absurdistan,* the novel's citation of Malcolm X directs us rather startlingly back to the social context of Roth's and Ozick's early fiction. Misha's use of the line suggests an itinerary of the concept of "multiculturalism" that may shed light on the preceding inquiry into the status of "culture." "By any means necessary" finally replaces the other prominent motto of *Absurdistan,* constantly deployed by Misha to justify his ridiculous attempts at saving the world, from funding the empty-promise foundation "Misha's Children" to agreeing to serve as the new Absurdi government's minister of multicultural affairs. The motto, adopted from Misha's Midwestern American liberal arts school, Accidental College, is "Think one person can change the world? We do." This was the actual slogan of Oberlin College when Shteyngart attended classes there in the 1990s, and it sums up the prevailing logic of humanitarianism as espoused on liberal campuses.[13] Individuals are the primary agents of change, and individual acts of humanitarian aid can be leveraged through already intact third-world cultural practices—think fair trade or Heifer

International or other culture-based commercial projects. The trick is to change the world but not the world's cultural diversity, and the corollary ethic is cultural respect and rights: let the minority cultures persist independently within host countries. As Misha puts it upon being named minister of multicultural affairs: "I would be in charge of minority relations. I would unite all the different people living in Absurdsvani. And together we would hold festivals and conferences almost every day. We'd celebrate our identities. It would look very good in the eyes of the world. *I would be a uniter*" (251).

If *Homebody/Kabul* recuperates the trend of "waving our credit cards and turning [culture] into junk," *Absurdistan* suggests that it was always junk to begin with and that the credit card only gives the illusion that there was any other value.[14] At the end of the novel, Misha realizes that everything he had believed was not simply a lie but also part of a vast global fraud engineered by sham oil companies and Halliburton executives. It turns out that Misha's Ministry of Multicultural Affairs has been established as part of an elaborate plan, first to stage a civil war, second to destroy the country's infrastructure, and finally to shine a happy multicultural face at the world to beckon Western reconstruction dollars. Misha's ministry, like Portnoy's "equal opportunity nights," turns out to be a pantomime serving the interests of the powerful under the pretense of saving the poor.

Compared with Alexander Portnoy, Misha's adoption of "by any means necessary" signals his self-conscious pivot away from a superficial devotion to multiculturalism and toward a stripped-down, brutal ethos of self-interest. Portnoy makes the same move when he flies to Israel and rapaciously attacks Naomi, relinquishing fantasies of being a do-gooder family man for brutal conquest and self-fulfillment. Portnoy's attempt to claim "the messianic Jewish hole" is thwarted by his inability to sustain an erection; that the impotence occurs in Israel suggests he desires difference. Similarly, at the end of *Absurdistan* Misha pledges to travel to the United States and his Bronx-based love Rouenna "by any means necessary" and declares—so like Portnoy—"the only time I feel safe is when my little purple half-*khui* [penis] is in your tender, tangy mouth" (332). Portnoy tries to kill his desire for difference and claim authentic Jewishness through Israeli sexual conquest, while Misha repairs the damage done to him by Jewishness through an imagined incorporation by Rouenna, a synecdoche for the Bronx and multicultural America.

Malcolm, Means, Multiculturalism

After Misha repudiates his faith in multiculturalism, he has nothing left to believe in. Political, geographical, and cultural nationalism are all tools for global capitalism at every turn. In the autonomous Jewish retreat of Absurdistan, Misha meets the "prehistoric" Mountain Jews, historical castaways who repel rather than inspire Misha: "*Haimosaurus rex* with the flabby little hands, the big roaring mouth, the broad muscular legs and sensual hindquarters. *So this is how it all began,* I thought to myself" (322). Here among the Mountain Jews, Misha finds the monument established in honor of his dead father, noting his accomplishments as a businessman and his fervent hatred of Arabs. At the base of the monument is Boris Vainberg's motto, "By any means necessary." Misha considers, "Had my papa known that he was plagiarizing Malcolm X? Papa's racism was a thing to behold, impenetrable, subsuming, all-encompassing, an epic poem. Could he have independently reached the same conclusion as the black leader of the Nation of Islam?" (329) To Misha's question I would rejoin, was that Malcolm's "conclusion" in the first place? "By any means necessary" is less a conclusion than an action plan. It is not clear if this is Misha's misstatement or Shteyngart's, but in any case, it raises the question, just what did Malcolm X mean, and what does it mean when we find his iconic line in a contemporary Jewish American satire?

Despite its standalone appearance in Malcolm X's speeches, the clause refers back to and is technically subordinated to whatever sentence, whatever stated goal precedes it: We will attain equality *by any means necessary*. Or, we will pass health care reform *by any means necessary*.[15] In this way, the clause simply signals that all tools are on the table. The clause announces the phrase preceding it as an absolute good to which all other actions may be subordinated. The stylized ambiguity of the clause gives it greater power, suggesting a set of means beyond what can be easily listed. Consider, for instance, that Malcolm X was quite clear and specific about the right and necessity of African Americans to use violence, specifying guns and dogs as apt tools to combat oppression, and in fact, several violent clashes between police and black Muslims had already occurred before Malcolm's speech in 1964. Thus, the power of "by any means necessary" is not simply its evocation of violence but also the more powerful suggestion that there are strategies and tools beyond the pale, outside of speech, possibly even beyond imagination that will be involved in the struggle. Finally, as a speech act, the clause announces an absolute commitment to a cause greater than all the "means" that would be mobilized to serve the clause. In this there is a special kind of power, because the commitment announced is transcendent without being Transcendent. It is a secular and not a sacred statement. It stands in place of a statement of faith in a higher power, while claiming the right to all available power.

Malcolm's rhetorical genius was to give the clause its standalone power, so that saying it conferred the power of faith on the speaker. "By any means necessary" subordinated everything—culture, religion, language; domestic and international law; peace and violence—to the absolute cause of equality. At the same time, rather than an exhortation—"I tell *you* the means by which to carry out *my* plan"—the clause invites the audience to fill in the rhetorical blanks—"imagine the most extreme actions and subordinate them to the just cause. There's your revolution." To assent to the clause meant to commit one's own version of radical action for transformational change.

One "means" Malcolm emphasized was the importance of Afrocentric history for orienting black Americans to the revolutionary cause of freedom and social equality. In the years after Malcolm's death, radical civil rights activism became increasingly steered by cultural nationalists, including Stokely Carmichael when he briefly led SNCC and then the Black Panthers; and the Afrocentrist academics at colleges and universities. Especially in education, black American intellectuals believed it important to have autonomy in schools and in curricular choice at the secondary and university levels. Ernestine Silk scoffs at this notion in Roth's *The Human Stain,* but Ilka takes it seriously at the end of *Her First American,* and whatever anyone thinks about it, February is still Black History Month.[16] However, after his African and Middle East visits and the formation of the Organization of Afro American Unity (OAAU), Malcolm's interest in Afrocentrism was practical, a means to an end. Contrary to many contemporary clichés of multiculturalism—including those satirized by Shteyngart—"culture" was quite decidedly an object of construction.

Malcolm did call for black history, and not just for one month a year, explaining, "Every little child going to school thinks his grandfather was a cotton picker. Why, your grandfather was Nat Turner; your grandfather was Toussaint L'Ouverture; your grandfather was Hannibal. Your grandfather was some of the greatest black people who walked on this earth" (43). Repeating "grandfather" instead of going up the chain of descent to great-grandfather and so on clarifies that his Afrocentrism is not one of allegories and metonymies, where students would be encouraged to identify with great black leaders throughout history. The repetition also yokes the singular noun to the plural "people," denaturalizing the very category and shifting Malcolm's audience from an epistemology of genetic racial descent to a pragmatism of racial constructedness. When Malcolm continues, "A race of people is like an individual man; until it uses its own talent, takes pride in its own history, expresses its own culture, affirms its own selfhood, it can never fulfill itself," ownership of history and culture means striking a claim on history, where cultural claims are performative: claiming it makes it yours (53). But beyond personal development, Afrocentrism will lead to worldwide activism. Finally, Malcolm makes clear that owning culture and history is not an end but a means: "We must recapture our heritage and our identity if we are ever to liberate ourselves from the bonds of white supremacy," because "once he realizes what was done, how it was done, where it was done, when it was done, and who did it, that knowledge in itself will usher in your action program. And it will be by any means necessary. A man doesn't know how to act until he realizes what he's acting against" (54–55). Malcolm was convinced that black Americans were living in dark ignorance, cloaked by their unthinking absorption with American culture, custom, and religion. Reclaiming "heritage" was not the goal per se but one of several means by which black Americans could throw off the cloak of ignorance and see their oppression for what it really was. Like violence, culture was a planing tool for leveling the hierarchical power differences between black and white.

We are a long way from Sartre's use of "by any means necessary," which originally appears in his play *Dirty Hands,* in a dramatic argument about how best to prompt Marxist revolution.[17] The play's hero, Hoederer, declares: "I'll lie when I must, and I have contempt for no one. I wasn't the one who invented lying. It grew out of a society divided into class, and each one of us has inherited it from birth. We shall not abolish lying by refusing to tell lies, but by using any means necessary to abolish classes" (120). The line does not call for violence per se but subordinates all tactics to the overall goal of the abolition of class. Hoederer's interlocutor replies, "All means are not good," but Hoederer insists, "All means are good when they're effective" (121). The pragmatism of "by any means necessary" is further complicated when Hoederer explains that one such effective means is to align with the ruling class for the sake of eventually overthrowing it: "We're not fighting against men nor against a policy, but against the class that produces this policy and these men" (121). The Marxist logic puts everything in its place and explains how all tactics can be mobilized in the dialectical process of class revolution. By the time we get to Shteyngart's Boris Vainberg, we see the line appended to just the opposite achievement. Boris, a *perestroika* kingpin, represents the failure of Hoederer's vision and suggests that, whether Marxian or capitalist, conquest is finally conquest.

If "by any means necessary" is endlessly adaptable, to the point of supporting contradictory aims, it is because it signals an absolute commitment to an unspoken ideal. The absolute, or the goal for which all aspects of living in the world are subordinate, could be communism, capitalism, or Misha's freedom to consume. But where would we place Malcolm X's use of the line? Malcolm is famous for his commitment both to a concept of freedom and to claims of cultural separatism, so he seems like a halfway point between Sartre and Shteyngart. Notably, Malcolm was assassinated at a point of political and not only religious transition, as his object of revolution was shifting from black American freedom to something hemispheric, even global. Malcolm's first "by any means necessary" speech was an address at the founding rally of the OAAU on June 28, 1964. Speaking at the Audubon Ballroom in Manhattan (where less than a year later, he would be assassinated) Malcolm declared the goal and the motto of the OAAU: "To fight whoever gets in our way, to bring about complete independence of people of African descent here in the Western Hemisphere, and first here in the United States, and bring about the freedom of these people by any means necessary" (37).[18] There is a conceptual strain between "independence" and "freedom" in this passage, the first term echoing the separatism of Malcolm's earlier speeches with the Nation of Islam, the second anticipating the expansion of his vision to encompass a worldwide struggle for human rights and dignity. Indeed, the speech continues in this mode, forecasting violence—"If you have a rifle, I must have a rifle. If you have a club, I must have a club. That's equality."—but also the prospect of seeing the Universal Declaration of Human Rights and the U.S. Bill of Rights "put into practice" in order to "represent the essence of mankind's hopes and good intentions" (40). Just a few days before his assassination, Malcolm explained to an interviewer that he was trying to "wake the people." The interviewer asked if he meant "wake them to their exploitation," but Malcolm replied "No…, to their own humanity" (Clark, xviii).[19]

Malcolm's revolutionary vision was still opaque when he was assassinated, and it leaves us wondering how he would cast a political philosophy that maintained his enduring commitment to black nationalism, on the one hand, and his expansive work for worldwide freedom and human dignity, on the other. Not that the two are not compatible, but it is not clear what, if *any,* means could accomplish both simultaneously. The wide conceptual space between the two goals has yet to be breached by any political philosopher at this point, and at least in academia it echoes with the noisy, contentious discussion between the fields of ethnic and multicultural studies and their detractors. Chapters 1, 2, and 4 addressed that gap and the way Jewish American writers have represented and responded to it. Philip Roth, though no friend of the multiculturalists, represented liberal commitments to human rights as in fact self-serving for how they sustain a status quo of unequal capitalist competition. The measure of liberalism's failure is Portnoy's self-loathing, which only increases as he succeeds on his own espoused terms, sequestering the poor and minority citizens of New York City under the logic of "equal opportunity," all the while opportunistically exploiting his fame as a rights champion in order to sleep with ever more women. Ozick's early fiction also addresses the struggle to reconcile universalism and particularity, arriving at a conclusion that could only make sense in fiction: Hebraic particularity is in fact the real universality, as all other forms of particularity are idolatrous. So say the characters of "The Pagan Rabbi," and Bleilip, the hero of Ozick's "Bloodshed," even more directly samples Malcolm X's version of "equality," carrying a gun on a visit to a Hasidic town in New York. Though Bleilip's motive for arming himself is never explained, we recall that not only Malcolm X but also Meir Kahane, founder of the Jewish Defense League in 1968, advocated the defense of Jews by any means necessary. Ozick's character is relieved of his defensive duty when he is told by his cousin's rebbe that by virtue of being a Jew, he is already involved in a much more enduring agonistic struggle, namely the responsibility of the Hebraic covenant.

By the time the clause "by any means necessary" shows up in Shteyngart's novel, Malcolm X's suggestive linking of ethnic or racial nationalism and global human rights is no longer plausible. The Homebody's diagnosis of the global disparity between Western liberal societies and the commodified third world, especially when read in light of *National Geographic*'s story about Sharbat Gula, which fetishizes the disparity at precisely the moment it illuminates it, suggests that there is no longer any possible reconciliation of nationalism and human rights. Even the old staple of cultural pluralism—that particular, privately experienced culture can find a universal place in the public sphere—is shown to be naive by Kushner and Shteyngart. For both, culture has become unhinged from particular nations or classes. Optimistically, in *Homebody/Kabul,* knowing cultures and making them strange through cross-cultural encounters—symbolized in the play by the reading and cataloguing of books—is the ethic that rehinges particularity to universality. As Priscilla says about her mother, "She demanded interpretation" (65). "Interpretation" helps explain the ethics of *Homebody/Kabul,* as it implies a phenomenal being open to and for the other, which is a much more complicated form of recognition than multiculturalism, which asks that we accept the other according to a prefigured cultural being. In Kushner's play, the being of culture is *transformation,* and it is precisely by being open to transformation that characters find a way out of the totalizing dilemmas of global capitalism outlined by the Homebody. Seen this way, we can see that *Homebody/Kabul* and *Absurdistan* complement rather than contradict each other. *Absurdistan*'s critique of multiculturalism clears the way for Kushner's recuperation of responsibility.

The Sacred Object of Culture

Between Malcolm and Misha comes multiculturalism, a theory and a practice elevating culture to both an object of study and an indelible way of being in the world. After the 1960s, culture became not just the means but also the object of many ethnic protest movements. Consider, for instance, the activism of La Raza, the Chicana/o rights organization that has significantly influenced the creation of university programs and departments of Chicana/o Studies. Prompted by the rubric of Chicana/o Studies, sociological, political, and legal analyses of the social predicaments of Mexican Americans over the last 150 years in the United States have produced not just an understanding of culture but also an understanding of culture as an epistemic resource, as Paula Moya puts it. More than just a way of knowing the world and certainly more than "a way of life," Moya claims that culture is a way of staying *alive*, of managing to survive within an ever-shifting landscape of white supremacy.[20] Among the founding legends—a true story, but a legend as well—that irrigates Chicana/o culture, at least from the 1960s through 1990s, is the story of Gregorio Cortez, and the mythopoetics of Cortez's famous resistance battle with Texas Rangers in 1901 traces the itinerary of "culture" in Chicana/o Studies. Cortez's self-defense killing of a Texas Ranger and his subsequent escape became the basis for a popular *corrido* (folk ballad) sung on the border to celebrate Cortez's victory. Cortez was acquitted of the killing, for, as the *corrido* puts it, "*la defensa es permitida,*" self-defense is permitted (Paredes 155).[21] Americo Paredes's monumental ethnography of the ballad of Gregorio Cortez, published as *With His Pistol in His Hand* in 1956, became a legend in its own right, retroactively deemed the first significant work of Chicana/o Studies, but a curious shift in the telling of the story occurred in the 1980s. While the ballad was originally sung to celebrate heroic Cortez, the very singing of the ballad—or writing about it, or innovating on it in poetry, film, theater, and criticism—became heroic. Culture shifted from a subject to an object, from a means to an end, to recall Malcolm, so that the poet Evangelina Vigil could innovate on Paredes, "*en que la defense* de cultural *es permitida*"—in defense *of culture* it is permitted (Vigil quoted in McKenna 199).[22] Vigil does *not* advocate killing for the defense of culture, but culture *is* installed as an exalted object in its own right, not simply as the means to record a salutary life.

In the last decade it has become popular for critics to attack this exaltation of culture, but that is not my aim here. Culture has become synonymous with identity and identity with life itself, and I would like to roll back that equation a bit, to recall culture as a pragmatic set of tools for living in the world, culture before its idealization. Walter Benn Michaels has attacked the sociological construction of minority cultures for the way "culture" is the twin of the discredited "race," doing all the work that race used to do for eugenicists and white supremacists.[23] More recently, Amy Hungerford and Christopher Douglas have critiqued artists, intellectuals, and critics who personify texts, giving them the status of historical or raced subjects.[24] These critiques helpfully break up the calcified concept of culture and recall that literature emerges from but is not the equivalent of a human being. With his critique of "literary multiculturalism," Douglas in particular helps demonstrate how and why the culture of culture is under attack. For example, analyzing Gloria Anzaldúa's exemplary study of Chicana/o culture's commitment to race, Douglas concludes, "Anzaldúa is an extreme example of a general and productive indistinction between race and culture in our current paradigm of multiculturalism" due to her constant recourse to anthropological sources and her rhetorical deployment of racialized discourse to ground her thesis of "the new mestiza" (301). However, Douglas falls into the same pattern for which he faults the practitioners of literary multiculturalism, of failing to take into account the affective, real-life circulation of experiences that pass between writers and readers. Readers of Anzaldúa did more than convincingly link her visionary border theory with a compelling history, just as Paredes's readers did not simply look to him for an instruction manual on how to be Chicana/o. No, Paredes's account of Cortez, amplified by José Limón, José David Saldívar, Teresa McKenna, John-Michael Rivera, and many more, was compelling because it provided a language and especially a metaphor to express the lives people were already living.[25]

At the same time, Ramón Saldívar's transnational reading of Paredes and the acrimonious critical debate between Saldívar and Limón on whether Paredes signifies a regional or a global critique of American hegemony raise the question: Who is reifying culture here?[26] Paredes and his acolytes? Or the critics who would isolate an ongoing, vibrant literary-critical discourse for the purpose of dismissing it? Similarly, Anzaldúa's border consciousness named the experiences of a diversity of men and women, not only Chicana/os but Jews too, including Irena Klepfisz.[27] Klepfisz's sympathetic identification with Anzaldúa should be evidence enough that whatever "border consciousness" means, it is not historically fixed, race-based, or even geographically settled, though race, history, and geography have *always* been a starting point for literature.

What Michaels and Douglas neglect in their assessment of multiculturalism are the scenes of reading and writing in which literature is produced and disseminated, and I mean not the rare upper echelons of the intellectual elite (Douglas begins and ends with Franz Boas as primogenitor of a century's worth of multiculturalism) but the thick and irreducibly complex experiences of authors and readers. Always, it is important to remember—though rarely acknowledged in academic criticism—that most literary writers are not pitching their tales to academicians, and most readers compare literature to their own life-worlds, however so defined, and not its place within a category. It may seem ironic and a bit late to critique categorization here, in the final chapter of a book based on a category, "Jewish American Literature," but I hope that the preceding readings have implied what I am getting at here: all categories are contingent modes of reading and may be good for revealing tendencies and trends, but they are never the last word.

If I had it my way, I would parenthetically append the question *what would happen if we called this...?* to every categorization of "Jewish American," "African American," "Asian American," what have you. True, like Misha Vainberg, college students often encounter writers packaged according to category, but the problem lies with categorization, not the writers themselves. Anzaldúa writes about and in response to her experiences, and readers are likewise in a fluid and not a fixed relationship to her text, so that her mythopoetics are best read as intervention and innovation and not whole-cloth invention. That is, Anzaldúa, along with any writer who attempts to think through and represent cultures and identities, must always already know that her or his depiction is far from the last word and always only an attempt at marking an experience and nothing more. So when Hungerford argues against personifying and thereby sacralizing texts, one must ask if the critical response to multiculturalism does not rely on a reification of texts at the expense of context, intellectual categories over living, breathing authors.[28] Whose account is fixed, whose fluid?

Returning to Jewish Literature study, there is nothing in the criticism of Jonathan Freedman, Eric Sundquist, or Caroline Rody that reifies, sacralizes, hypostasizes, or otherwise commits to some concrete notion of race, culture, or "multiculturalism," and all focus significantly on Jewish writers' dialogic engagement with other minority writers.[29] In notable contrast, Douglas excludes Jewish American writing from his "genealogy of literary multiculturalism," because "social science did not crucially provide them with the enabling concept of culture that it provided to the other racialized minority writers. It may be that the reconceptualization of Jews as racially white meant that such social science concepts of culture had less appeal than they did to their still-racialized contemporaries" (327n2). Well, the cart *could* come before the horse, certainly—Jews became white and so did not need social science concepts of culture to evince their particularity. Or, more logically, it was these very concepts, from Boas's anthropology to Kallen's cultural pluralism, that allowed Jews to interrogate the very basis of racialization and so recast themselves as white. It is hard to imagine "I am American, Chicago-born," Saul Bellow's famous opening lines in *The Adventures of Augie March,* as not underwritten by sociology, especially when followed up with, "and go at things as I have taught myself, free style, and will make the record in my own way," a declaration that combines Horace Kallen's cultural pluralism and Charles Peirce's inductive pragmatism. Bellow studied Sociology and Anthropology at the University of Chicago and Northwestern, and though he has frequently rejected the social sciences' representation of man-in-society, his work is clearly informed by and at times shaped in contra-distinction to the social sciences[30] Notably absent in the opening line is any mention of being Jewish—which Augie *is*—but this notability is also notable: the unspoken identity remains an absent presence, as Jewishness is an American type. Roth's *Portnoy's Complaint* is an explosion of that type, the consequence of a prior generation's attempt to fit in too well, and for both writers, the sociology of American ethnicity, race, and class fed their representation of Jewish ways of being in the United States.

Bringing the discussion back into the orbit of this book, consider the apparently contradictory themes of Cynthia Ozick's story "The Pagan Rabbi," which depends on an essential Jewishness, and her novel *The Messiah of Stockholm,* which seems to deconstruct it. Against the lures of Hellenistic, hedonistic social movements, Ozick's story depicts a Jewishness that is bound by a covenant resistant to the changing values of the material world. Against a tendency toward a facile identification with historical trauma, Ozick in *The Messiah of Stockholm* depicts history as a fraud. These observations do not straighten out the curve in Ozick's career but suggest that the curves are the very stuff of a career, precisely what critics miss when they take snapshots of literature and respond as if the frozen literary text were intended to be a theoretical monument. Covenant, identity, history, geography—all comprise the category "Jewish," and it should not surprise us that in any given category there is an incoherence between the fixity of some aspects of Jewishness (covenant) and the fluidity of others (identity). This is the reason that Philip Roth's magisterial *Operation Shylock* is typically described as "postmodern" for the way it realistically and

credibly coheres the several contradictory aspects of being Jewish. Roth's
"Jew" is broad enough to include secular Americans and religious Israelis,
Holocaust survivors, and Jews who would rather opt out of history. The
narrative becomes increasingly anxious and paranoid as it accrues its contradictions, but it nonetheless ends with nostalgic-seeming depiction of the
most *haimisch* sort of Jewish American ethnicity, the Upper East Side New
York Jewish delicatessen, a veritable living museum of Jewish American
culture.

Roth's delicatessen, much remarked upon in Roth criticism, appears as
the very essence of Jewish culture in America, and his evocation of bagels,
cold cuts, and formica counters is seductive.[31] But readers should recall
that it appears after three hundred pages' worth of Roth unraveling the
very concept of Jewish essence, against the notion of cultural authenticity.
The delicatessen at the end is a simulacrum, a sign for which there is no
referent, not because it is ersatz but because it has reified into a symbol of
Jewishness in the absence of any coherent or consistent culture of the Jews.
Even I, a Sephardic Jew who grew up in Orange County, California, feel
nostalgic for Roth's deli, though I've never been there, my parents didn't
eat there, and my grandparents never enjoyed the rare treats of eastern
European peasants.

Is this false consciousness, phony identification, or misplaced nostalgia?
Would it be better to start up a more historically true set of identifications—
to find the Sephardic equivalent of the deli and cathect Jewish longing and
memory onto it? Well, yes, on the one hand. Sephardic historiography and
literature recovery projects are tremendously worthwhile, and insofar as
they chart new stories of immigration, racialization, and interethnic cooperation and conflict—especially prior to the seventeenth and eighteenth
centuries, as Jews and Mexicans in the West separately and mutually ne-
gotiated their status in relation to the Spanish crown—these projects plu-
ralize and globalize "American" history. However, historiography and
cultural history are not exactly the same thing. Cultural history, attempting to trace the lineage of a set of ideas, habits, practices, or values in a
given society, requires idiosyncratic choices, ways of reading, and value
assumptions that align the present with the past through implicitly imagined associations. To put it bluntly, and thereby recall Malcolm X, asking
"Was my grandfather related to Toussaint L'Ouverture?" may prompt
historiography, but "My grandfather *was* Toussaint L'Ouverture, and he

was among the greatest black people that walked the earth" prompts or draws upon cultural history. In this spirit, Roth's delicatessen may not be the true essence of Jewishness, centuries of experience distilled in a pickle barrel, but it may signal a moment of equilibrium between ethnicity and assimilation for Jews in the United States and thereby index current Jewish cultural sensibilities. In short, the myth of the *haimisch* deli is one that Jewish American culture, and American culture at large, still draw upon no matter what preceded it or what came after. Shteyngart's *Haimosaurus Rex* mocks authenticity and severs any notion of Jewish "roots" for Misha, but Roth's deli quite differently exhibits nostalgia as a grand performance that produces rather than reproduces diasporic sensibility.

Granted, in the real, material world, we may be prey to myths of authenticity, not to mention autochthony, both of which subtly align race and place, producing "identity" and often thwarting recognition. Cayton's claim to Lore that New York is a Jewish town or Carter's emphatic announcement of Alabama as the most Southern of places may strike us as true, and we consequently find a more provincial, more static, less fluid America for all its plurality. I am reminded of a cartoon map of the United States published in an early issue of the pop-zeen *Heeb,* with sections of the country tagged according to New York Jewish provincial tastes. California, for instance: "No one should be this far from a bagel."[32] The map suggests a pluralism that is the opposite of cosmopolitanism, a form of recognition that fixes on and then turns its back on difference. What we need are stories—which are finally representations of people in places—that give deeper accounts of where we come from and that enable more and better ethical ways of charting the future.

Whose future? The headline "The Future of American Judaism" appears every few years in major Jewish periodicals, and the stories often chart declining rates of observance, increases in mixed marriage, and most recently, waning support for and identification with Israel among younger American Jews.[33] Without wading into a discussion of those trends—which may appear from a distance as one long, enduring trend across the twentieth century into the present—I would counter that better than pondering the future of American Jews, we might inquire into the future of Jews' America. Chapters 1 and 2, which rotated Roth and Ozick 180 degrees from a diachronic to a synchronic axis, read those two authors as interested in just this question: what kind of America was coming into being in the late 1960s through the mid-1970s, and how might they address it, as Jews? Shteyngart's satire of his Jewish origins and his appropriation of Malcolm X makes him the heir to Roth, or at least the latest, best Jewish American writer to link sex and race in a critique of rights and opportunism. As with *Portnoy's Complaint,* there is little to salvage from *Absurdistan,* and even Roth's hint that the eradication of psychologically impacted social identities might open a path for better ethical relations finds no hold in Shteyngart, where the logic of global capitalism is so ingrained that commodification precedes ethics. Still, if Ozick held fast (and still does) to an ethics outside of politics in contrast to Roth's satire, we find Kushner, too, imagining an ethics of recognition and responsibility that passes through but does not naturalize the political. Kushner's Priscilla cashes in on her British citizenship at exactly the moment she comes to recognize it as subject to revision. At the beginning of the play the Homebody tells the audience that "love has only to do with home," and Priscilla comes to learn more precisely that love may mean losing proprietary claims for home or recognizing another's place within it. Unhinging religion, nation, and culture but still allowing for the emotional, political, and ethical salience of each, Kushner's play reestablishes home as the future we must invent for ourselves and others.

EPILOGUE

Less Absurdistan, More Boyle Heights

Not Your Mother's Melting Pot

Risking nostalgia, I close by rolling back time to the origin of the melting-pot myths and the cultural pluralist penumbra with a look at Jewish American "frontier" writing, Rachel Calof's memoir *Rachel Calof's Story*, and Harriet Rochlin's contemporary novels comprising her *Desert Dwellers* trilogy.[1] Calof's and Rochlin's stories are quite different, but together they may hint at how to think about a deracinated and dynamic pluralism. Calof's memoir describes her life on a North Dakota homestead between the 1890s and 1940s and seems wholly uninfluenced by either literary trends or prevailing social theories of pluralism, even though her life and the composition of her memoir overlap the sociological spread of terms like *melting pot, assimilation,* and *cultural pluralism.* In contrast, Rochlin is a contemporary novelist, amateur historian, and, along with her late husband Fred, archivist of Western Jewish life. Rochlin, unlike Calof, was influenced by the politics of pluralism and indeed of the radical cultural nationalism of the 1960s, and she regards her novels as contributing to a revised understanding of the place of Jewishness in American cultural life. Both writers represent a Jewishness that depends on structures of racial feeling, including family loyalty, commitment to cultural traditions, and above all, reproduction, but that pragmatically looks at just what counts as "family" and Judaism itself.

Rachel Calof was a Ukrainian Jewish immigrant who homesteaded in North Dakota in the 1890s and whose memoir, written in the 1950s, was published as *Rachel Calof's Story* in 1995. The memoir has been published in a gripping English translation that retains much of the original Yiddish language's capacity to swing between tragedy and comedy, as Rachel battles—pardon the yiddishy melodrama—for life's joys and in the face of death's constant menace. While she was still a child, her mother died, and her heedless father remarried and pawned her off as a servant to her extended family. Wanting out of this exploitative setup and hoping to make some money to help her orphaned younger siblings, Rachel agreed to an arranged marriage with twenty-two-year-old Abraham Calof, who had himself only recently emigrated to the United States, along with his family, to homestead.

Rachel Calof's passage to the United States begins archetypically and develops with familiar immigrant plot points: the boat journey to America, fear and then relief at Ellis Island, and the greenhorn's wonder at New York. For about two pages, *Rachel Calof's Story* overlaps the opening of Henry Roth's *Call it Sleep* or the immigration scenes from Jacob Cahan's "Yekel" and Anzia Yezierska's *Hungry Hearts*. However, New York is instantly a terror to Rachel. In two brief scenes she finds her virtue questioned and her health imperiled by vermin, and she and Abraham quickly beat it for North Dakota. There they meet Abraham's family, and Rachel learns that she will be living for the foreseeable future in a one-room shack, bunking with the family's livestock with the arrival of winter: "A pit had been scooped out in the center of the dirt floor. This was the private space which we had been promised. Looking about at the people and the space provided for our living, I knew that I was very close to the living level of an animal....I was urged to make myself at home" (26–27). The situation is bleak, the weather deadly, her place in "America" but a blank spot on the map.

Between the danger and her despair, neither Rachel nor her new family give any thought to questions of identity. There is no American community into which she can assimilate, nor a public sphere in which to practice cultural pluralism. Mental and physical survival are Rachel's overriding priorities instead. However, she immediately refuses the rest of the family's concession to the environment, especially their habit of going to sleep when the sun sets, like badgers. That her matrimonial suite is in a dug-out pit is bad enough; that it is located in her in-laws' shack is something else. Refusing relegation to animal status, Rachel fashions a simple candle made of dried mud, a bit of rag, and some butter. The light allows her to stay up past sundown, and the candles can be used to mark the Jewish Sabbath, which presumably had heretofore passed unnoticed.

Jewish observance is not minimized in Rachel's life, but it exists on a separate axis from the daily business of survival. Jewish law allows for a state of exception, the violation of law for the sake of preserving human life, with the perpetuation of life being the foundation of all other law. Unlike, say, Christian missionaries, for whom suffering and deprivation may be consonant with their transcendent mission, and likewise unlike those Jewish immigrants who converted to Christianity or simply dropped Jewish observance as a means of easy social acceptance, the Calof family has no religious "purpose" on the prairie, nor is there a society into which it might be advantageous to assimilate. Consequently, their struggle with Judaism is not metaphysical, and neither is it a matter of social expediency. Rather, Judaism is resolved pragmatically and not ideally. For example, Calof does not comment on the specific kosher properties of the butter candle, nor does she observe a scene of Sabbath transcendence following her invention. Rather, marking the Sabbath is but one of the many pleasing functions of the candle. The candle rescues Rachel from a state of animal being, which is entirely congruent with the symbolic meaning of the Jewish Sabbath, but Calof sets this up as a felicitous effect of her basic need to live a self-directed life, not her religious purpose per se.

Calof's frontier innovations, born of desperation and deprivation and not primarily political, help us think freshly about the myths of Jewish assimilation that may overdetermine our literary-critical assumptions. The melting pot in particular is the sovereign motif of immigrant literature, the assimilating experience of acculturation, burning off superficial culture and revealing the American inside the ethnic immigrant. Metaphorically speaking, Calof does indeed have the crucible-like experience of having to examine each custom and ritual and to decide on what makes the most sense for her and her family in this new world. But she also literally re-inscribes the melting pot when she describes how her first daughter was accidentally burned to the bone by a cast-iron pot lid, which had heated in coals to radiate warmth in the frigid early spring. The baby's flesh initially decays, but she recovers, and Calof sums up the moment with an echo of Willa Cather, that the "children of pioneers came into the world with a certain hardiness of nature in preparation for the harsh conditions awaiting them" (67).[2] Following another birth, Rachel suffers postpartum psychosis after her mother-in-law relentlessly refuses to heat water for her to wash herself and her baby. Because it is the Sabbath, she will not light a fire to heat the water or even the home; then she warns Rachel that in the first days of the newborn's life, she must carry a knife with her at all times to fend off the devil, who will inevitably come to snatch the child away. Stimulated by her mother in law's superstition and impractical piety, Rachel becomes sick and then is convinced she sees devils dancing on her windowsill and preparing to break in and steal her new baby. After weeks of solitary suffering—her husband is working as a contract laborer on another farm—her sister-in-law moves in with her and coaxes her back to health and sanity.

The pragmatics of living a Jewish life are highlighted more directly in another instance, after Rachel gives birth to Mac, her first boy. The birth of a first son provides the occasion for celebration, and the family decides to slaughter an ox to make a feast. They hire a *sochet*—a Jewish ritual slaughterer—to kill the ox according to kosher practice, but upon butchering the animal, the *sochet* discovers something about the ox that renders it unkosher. However, the *sochet,* observing that Rachel was anemic and weak and in need of nourishment, insists that she eat the meat anyway, explaining "that according to his interpretation of Jewish law [she] was obliged to eat the meat because [she] was sick and needed nourishment...as a mother of small children [she] was morally bound to keep...as healthy as possible" (72). Aghast, Rachel's oppressive mother-in-law, the bane of her life up till that point, hereafter refuses to enter her no-longer-kosher home. Until this moment, Rachel's mother-in-law has been the family's keeper of religious custom, a role typically occupied by the family matriarch. Without a mother of her own and her Jewish education largely neglected by her father, Rachel has deferred to her mother-in-law. However, this moment of law-breaking likewise becomes one of law-making, as Rachel gets what she has so long desired, sovereignty in her own home. Calof explains, "She promised that she would not even drink water in my house which would now be considered polluted. What a wonderful bonus.... It would be an understatement to say that I was pleased" (73). The humor attending the episode cuts off any broader analysis of the religious or identitarian implications of Rachel going non-kosher, and Jewishness accommodates and advances daily life without becoming the sacred object of the Calofs' existence.

Calof's enduring quest, established early on in the memoir, is the desire for privacy: "Of all the privations I knew as a homesteader, the lack of privacy was the hardest to bear" (24). Indeed, a recurring theme throughout the memoir is Rachel's constant battle for private space and freedom from her imposing mother-in-law and her growing sense of self-possession and agency. However, Calof clarifies that her sense of autonomy occurs not through domestic accomplishment but through an affirmation of her individual worth. She recalls that for the first half-year that she lived with Jacob and his family, she was not formally married to him, apparently a tactical decision that allowed her to claim homestead land in her own name and thereby double the family's claim: "Single women had the same rights as men. Abraham's land would be in his name but mine would be in my maiden name" (35). Though the family effectively merged the two properties, Calof reflects on how the land claims engender her growing sense of self-worth and entitlement to make decisions on behalf of herself and the family. After making a trip to Devils Lake to file their land claims, Jacob and Rachel camp at their "hotel"—beneath their horse-drawn wagon—where the "floor was the never-ending prairie and the ceiling the vast vault of the sky" (34). Having broken free of the squalid homestead and her oppressive in-laws and having acquired a legal claim on land in her own name, Rachel becomes increasingly confident in her capacity to evaluate and direct her own life:

This trip to Devils Lake had heightened my resentment and discouragement at the prospect of returning to the depressing conditions [of the homestead]. Abraham sighed regretfully. He was very sympathetic and vowed that some day our lives would be better. I did not take much comfort in the phrase "some day," but I was pleased by his concern and sensitivity. I told [Abraham] not to worry about me anymore, that I stood by his side and

together we would attain a decent life. Of course, I knew that the problems
ahead were as deep as an ocean, but our talk under the stars fortified me and
by the time we reached our destination I felt pride of ownership in the land
which we had claimed. (36)

Rachel impressively outlines a problem and proffers her own fidelity as a
solution, more or less relegating Abraham to a bit player in his own drama.
Her commitment is not subordination but allegiance, framed as a choice
and not compulsory. Her land claim establishes her material equality with
Abraham, the basis for her renewal of their partnership.

Calof's memoir ends surprisingly. Year by year, her family faces more
perils but also becomes more rooted until they have established a successful, sustainable farm. Having built and furnished a house and garnering enough income from farming for plenty of food and heat, Abraham
becomes something of a community leader, both in Jewish and local
community circles. However, Rachel's enduring desire for privacy and
self-direction persists, beyond the accumulation of material comfort. In
the afterword to the memoir, Rachel's youngest child, Jacob, delicately
suggests that his parents' allegiance ended along with their hardships and
that his mother became increasingly resentful of his father's use of their
house for communal gatherings. Where once Rachel's domestic role had
intrinsic worth as part of the family's struggle to survive, the very same
duties—cooking, cleaning, and general domestic upkeep—came to seem
like patriarchal impositions. Though it does not appear that the Calofs di-
vorced, their son Jacob reports that when his parents came to visit children
and grandchildren, it was always separately.[3]

Though I am reluctant to submit Calof's memoir to the same level of
scrutiny as Cayton's autobiography in chapter 4—primarily because Calof
was evidently not writing for publication and secondarily because her
thoughtfulness about being Jewish does not approach the complexity of
Cayton's on being African American—it is worth noting that she weaves
her story with three dominant threads but does not tie them off at the end.
The material, domestic, and labor struggles of her family, her personal
fidelity to Judaism, and her desire for an autonomous life are the dominant themes of the memoir, but at the end there is no harmony, no unified theory of how the three cooperate. Indeed, Rachel and Abraham pull
up stakes after their children grow up and move out, and they move into

the city, where Abraham starts a grocery business, an unsatisfying denouement if we are looking for the sort of narrative closure found in Cather.

The open end of Calof's memoir suggests a pluralism-in-progress: the frontier is not subordinated to American identity, as in Frederick Jackson Turner's frontier thesis; rather, it is a mode of being American along with being Jewish and in addition to the struggle for personal autonomy.[4] There is no announcement of what it means to be Jewish, primarily because Jewishness was never in doubt for Calof and her clan, and religion, culture, and identity are the performative mode and effect of surviving in America.

The memoir was published in 1995, right at the beginning of a new wave of scholarship and criticism in Jewish cultural studies, and this interesting anachronism yields a distinctive sort of pluralism. The editors of the 1998 collection *Insider/Outsider: American Jews and Multiculturalism* observe in their introduction that "it is no secret that Jews confront contemporary multiculturalism with great ambivalence, trepidation, and even hostility," but Calof's memoir hails from a period before multiculturalism's anxious theorization, offering a portrait of pluralist America that refuses facile formulation (4). Yes, as Jews she and her family would eventually "become white folks," as Karen Brodkin has explained, and the narrative makes no mention of other immigrant cultures or native claims to the land.[5] But Calof's emphasis on difficulty and her lack of celebratory pangs for assimilation suggests how aware she is from the beginning that her life will be a gradual trade-in of greater difficulties for lesser ones. This is not a memoir of the American Dream, the Promised Land, or even, as Norman Podhoretz titled his memoir, "Making It," and so Jewish America remains a work in progress.[6]

Where Is Boyle Heights?

Harriet Rochlin may be the best contemporary Jewish American writer you have never heard of. The author of three novels comprising the *Desert Dwellers* trilogy and the Western historiography *Pioneer Jews,* Rochlin writes about Jews who are outside the typical frameworks and plot points of American Jewish literature.[7] Though set in the nineteenth century, there is no Ellis Island, Delancey Street, or East Coast geography in her fiction, and she has no place for either humorous or woeful tales of immigrant assimilation and religious reformation characteristic of her turn-of-the-century precursors. Instead, her characters are pioneer settlers and land speculators, and though they are Jewish, stock "ethnicity" plots generally do not appear. For this and several other reasons, she is a hard writer to place—not typically Jewish, not typically Western—and her work is significantly underread. In the spirit of rolling back the debates on multiculturalism and pluralism, Rochlin's work springs from and exemplifies a form of pluralism rarely seen in literature and certainly underdeveloped by professional practitioners.

Rochlin grew up in Boyle Heights in the 1920s and 1930s, when that East Los Angeles neighborhood was a startlingly vibrant, multiracial, leftist enclave of social progressivism and political cooperation. Perhaps like many, Rochlin did not fully realize just how unusual Boyle Heights was until she left in the 1940s, first to attend U.C. Berkeley, where she earned a B.A. in Hispanic literature, and then when she settled in the San Fernando Valley with her husband Fred Rochlin. Fred, who grew up in Nogales, Arizona, in a secular Jewish socialist family, was an architect but also an amateur historian and an industrious collector of nineteenth- and early twentieth-century border-area photography.

Harriet Rochlin was inspired by her husband's passion for the southwest, and though her own family emigrated from eastern Europe, she too came to identify with the West, including its history of ethnic mingling and feminist reform. She has explained, "I was desperately seeking some means to unite, to articulate my visceral feelings, to in some way objectify my attachments [to the images of western Jewish settlers]," and she found her warrant for writing in the 1960s "new pluralism."[8] Of the new pluralist appeal for ethnic history, Rochlin explains, "It just happened to come at a time when I very much needed it...during that whole period I myself didn't know where to firmly put my feet down, as a Jew, as a Westerner, as a woman."[9] The multiple draws on her sense of self could only partially be fulfilled through historiography, and Rochlin turned to writing as a way not to prove her origins but to produce them: "I was seeking some kind of identity, some kind of evidence of origins that I could really attach to."[10] Rochlin was *not* seeking a misty, ersatz ethnicity, as evidenced by the work she ended up producing, which has more in common with T. Coraghessan Boyle's *Tortilla Curtain* than with Irving Howe's *World of Our Fathers*.[11] Rather, she set about inventing origins, largely based on her and her husband's historiography, her love of the West, and her inculcated belief in cultural pluralism. Though social histories of the new pluralism tend to sort ethnic movements into nonwhite and white reactionary camps, Rochlin was equally inspired by Chicana/o, African American, and Native American cultural movements as she was by the return of Irish, Italian, and Slavic cultural identification. In this way, Rochlin is like Lillian Cohen, the dentist's wife from Syracuse who cited Eldridge Cleaver in a letter to Philip Roth, and probably like a significant many progressive Jews who were not only not cowed by cultural nationalists of color but also found common cause with them.

Rochlin's trilogy reads as if it were modeled on Leon Uris's famous novel of Jewish repatriation, *Exodus* (1958), itself a source of ethnic pluralist pride for Jews in America, especially after 1967.[12] With the American Southwest standing in for the Promised Land and Arizona territory settler Benny Goldson for Ari Ben Canaan, Rochlin represents the Arizona territory as a borderland, where Mexican and U.S. populations merge. When protagonist Frieda Goldson approaches her new home, the Arizona settlement of *Dos Cacahuates,* her husband points out, "'Look, you can see Mexico,'... pointing south. Frieda peered into the distance, unable to detect an iota of difference between the Mexican and American desertscapes" (31). Subsequently, Mexicans and the Arizona settlers cross the border regularly and with minimal regulation in order to trade provisions and supplies. Contact is common enough to result in mixed marriages, and at the Passover seder, the Haggadah, the traditional retelling of the Jewish exodus, is translated from Hebrew into English and Spanish for the sake of the mixed Mexican and Jewish guests. The meal includes "tortillas for matzah; chiles for bitter herbs; wine sanctified, not by a rabbi, but by the Brothers of the Holy Cross" (47). The menu might give Orthodox Jews fits, but Rochlin's characters are Jewish settlers, not settler Jews, to paraphrase the old identity conundrum. Rochlin practices a pragmatic Judaism that favors ethics and worldly action over esotericism, and she eschews the notion of "chosenness" that looks backward in favor of Western spirit of cultural adaptation, reconstruction, and invention.[13]

The *Desert Dwellers* trilogy slashes through several sociological accounts of American acculturation. Like Calof's memoir, Rochlin's novels hearken to American frontier myths, only Rochlin's frontier, with an already existing ethnic plurality of Mexicans and Native Americans, and with a productively blurred border rather than a blank space on the map is already pluralized. Benny and Frieda do not question what it means to be American, but Frieda is particularly keen to flee from the old-world Jewishness of her relatives. In the opening novel *The Reformer's Apprentice,* Frieda lives in her family-run boarding home for immigrant Jewish men, where she chafes at her relatives' religious conservativism and the boarders' sexist attitudes. The tone of the early chapters of *The Reformer's Apprentice* is similar to Calof's at the beginning of her memoir and recalls Anzia Yezierska's depiction of forlorn and oppressed immigrant women. But like Calof, Rochlin's Frieda does not assimilate, "melt," or otherwise transform into something recognizably different and American as a result of deprivation, hardship, and cultural contact. In this way, Frieda also swerves from Horace Kallen's anticipation of Jewish revival in the United States. She does not become "more the Jew," as Kallen forecasts, but a different sort of Jew, whose ethics and practice are a virtual contact zone between intrinsic faith and extrinsic plurality.

The reconciliation between individuality and plurality, and between European Jewish ethnicity and American southwest culture, occurs in the trilogy's final novel, *On Her Way Home,* when Frieda recommits to her husband and to their settlement. The novel is dark, as Frieda spends much of the plot visiting a Nogales jail, where her sister Ida is awaiting trial for murder. Though she is falsely accused and is finally freed, her experience causes Frieda to reflect again on her choice to live in the desert, on the margins of the law and outside the boundaries of a stable, if restrictive, paternal culture. Why has she chosen to live among speculators and outlaws? Why is she risking her life to build a settlement when her family in San Francisco is already comfortably, if restrictively, established? Finally, if a bit sentimentally, Frieda concludes that her covenant is with the possibility and promise of reinvention, social progress, and cultural improvisation, and Rochlin concludes the trilogy with a gesture that ritualizes this commitment. In a surprising revision of the Jewish practice of hanging a mezuzah on the doorpost, Frieda tells her husband, "I'll carve it on the doorpost. *Aqui me quedo.* I'm here to stay" (270). Ritually Jewish, pragmatically local, personal, present-tense, and culturally hybrid, Frieda's covenant marks a borderlands diasporic consciousness, where Jewishness is malleable and protean and at home.

The cultural pluralism of Rochlin's novels is closer to William Connolly's theorization of "creedal ventilation" where internal differences within the group and contact with other group's values prompt cultural revision, than it is to Horace Kallen's static "symphony" of cultural difference, where each instrument is always the same, in the same seat, and always an instrument.[14] While Kushner and Shteyngart position their representation of multiculturalism on the precipice of the future, suggesting the inevitability of their (optimistic or depressing) visions, Rochlin anachronistically lodges her vision in America's past—not as the missed opportunity to get it right, as with Segal or (perhaps) Goodman, but with the historiographer's assumption that rewriting the past is nothing but getting it right, is always a stab at a clear, accurate, and thus path-charting prolegomena to present possibility.

In addition to her research, Rochlin casts her revisionary literature by drawing on her experience growing up in Boyle Heights to imagine an innovative, active cultural pluralism. Recalling her childhood, Rochlin explains that pluralism was "vigorously taught" in the schools and gave a "feeling of exhilaration," emphasizing that people who have the experience "remember it with a sense of vibrancy."[15] Rochlin recalls being thrilled by the different languages, foods, modes of dress, and daily cultural customs of her classmates; lest this seem like nothing more than a nostalgic child's point of view that misses the more complicated world of adult conflict and contention, historian George Sanchez's recent work on Boyle Heights affirms Rochlin's childhood reminiscences. Sanchez explains that this East Los Angeles neighborhood's multiculturalism was substantially constituted by two racially motivated government policies in the 1930s and 1940s: racial redlining and, after World War II, the inclusion of Jews under the category "Caucasian." As migrants increasingly came to California in the late nineteenth and early twentieth centuries, local government officials distinguished between midwestern migrants and ethnic newcomers, including Jews, Mexicans, and Japanese (635). Zoning ordinances and real estate covenants segregated East Side and West Side neighborhoods, effectively creating a multiracial, multicultural East LA. By 1940, there were about 35,000 Jews, 15,000 Mexicans, and about 5,000 Japanese in Boyle Heights, as well as smaller populations of African Americans and Italian, Armenian, and Russian immigrants (635).

The Jews in particular were left-leaning, and the neighborhood established an early tradition of multiracial cooperation for advancing schools,
public health, and local representation on city council. By the 1940s, however, mixed ethnic neighborhoods appeared politically frightening to local
government leaders, as well as somehow un-American, and state-level
politicians mobilized "social science research, fiscal policy, and direct intervention" to re-form "local communities through housing and transpor-
tation policy" (636). Officially reclassified as "Caucasian," many Jews left
Boyle Heights for the West Side, but one result was to concentrate further
and radicalize the remaining Jewish population who persisted in their
commitment to the neighborhood and its ethos.

In the 1940s and 1950s, Boyle Heights became even more actively committed to left-leaning social causes, labor, and multicultural cooperation in
response to postwar suburbanization and state-level McCarthyism. The
Soto-Michigan Jewish Community Center (named after its cross streets,
Soto and Michigan) turned its attention to "innovative programming
aimed at addressing the changing nature of the Boyle Heights community and the need for increased intercultural work in the neighborhood"
(642). The center organized a "festival of friendship" and special celebration nights for the various ethnic groups in the neighborhood. Later came
a Negro History Week and a celebration for Mexican Independence Day.
Though this sort of programming now seems hokey and fit for Shteyngart's mockery, in the 1940s these were anomalous, countercultural activities. More important, the cultural celebrations were the festive counterpart
to more politically salient activities emerging from the neighborhood such
as the Los Angeles Committee for the Protection of the Foreign Born
(LACPFB), which fought ramped-up immigrant deportation policies
under J. Edgar Hoover, and active support for left-leaning city council-
man Edward Roybal (653).

Over time, Jews who moved to California chose the suburbs, and as the
remaining population aged, Boyle Heights became an increasingly Hispanic
neighborhood. According to Sanchez, subsequent McCarthyism and racist
social policies destroyed the multiracial political and social cooperation that
reigned in Boyle Heights, and he blames the 1960s ethnic nationalisms—
focused solely on single group identity—for eclipsing the legacy of Boyle
Heights. The version of multiculturalism that emerged in corpora-
tions, public schools, and government programs in the 1970s repeated

many of the intellectual fallacies of Kallen-esque cultural pluralism, but the multiculturalism of Boyle Heights assigned rich meaning to groups-in-partnership, where having a cultural or racial identity was the beginning and not the end of multiculturalism and affiliation was the necessary means for fighting against racism and for social and economic justice and immigrant rights.

Boyle Heights still exists, of course, and community leaders are attempting to rekindle the cooperative multiracial spirit, but culture has lost much of its political value for everyday activism—as shown in Shteyngart's novel. Rochlin still draws inspiration from her multicultural childhood, but for the rest of us, there may no going back. But what about forward? If the city Sanchez describes no longer exists as such, and if attempts to reconstruct it are mere fronts for global capitalism as Shteyngart represents it, can there be a place, a site, a source of multicultural and multiracial cooperation? A community committed to art, culture, politics, and ethics? Committed not to static museum-piece culture but to an improvisatory cultural practice that gives life to irreducible and transformative art? A place less like Absurdistan and more like Boyle Heights? Reader, I suggest that such a place exists; that you are holding this book in your hands and reading it means that you are already there. The place I refer to is—or can be—academia itself.

Writing this, I trust that academic communities may resemble mid-century Boyle Heights in a number of ways. The denizens of academia "reside" there because of a commitment to culture, art, ethics, and politics and not just for the low rent. Academics, especially humanists and those who research and write on race, religion, ethnicity, and culture, often identify deeply with their objects of study, while scholarly convention requires critical distance sufficient for the kind of revisionary work necessary for a refurbished multiculturalism. Though there is an incipient politics within ethnic studies that pushes scholars toward a defensive, monocultural scholarship, we tend to read across those lines in order to mine critical paradigms as well as to satisfy personal interests. Our friends and colleagues are often doing the sort of work we value and aspire to within their own ethnic "slot," and if that sounds too upbeat, I would at least suggest that even the disarming interrogations that do occur at conferences and symposia, where one ethnic group's scholar reveals how another scholar has neglected her group's experience, history, or point of view can nonetheless be taken as a potential invitation for virtual collaboration that will draw the broadest, most comprehensive account of the experiences of minorities in the United States. Ultimately, I trust that most of us writing in ethnic studies seek to deconstruct the sorts of prevailing intellectual hegemonies that minoritize, racialize, and marginalize ethno-racial groups in the first place and to bring to light long-neglected histories, experiences, and cultural artifacts.

Programs and departments of ethnic, Chicana/o, Native American, African American, Asian American, and Jewish Studies are often the result of bitter campus battles. From grassroots, student-led hunger strikes to top-down acts of administrative concession and contrition to off-campus community-building and fundraising endeavors, the very fact of such programs traces a victory for ethnic solidarity and protest, not to mention scholarship. And once established, such programs are charged with a broad mission of community outreach, minority student and faculty mentoring, and social activism in addition to teaching and scholarship. Unusual among campus academic units, ethnic studies programs often attract students seeking cultural community and social and political validation. Necessarily, then, Chicana/o Studies represents the interests of Chicana/os on and off campus, and Jewish Studies does the same for Jews, and so forth. At the same time, such programs may serve as the "conscience" of a university's curriculum, offering the courses that fulfill diversity or multicultural requirements. The result is a highly politicized academic mission, where ethnic studies programs are often on the defensive, rightfully fighting to protect their original mission, on the one hand, and struggling to work within the general curricular norms that, intentionally or not, commodify ethnic studies for its "multicultural insight" on the other. Shteyngart mocks curricular pieties through Misha's multiculturalism, but I suspect many scholars working within ethnic studies get the satire, as discipline specific, deep-reaching research is pressed into ready-molds of multicultural celebration. All touch corrupts, as Kushner's Homebody says, and the interface of ethnic studies research and a marketplace-like curriculum is the tepid celebratory homage to the ethnic underdog.

Still, *Absurdistan*'s satire of academic multiculturalism may be a starting point for reinvigorating ethnic studies and specifically Jewish Studies.

To the extent that Jewish Studies or any other identity-rooted academic program exists solely to produce monuments to that identity, it will find itself the subject of satire. But as Sanchez has said about Boyle Heights, celebrating identity is the beginning and not the end of a vigorous ethnic pluralism, and given the longstanding Jewish reckoning with identity, a self-reflexive, interethnic Jewish Studies may respond to satires (or worse) of "culture" with more complex accounts of culture's origins and transformations. Following Sanchez's overview of how a pluralist Boyle Heights combatted racism and illegal deportations and battled for political recognition and representation, I suggest that Jewish Studies may draw inspiration from such a model and seek out interethnic community for the analysis of racial formation and the advocacy of rights and recognition.

For over a decade now, Jewish Cultural Studies has lamented its relegation outside the family of multicultural or ethnic studies racial and ethnic groups, asking why the Jewish study of Jewish life is not regarded as having the same curricular or research worth as the African American study of black life or the Native American study of Native American life.[16] Recently, however, an interesting and provocative shift has occurred in Jewish Studies: the Jewish study of American life in Jonathan Freedman's masterful *Klezmer America,* the Jewish study of Native American life in Rachel Rubinstein's *Members of the Tribe,* and Dalia Kandiyoti's Jewish study of Latino life, *Migrant Sites.*[17] These are books that explore how Jewish history, literature, and culture interface with, borrow from, or otherwise suggest models for how to read America's cultural pluralism, and this book is my own attempt to work in this mode. *Race, Rights, and Recognition* not only presumes that Jewish American literature is responsive to the politics and ethics that emerge from new social and cultural alignments after the 1960s, it also demonstrates how Jewish American literary criticism can reflect upon, revise, or perhaps even advance a broad social understanding of how we narrate difference in the United States. Admittedly, hashing through U.S. ethnic identity issues can seem like sifting through the ruins of a never-completed, derelict monument to a worthy cause, but I am convinced that a globalized approach to Ethnic Studies that returns to the core questions of recognition, citizenship, and human rights will discover the insights necessary for engaging our current global moment. If Ethnic Studies missed out on the Jewish American literary critique of the 1960s and 1970s formations of multiculturalism and the concomitant politics of race, we dare not now miss out on Jewish American literature's dynamic critique of global human rights and the politics of international recognition and its revisionary modeling of an ethics of intervention.

Acqui me termino: here, I'll end.

NOTES

Introduction

1. Saul Bellow, *Mr. Sammler's Planet* (New York: Viking, 1970).

2. Saul Bellow, "Mr. Sammler's Planet," *Atlantic Monthly,* November 1969, 95–150, December 1969, 99–142.

3. Hannah Arendt, "Reflections on Violence," *New York Review of Books,* February 27, 1969. Available at www.nybooks.com/articles/archives/1969/feb/27/a-special-supplement-reflections-on-violence/, accessed June 15, 2011.

4. "Critical Post-Judaism" is Jonathan Boyarin's inspiring if clunky term for a new mode of Jewish-informed cultural critique. See *Thinking in Jewish* (Chicago: University of Chicago Press, 1996).

5. In this respect, I distinguish my work from an important list of books preceding it, beginning with Emily Miller Buddick's *Blacks and Jews in Literary Conversation* (New York: Cambridge University Press, 1998) and continuing with Adam Zachary Newton's *Facing Black and Jew: Literature as Public Space in Twentieth Century America* (New York: Cambridge University Press, 1999) and Eric Sundquist's *Strangers in the Land: Blacks, Jews, and Post-Holocaust America* (Cambridge, MA: Harvard University Press, 1995). All three books are rich comparative studies on the black/Jewish literary "interface" (Newton).

6. See, for instance, Eduardo Cadava and Ian Balfour, "The Claims of Human Rights: An Introduction," *South Atlantic Quarterly* 103 (Spring/Summer 2004): 277–96.

7. Horace M. Kallen, *Culture and Democracy in the United States* (New Brunswick, NJ: Transaction Publishers, 1998).

8. For example, see "The Census Form: Send it Back!" *San Francisco Bay View,* March 10, 2010. Available at http://sfbayview.com/2010/the-census-form-send-it-back/, accessed August 24, 2011.

9. Will Herberg, *Protestant, Catholic, Jew: An Essay in American Religious Sociology* (Garden City, NY: Doubleday, 1955).

10. Clifford Geertz, *The Interpretation of Cultures: Selected Essays* (New York: Basic Books, 1973).

11. G. W. F. Hegel, *The Phenomenology of Spirit,* trans. A. V. Miller (London: Clarendon Press, 1977), 111–15.

12. See Charles Taylor, "The Politics of Recognition," in *Multiculturalism: Examining the Politics of Recognition,* ed. Amy Gutman (Princeton, NJ: Princeton University Press, 1994), 25–74. Noteworthy for its condescending tone is Brian Barry's *Culture and Equality: An Egalitarian Critique of Multiculturalism* (Cambridge, MA: Harvard University Press, 2001). Barry's unselfconscious assumption of the role of consuming chooser who can adopt or shed any identity associations at will seems especially remote from the way people of color live, embedded in regimes of cultural chauvinism. On the other hand, Kwame Anthony Appiah's celebration of cosmopolitanism, while nominally more open to cultural difference and written from the point of view of an African immigrant to the United States, nonetheless conflates social privilege—Appiah was the son of a tribal chief—with cosmopolitan choice. Appiah, *Cosmopolitanism: Ethics in a World of Strangers* (New York: W. W. Norton, 2007).

13. Elizabeth Povinelli, *The Cunning of Recognition: Indigenous Alterities and the Making of Australian Multiculturalism* (Durham, NC: Duke University Press, 2002).

14. Fred Kaplan gets the gist of both sides of the debate in his article, "Was George Bush Right about Freedom and Democracy?" *Slate,* March 2, 2005.

15. Michael Kramer, "Race, Literary History, and 'the Jewish Question,'" *Prooftexts* 21.3 (Fall 2001): 287–321.

16. Henry Louis Gates Jr. famously explored the link between human being, race, and writing in "Writing 'Race' and the Difference It Makes," his editor's introduction to *"Race," Writing, and Difference* (Chicago: University of Chicago Press, 1986). See also Robert Dale Parker, *The Invention of Native American Literature* (Ithaca, NY: Cornell University Press, 2003).

17. Franz Boas, *Race, Language, and Culture* (Chicago: University of Chicago Press, 1995).

18. Over and above the neoconservative Jews with ties to the Bush administration, including Ari Fleischer and Paul Wolfowitz, see, for instance, Alan Dershowitz, *The Case for Israel* (New York: John Wiley and Sons, 2004).

19. David Domke, "George W. Bush and the Gospel of Freedom and Liberty," *Seattle Times,* May 1, 2005. Available at http://seattletimes.nwsource.com/html/opinion/2002257816_sunday domke01.html, accessed August 1, 2010.

20. Paula M. L. Moya, *Learning from Experience: Minority Identities, Multicultural Struggles* (Berkeley: University of California Press, 2002), 38.

21. Boyarin, *Thinking in Jewish.*

22. Matthew Arnold, preface to *Culture and Anarchy* (New York: Oxford University Press, 2006).

23. Horace Kallen, *Culture and Democracy in the United States* (New Brunswick, NJ: Transaction Publishers, 1998).

24. William Connolly, *Pluralism* (Durham, NC: Duke University Press, 2005).

25. Werner Sollors, *Beyond Ethnicity: Consent and Descent in American Culture* (New York: Oxford University Press, 1987).

1. Portnoy's Complaint

1. Philip Roth, *Portnoy's Complaint* (New York: Vintage, 1994).

2. Wendy Brown explains that the ethos of "tolerance" that emerged from 1960s pluralism amounts to the regulation of aversion and the production of "race" attached to individual bodies,

a practice she compares to the French strategy for regulating Jewish participation in public life in the nineteenth century. Brown, *Regulating Aversion: Tolerance in the Age of Identity and Empire* (Princeton, NJ: Princeton University Press, 2006).

3. See chapters one and two of Carol Anderson's excellent and richly archival history, *Eyes off the Prize: The United Nations and the African American Struggle for Human Rights: 1944–1955* (New York: Cambridge University Press, 2003).

4. See Arthur Goren, *The Politics and Public Culture of American Jews* (Bloomington: Indiana University Press, 1999), 197–200.

5. Goren, *Politics and Public Culture,* 200.

6. Among the few and first to discuss how race operates in Roth's work is Barry Gross, "American Fiction, Jewish Writers, and Black Characters: The Return of 'The Human Negro' in Philip Roth," *MELUS* 11.2 (1984): 5–22. See also the special issue of *Philip Roth Studies* on Roth and race (Fall 2006). Of course, there are too many articles on *The Human Stain* to mention here, but this 2000 novel initiated a lively conversation about Roth and race. Eric Sundquist's chapter on *The Human Stain* is perhaps the most comprehensive, while Timothy Parrish's essay on Roth and Ellison is the most compelling. Sundquist, *Strangers in the Land: Blacks, Jews, Post-Holocaust America* (Cambridge, MA: Harvard University Press, 2005); and Parrish, "Ralph Ellison: *The Invisible Man* in Philip Roth's *The Human Stain,*" *Contemporary Literature* 45 (2004): 421–59. Adam Newton's unique "facing" of Roth with David Bradley is also original. Newton, *Facing Black and Jew: Literature as Public Space in Twentieth-Century America* (New York: Cambridge University Press, 1999). Jeffrey Rubin-Dorsky's treatment does not touch on race, but his argument that Roth's work demonstrates that America is the "homeland" of the Jews can be understood in terms of the eclipse of race for Jews between 1969 and the present. Rubin-Dorsky, "Philip Roth and American Jewish Identity: The Question of Authenticity," *American Literary History* 13 (2001): 79–107. More to the point, Ranen Omer-Sherman discusses Roth's work as a "lamentation" for the lost revolutionary potential of Jewish American culture, a conclusion matching my own here. Omer-Sherman, *Diaspora and Zionism in Jewish-American Literature* (Hanover, NH: Brandeis University Press, 2002). My own lament: the recently published *Cambridge Companion to Philip Roth* (New York: Cambridge University Press, 2007) has little to say about race.

7. Eldridge Cleaver, *Soul on Ice* (New York: Delta Press, 1999).

8. Roth, "How Did You Come to Write That Book, Anyway?" *Reading Myself and Others* (New York: Vintage, 1985).

9. The scene calls to mind the biblical Zipporah, wife of Moses, and the troublingly ambiguous scene of circumcision in Exodus (4:24). Commentators debate whom Zipporah circumcises in this passage, Moses or her son, as she calls the recipient of her cut "a bridegroom of blood." Portnoy makes the connection himself (253). See Jacques Derrida, "Circumfession," in *Jacques Derrida,* ed. Geoffrey Bennington (Chicago: University of Chicago Press, 1991); and Gil Anidjar, "On the (Under)Cutting Edge: Does Jewish Memory Need Sharpening?" in *Jews and Other Differences: The New Jewish Cultural Studies,* ed. Jonathan Boyarin and Daniel Boyarin (Minneapolis: Minnesota University Press, 1997).

10. See Jonathan Boyarin, "Self-Exposure as Theory," in *Thinking in Jewish* (Chicago: University of Chicago Press, 1997), 53.

11. Horace Kallen argued throughout the 1930s and well into the 1950s that Jews were a "race." Kallen, *Culture and Democracy in the United States* (New York: Transaction, 1998).

12. Thanks to Arthur Nelson for research assistance on the NYCCHR.

13. Cheryl Greenberg, *Troubling the Waters: Black-Jewish Relations in the American Century* (Princeton, NJ: Princeton University Press, 223).

14. Gerald Benjamin, *Race Relations and the New York City Commission on Human Rights* (Ithaca, NY: Cornell University Press, 1974), 203.

15. All materials cited in this paragraph are from the Philip Roth Papers, Library of Congress, container 188, folder 3.

16. Emphasis added.

17. Quoted in Anderson, *Eyes off the Prize,* 1.

18. Ernest van den Haag, *The Jewish Mystique* (New York: Stein and Day Press, 1969), 82.

19. Greenberg, *Troubling the Waters,* 16.

20. Glazer,Nathan. "Negroes and Jews: The New Challenge to Pluralism." *The Commentary Reader.* ed, Norman Podhoretz. New York: Atheneum, 1966. 390.

21. "Readers' Reactions 1968–1969," Philip Roth Papers, Library of Congress, container 188, folder 5.

22. Letters, research notes, and drafts cited here are from the Philip Roth Papers, Library of Congress.

23. Sundquist, *Strangers in the Land,* 357.

24. Philip Roth Papers, Library of Congress, container 188, folder 5.

25. This is from the unnumbered front matter to *Portnoy's Complaint.*

26. Kathryn Stockton, *Beautiful Bottom, Beautiful Shame: Where Black Meets Queer* (Durham, NC: Duke University Press, 2006), 5.

27. Sigmund Freud, "The Economic Problem of Masochism," *The Standard Edition of the Complete Psychological Works of Sigmund Freud, Vol. 19,* ed. James Strachey (New York: W. W. Norton, 1976), 169.

28. See, for example, Ozick's story "Bloodshed," *Bloodshed and Three Novellas* (Syracuse, NY: Syracuse University Press, 1995) and her essay, "Toward a New Yiddish," *Art and Ardor* (New York: Dutton, 1984).

29. David Savran, *Taking It Like a Man: White Masculinity, Masochism, and Contemporary American Culture* (Princeton, NJ: Princeton University Press, 1998), 33.

30. Jennifer Travis, *Wounded Hearts: Masculinity, Law, and Literature in American Culture* (Chapel Hill: University of North Carolina Press, 2009), 9.

31. Carla Kaplan, *The Erotics of Talk: Women's Writing and Feminist Paradigms* (New York: Oxford University Press, 1996).

32. See Freud, *Interpreting Dreams,* trans. and ed. James Strachey (New York, Avon Books, 1965). 212. Freud explains a dream by recalling his secret shame when learning that his father was forced off the sidewalk by a German officer. Roth's more explicit paraphrase of this moment in Freud appears in *The Ghost Writer,* when Nathan Zuckerman admits feeling a measure of shame and anger on behalf of his father, who had to settle for podiatry when denied acceptance to medical school during the age of anti-Semitic quotas. Roth, *The Ghost Writer* (New York: Farrar Straus Giroux, 1979), 84-85.

33. Philip Roth Papers, Library of Congress, container 188, folder 2.

34. Lynn Hunt, *The Invention of Human Rights: A History,* appendix (New York: Norton, 2007), 221.

35. Shmuel Trigano, "The French Revolution and the Jews," *Modern Judaism* 10.2 (1990): 171–90.

36. Norman Podhoretz, "My Negro Problem—and Ours," in *The Commentary Reader,* ed. Norman Podhoretz (New York: Athenaeum, 1966), 376–87.

37. Jacques Lacan, "Kant avec Sade." *October* (Winter 1989): 55–75, 69.

38. Lacan. "Kant avec Sade," 55–79.

39. Marquis de Sade, *Justine, Philosophy in the Bedroom, and Other Writings,* trans. Richard Seaver (New York: Grove, 1990).

40. De Sade, *Justine,* 58.

41. De Sade, *Justine,* 60.

42. Lacan quoted in Kenneth Reinhard, "Kant With Sade, Lacan With Levinas." *Modern Language Notes* 110.4, Comparative Literature Issue (September 1995): 786.

43. Reinhard, "Kant With Sade, Lacan With Levinas," 787.

44. Ibid., 799.

45. Roth, *Ghost Writer;* Philip Roth, *The Counterlife* (New York: Vintage, 1986); Roth, *Operation Shylock: A Confession* (New York: Vintage, 1993); and Roth, *The Human Stain* (New York: Vintage, 2001).

46. Omer-Sherman, *Diaspora and Zionism.*

2. Rereading Cynthia Ozick

1. See, for example, Harold Bloom, "Introduction," *Cynthia Ozick: Modern Critical Views,* ed. Harold Bloom (New York: Chelsea, 1986), 1–8; Elaine Kauvar, *Cynthia Ozick's Fiction: Tradition and Invention* (Bloomington: Indiana University Press, 1993); Victor Strandberg. *Greek Mind/ Jewish Soul: The Conflicted Art of Cynthia Ozick* (Madison: Wisconsin University Press, 1994); and Timothy Parrish, "Creation's Covenant: The Art of Cynthia Ozick," *Texas Studies in Language and Literature* 43 (2000): 440–64.

2. Cynthia Ozick, "Preface," *Bloodshed and Three Novellas* (New York: Dutton, 1983); Ozick, "Metaphor and Memory," *Metaphor and Memory* (New York: Vintage, 1991), 265–83; Ozick, "The Dock-Witch," *The Pagan Rabbi and Other Stories* (New York: Knopf, 1971), 173–206; and Ozick, *Heir to the Glimmering World* (New York: Houghton, 2004).

3. Cynthia Ozick, "The Pagan Rabbi," *The Pagan Rabbi and Other Stories* (New York: Knopf, 1971), 1–38.

4. To illustrate the exclusion of Jewish literature from academic studies of ethnic literature, consider the collection of critical essays edited by David Palumbo-Liu, *The Ethnic Canon: Histories, Institutions, and Interventions* (Minneapolis: Minnesota University Press, 1995). There is no mention of Jews or Jewish literature in the entire collection. In *Ethnic Studies and Multiculturalism* Thomas La Belle and Christopher Ward demonstrate how the civil rights activism and ethnic consciousness-raising of the 1960s served as the basis for academic and corporate multiculturalism (Albany: State University of New York Press, 1996). For a commentary on American Jews and multiculturalism, see Michael Walzer's essay "Multiculturalism and the Politics of Interest" articulates modern multiculturalism with the Jewish advocacy for cultural pluralism in the early twentieth century, in David Biale, Michael Galchinsky, and Susannah Heschel, eds., *Insider/Outsider: American Jews and Multiculturalism* (Berkeley: University of California Press, 1995), 88–98.

5. Cynthia Ozick, *The Messiah of Stockholm* (New York: Knopf, 1987).

6. Amy Hungerford notes that in a speech to undergraduates at Yale, "Cynthia Ozick discouraged them from reading her novella *The Shawl*...because she herself is not a survivor. She advised them that they should read all the factual literature there is on the Holocaust before they look at her story." Hungerford, *The Holocaust of Texts: Genocide, Literature, and Personification* (Chicago: Chicago University Press, 2003), 155.

7. Emily Miller Buddick's discussion of Ozick's critical writing on race and ethnicity in her important book *Blacks and Jews in Literary Conversation* is an exception. Likewise, Adam Zachary Newton's innovative *Facing Black and Jew* explores how Ozick's essay "Literary Blacks and Jews" aims for ethical analysis but instead resorts to a common if subtle arrogation of the very grounds for ethical encounter to Jews and Jewish literature.

8. Arthur Goren describes this political turn in terms of Jewish institutional efforts at assimilation to American public culture. Goren, *The Politics and Public Culture of American Jews* (Bloomington: Indiana University Press, 1999). Marc Dollinger explains the Jewish commitment

to pluralism as a pragmatic strategy of progressive politics. Dollinger, *Quest for Inclusion: Jews and Liberalism in Modern America* (Princeton, NJ: Princeton University Press, 2000). Karen Brodkin describes Jewish perspectives on liberalism in terms of the benefits Jews gained from affiliations with whiteness. Brodkin, *How the Jews Became White Folks and What That Says about Race in America* (Newark: Rutgers University Press, 1998).

9. Taylor, "The Politics of Recognition," in *Multiculturalism: Examining the Politics of Recognition,* ed. Amy Gutman (Princeton, NJ: Princeton University Press, 1994), 25–74; and Will Kymlicka, *Multicultural Citizenship: A Liberal Theory of Minority Rights* (New York: Oxford University Press, 1995).

10. *Commentary* is a journal of ideas and critique published by the American Jewish Committee, the organization responsible for describing and promoting the concept of "the new pluralism" from 1968 forward. By the late 1960s, under the direction of Norman Podhoretz, *Commentary* completed its turn from support for organized labor and socialism to a commitment to liberal republicanism, critiquing first communism and then the cultural revolution of the 1960s and 1970s. By 1970, the journal, once a forum for ideas that would become central to progressive politics, had become a forum for dissent and protest against progressive social and academic policies on ethnicity, culture, and race. It may seem surprising that the American Jewish Committee should publish a journal so antipathetic towards its stated goals; however, that *Commentary* excoriated the politics and policy of multiculturalism indicates the breadth and variety of Jewish intellectual response to the politics of ethnicity and race during the 1960s and the value of exploring the ambivalence that preceded this shift.

11. Mark Shechner has described the Jewish turn away from leftist ideals in the 1960s as one from "socialism to therapy," cannily noting the cultural turn inward and the growing Jewish obsession with third-generation identity issues, but the need for therapy might also appropriately point to (take your pick) the euphoria, paranoia, or transferential dynamics between Jews and other ethnic groups. Shechner's view that Jewish writers including Roth, Trilling, and Mailer—and, we might add, Ozick—are concerned with the nature of identity from a psychoanalytic viewpoint is on the mark, though his implicitly diachronic analysis burrows downward into Jewish American history without seeking for answers laterally in the social developments contemporaneous with the literature itself. This diachronic view needs to be supplemented with a synchronic approach that acknowledges that Ozick's character-driven fiction is always set in the writer's present moment. Her characters may be second- and third-generation American Jews or perhaps Holocaust survivors and refugees, but they are also Americans and, in her early fiction, subject to contemporaneous social pressures of identity and ethnicity. Shechner, *After the Revolution: Studies in Contemporary Jewish American Literature* (Bloomington: Indiana University Press, 1987).

12. Michaels refers to Isaac Berkson's 1927 text, *Theories of Americanization: A Critical Study, with Special Reference to Jewish Groups* (New York: Arno, 1969).

13. Walter Benn Michaels, *Our America: Nativism, Modernism, and Pluralism* (Durham, NC: Duke University Press, 1995).

14. Robert Alter, "Jewish Dreams and Nightmares," *Commentary,* January 1968, 48–54.

15. Kauvar, *Cynthia Ozick's Fiction;* and Michael Galchinsky, "One Jew Talking: Jacob Glatstein's Diminished Imperative Voice," *Prooftexts* (September 1991): 241–57.

16. Susannah Heschel explains that nineteenth-century Christian historiography on Judaism "was a necessary element in constructing the hegemony of Christian scholarship. Studies of first-century Judaism provided information about the historical background of the New Testament, but, more important, they established the preferred Christian interpretation under the pretense of an objective, scholarly gaze." Heschel, "Jewish Studies as Counter-History," *Insider/Outsider,* ed. Biale, Galchinsky, and Heschel, 110.

17. For a critique of the methodologies of early twentieth-century "race science," see Franz Boas, *Anthropology and Modern Life* (New York: Norton, 1928).

18. The phrase comes from Lothrop Stoddard's work of "race science," *The Rising Tide of Color against White-World Supremacy* (New York: Scribner, 1921).

19. Charles Taylor develops this argument at length through Kant-derived claims about "the good life" in "The Politics of Recognition."

20. Herberg, *Protestant, Catholic, Jew.*

21. Brodkin, *How the Jews Became White Folks.*

22. Cynthia Ozick, "Letter," *Commentary,* September 1976, 8–10.

23. Cynthia Ozick, "Toward a New Yiddish," *Art and Ardor: Essays* (New York: Dutton, 1984), 151–77.

24. Cynthia Ozick, "Literary Blacks and Jews," *Art and Ardor,* 90–112.

25. The term *multiculturalism* has surprisingly different definitions in political philosophy and literary studies, eliciting startlingly different reactions from practitioners of both. In political philosophy, multiculturalism is a theory of cultural formation that asserts the rights of cultural groups to participate *as* groups in a democracy. To the extent to which they are multicultural, democratic countries like Canada, Great Britain, and the United States foster diverse cultural practices and even sanction radical cultural difference in public institutions such as schools and prisons. In contrast, multiculturalism in ethnic literary studies has come to mean the banal celebration of cultural difference, where the inclusion of diversity amid mainstream literary trends leaves cultural centers and margins intact. For a trenchant exchange on multicultural political philosophy emerging from and extending well beyond the Canadian question, see the essays by Charles Taylor and respondents in Amy Gutman's *Multiculturalism.*

26. Daniel O'Neill, "Multicultural Liberals and the Rushdie Affair: A Critique of Kymlicka, Taylor, and Walzer," *Review of Politics* 61 (1999): 219–50. In addition to Taylor, "Politics of Recognition," see William Connolly, *Pluralism* (Durham, NC: Duke University Press, 2005). Where Taylor argues for the importance to minority groups of sustaining cultural distinctness in order to promote democratic freedom, Connolly argues that cultures necessarily overlap and influence one another—also for the good of democracy.

27. For an interdisciplinary study of how Jewish culture interfaces with academic multiculturalism and ethnic studies, see Biale, Galchinsky, and Heschel, eds., *Insider/Outsider.*

28. Michael Kramer has suggested that the category "Jewish literature" always presupposes Jewishness as a racial designation. Kramer was roundly attacked by critics, among them Brian Cheyette and Morris Dickstein. Still, authors as various as Jonathan Boyarin and Eric Sundquist acknowledge either a political-racial status of Jews in American and world literature or find the category of race salient for making cross cultural comparisons. Kramer, "Race, Literary History, and the 'Jewish' Question," *Prooftexts* 21.3 (Fall 2001): 287–321.

29. Cynthia Ozick, "Usurpation (Other People's Stories)," *Bloodshed and Three Novellas,* (Syracuse, NY: Syracuse University Press, 1995), 129–78.

30. Jonathan Boyarin, "Circumscribing Constitutional Identities in *Kiryas Joel,*" *Powers of Diaspora: Two Essays on the Relevance of Jewish Culture* (Minneapolis: Minnesota University Press, 2002), 103–27.

31. Bernard Malamud, "Angel Levine," *The Magic Barrel* (New York: Farrar Straus Giroux, 2003), 43–56.

3. The New, New Pluralism

1. Allegra Goodman, *Kaaterskill Falls* (New York: Delta, 1999).

2. Stanley Fish, "Boutique Multiculturalism, or Why Liberals Are Incapable of Thinking about Hate Speech," *Critical Inquiry* 23.2 (1997): 387–95.

3. Werner Sollors, *Beyond Ethnicity: Consent and Descent in American Culture* (New York: Oxford University Press, 1986).

4. See, for example, Joseph Hough, *Black Power and White Protestants: A Christian Response to the New Negro Pluralism* (New York: Oxford University Press, 1968).

5. My understanding of Olana is largely based on immensely helpful conversations with art historian Jennifer Raab and a reading of the final chapter of her Ph.D. dissertation "Frederic Church and the Culture of Detail," Yale University, 2009.

6. Vivian B. Mann, Thomas F. Glick, Jerrilynn D. Dodds, eds., *Convivencia: Jews, Muslims, and Christians in Medieval Spain* (New York: George Braziller, 1992).

7. This phrase came out of a conversation with Jennifer Raab about *Kaaterskill Falls,* but I no longer recall which of us came up with it.

8. Jonathan Boyarin, *Thinking in Jewish* (Chicago: Chicago University Press, 1996).

9. Wendy Brown, "Tolerance as Supplement: The 'Jewish Question' and the 'Woman Question,'" *Regulating Aversion: Tolerance in the Age of Identity and Empire* (Princeton, NJ: Princeton University Press, 2006), 48–77.

10. Laura Levitt, "Impossible Assimilations, American Liberalism, and Jewish Difference: Revisiting Jewish Secularism," *American Quarterly* 59.3 (2007): 807–32.

11. Levitt, "Impossible Assimilations," 815.

12. Michael Warner, *Publics and Counterpublics* (Brooklyn: Zone Books, 2002).

13. Connolly, *Pluralism* (Durham, NC: Duke University Press, 2004).

14. Ralph Ellison, "The World and the Jug," *Shadow and Act* (New York: Vintage, 1995).

4. Recognition and Effacement in Lore Segal's Her First American

1. Lore Segal, *Her First American* (New York: New Press, 2004).

2. Lore Segal, *Other People's Houses* (New York: Harcourt, 1963).

3. Ralph Ellison, *Invisible Man* (New York: Vintage, 1995).

4. Barack Obama, *Dreams from My Father: A Story of Race and Inheritance* (New York: Crown, 2007).

5. Comte Stanislas de Clermont-Tonnerre, quoted in Lynn Hunt, *Inventing Human Rights: A History* (New York: Norton, 2007), 158.

6. Jacques Rancière, *Disagreement: Politics and Philosophy,* trans. Julie Rose (Minneapolis: Minnesota University Press, 1999), 27.

7. Horace Cayton, *Long Old Road: An Autobiography* (Seattle: University of Washington Press, 1963).

8. Drake St. Claire and Horace Cayton, *Black Metropolis: A Study of Negro Life in a Northern City* (New York: Harcourt, 1945).

9. Lore Segal, personal email, January 8, 2010.

10. In addition to Ellison, "World and the Jug," see James Baldwin, *The Fire Next Time* (New York: Vintage, 1992); and Richard Wright, *Black Boy* (New York: Harper Perennial Classics, 2008).

11. Roth, *Human Stain,* 108.

12. Hannah Arendt, *The Origins of Totalitarianism* (New York: Harcourt, 1951).

13. Jacques Rancière, *Disagreement: Politics and Philosophy,* trans. Julie Rose (Minneapolis: Minnesota University Press, 1999).

14. See Anderson, *Eyes off The Prize.*

15. Kara Solarz provided extraordinary research assistance in gathering Cayton's columns.

16. Al Nall, "King Says More Interest in Hungarians Than Al. Negroes," *Amsterdam News,* December 22, 1956.

17. Horace Cayton, "Any Negro Delegate to the United Nations Must Follow Policy of State Department," *Pittsburgh Courier,* February 23, 1953.

18. Cayton, "World At Large." *Pittsburgh Courier,* August 11, 1956

19. Ibid.

20. Later, Cayton will credit this line to Ralph Bunche (360).

21. Tanganyika was an independent nation between 1961 and 1964 and is now part of the territories of Rwanda, Burundi, and Tanzania.

22. Stanley Crouch, "Foreword: An American First," *Her First American* (New York: New Press, 2004). iv–xiv; and Philip G. Cavanaugh, "The Present Is a Foreign Country: Lore Segal's Fiction," *Contemporary Literature* 34.3 (1993): 474–511.

23. Paul de Man, "Autobiography as Defacement," *Modern Language Notes* 94.5 (1979): 919–30.

24. Judith Butler, "Giving an Account of Oneself," *Diacritics* 31.4 (2001): 22–40.

25. Ellison, "World and the Jug."

26. Sollors, *Beyond Ethnicity;* Matthew Frye Jacobson, *Whiteness of a Different Color: European Immigrants and the Alchemy of Race* (Cambridge, MA: Harvard University Press, 1998); and Brodkin, *How Jews Became White Folks.*

27. Henry Louis Gates Jr., *In Search of Our Roots: How Nineteen Extraordinary African Americans Reclaimed Their Past* (New York: Crown Publishers, 2009).

5. Responsibility Unveiled

1. Tony Kushner, *Homebody/Kabul* (New York: Theatre Communications Group, 2004). See the afterword for Kushner's humorous response to recurrent claims of his "eerie prescience" (144).

2. Tony Kushner, interview, "All Things Considered," National Public Radio, December 3, 2001. Available at www.npr.org/programs/atc/features/2001/dec/kushner/011203.kushner.html, accessed August 24, 2011.

3. Kushner, afterword, *Homebody/Kabul,* 144.

4. Kushner, afterword, *Homebody/Kabul,* 144.

5. Embassy of Afghanistan, "Business and Investment in Afghanistan: A Resource Guide," Washington, D.C., 20.

6. See Larry Diamond, "Universal Democracy?" *Policy Review,* Hoover Institute at Stanford University. Available at www.hoover.org/publications/policy-review/article/8078, accessed August 24, 2011.

7. Judith Butler, *Precarious Life: The Powers of Mourning and Violence* (New York: Verso, 2004).

8. Shoshana Felman and Dori Laub, *Testimony: Crises of Witnessing in Literature, Psychoanalysis, and History* (New York: Routledge, 1992); and Cathy Caruth, *Unclaimed Experience: Trauma, Narrative, and History* (Baltimore: Johns Hopkins University Press, 1996).

9. Debra Denker, "Along Afghanistan's War-Torn Frontier," *National Geographic* 167.6 (1985): 772–97.

10. Cathy Newman, "A Life Revealed," *National Geographic,* April 2002.

11. Jacques Rancière, "Who Is the Subject of the Rights of Man?" *South Atlantic Quarterly* 103.2/3 (2004): 297–310.

12. Slavoj Žižek, *Tarrying with the Negative: Kant, Hegel, and the Critique of Ideology* (Durham, NC: Duke University Press, 1993).

13. See David Braun, "How They Found National Geographic's 'Afghan Girl,'" *National Geographic News,* March 7, 2003. Available at http://news.nationalgeographic.com/news/2002/03/0311_020312_sharbat.html, accessed August 24, 2011.

14. Iris scanning systems have been experimentally installed in several locations throughout the United States—including Charlotte/Douglass International Airport, just down the road from my home—with the mission of identifying and preventing a would-be terrorist from entering a building or boarding a plane. Travelers and airport visitors automatically have their irises scanned and compared against a database of suspected terrorist's scans. Daniel Sieberg, "Iris Recognition at Airports Uses Eye-Catching Technology," CNN.com, July 24, 2000. Available at http://archives.cnn.com/2000/TECH/computing/07/24/iris.explainer/, accessed August 24, 2011.

15. See Braun, "How They Found."

16. "Afghan Girl Revealed," audio recording. Available at http://ngm.nationalgeographic. com/2002/04/afghan-girl/sight-and-sounds-interactive, accessed August 24, 2011.

17. Deborah Cohler, "Keep the Home Front Burning: Renegotiating Gender and Sexuality in U.S. Mass Media after 9-11," *Feminist Media Studies* 6.3 (2006): 245–61.

18. Saba Mahmood and Charles Hirschkind also observe that a group financed by Hollywood celebrities, the "Feminist Majority," made the liberation of Afghani girls and women its celebrated cause, advocating for education, western dress, and domestic rights for women. Against all other values, these are the most prized, worth the price of war. But as Mahmood and Hirschkind note, the 2002 war would do little to change the lives of the vast majority of Afghan women, most of whom lived outside of the "liberated" capital, Kabul. Mahmood and Hirschkind, "Feminism, the Taliban, and the Politics of Counter-Insurgency," *Anthropological Quarterly* 75.2 (2002): 339–54.

19. David Brooks argues for benevolent imperialism in his January 14, 2010, *New York Times* column, "The Underlying Tragedy." Available at www.nytimes.com/2010/01/15/opinion/ 15brooks.html, accessed August 24, 2011. See also Michael Ignatieff, *Human Rights as Politics and Idolatry* (Princeton, NJ: Princeton University Press, 2001); and Wendy Brown's rejoinder, "'The Most We Can Hope For': Human Rights and the Politics of Fatalism," *South Atlantic Quarterly* 103.2/3 (2004): 451–63.

20. Anne McClintock observes that this solipsism reinstantiates western priority. Reviewing American political and moral discourse over the release of torture photos from Abu Ghraib, Mc-Clintock concludes that the photos "turned the question of torture abroad back to a question about us in the United States: *our* morality, *our* corrupt sensibilities, *our* loss of international credibility, *our* gender misrule" (58). Likewise, Philip Gourevitch argued against the release of still more photos by the Obama administration—not out of a desire to protect America but out of concern that the conversation would shift from the pain of the victims of torture to self-reflexive forms of inquiry. McClintock, "Paranoid Empire: Specters from Guantanamo and Abu Ghraib," *Small Axe* 28 (March 2009); and Gourevitch, "The Abu Ghraib We Cannot See," *New York Times,* May 24, 2009. Available at www.nytimes.com/2009/05/24/opinion/24gourevitch.html, accessed August 24, 2011.

21. See Susan Moller Okin, ed., *Is Multiculturalism Bad for Women?* (Princeton, NJ: Princeton University Press, 1999).

22. See Emmanuel Levinas, "Peace and Proximity," in *Emmanuel Levinas: Basic Philosophical Writings,* ed. Adriaan T. Peperzak, Simon Critchley, and Robert Bernasconi. (Bloomington: Indiana University Press, 1996).

23. Cain wails, "'You have banished me this day from the soil, and I must avoid Your presence and become a restless wanderer on earth—anyone who meets me may kill me!' the Lord said to him, 'I promise, if anyone kills Cain, sevenfold vengeance shall be taken on him.' And the Lord put a mark on Cain, lest anyone who met him should kill him" (Genesis 4.13–4.16). *Tanakh: A New Translation of the Holy Scriptures According to Traditional Hebrew Text* (Philadelphia: Jewish Publication Society, 1985).

24. Jacques Rancière, "Who Is The Subject?" 305.

25. For a critical discussion of a broader idea of European citizenship, see Etienne Balibar, "World Borders, Political Borders," *We the People of Europe?: Reflections on Transnational Citizenship,* trans. James Swenson (Princeton, NJ: Princeton University Press, 2004), 101–14.

26. Jacques Derrida, *The Gift of Death,* trans. David Willis (Chicago: Chicago University Press, 1992).

27. The stage direction for the final scene has Milton helping Mahala remove her coat, as the scene dissolves from the Khyber Pass to London. Then "he watches her as she adjusts her hair and clothes, becoming an English Woman" (136). Presumably, though not certainly, Milton subsequently exits the stage before the scene commences.

28. Gayatri Chakravorty Spivak, "*Frankenstein* and a Critique of Imperialism," in *Frankenstein: A Norton Critical Edition,* ed. J. Paul Hunter (New York: Norton, 1996), 262–70. Thanks to David Siglar for pointing out the similarities between *Homebody/Kabul* and *Frankenstein* and for directing me to Spivak's essay.

29. Emmanuel Levinas, "Substitution" in *The Levinas Reader,* ed. Sean Hand (Cambridge, MA: Blackwell Publishers, 1994), 88–126.

30. Reinhard, "Kant with Sade, Lacan with Levinas," 785–808.

31. Ibid.

32. Roth, *Ghost Writer.*

6. Globalization's Complaint

1. Kushner, *Homebody/Kabul,* 59.

2. Gary Shteyngart, *Absurdistan* (New York: Random House, 2007).

3. Jacques Derrida. "Structure, Sign, and Play in the Discourse of the Human Sciences," in *Writing and Difference,* trans. Alan Bass (London: Routledge, 1967), 278–94.

4. Geertz, *Interpretation of Cultures;* and Peter Berger, *The Sacred Canopy: Elements of a Sociological Theory of Religion* (New York: Doubleday, 1967).

5. Franco, *Ethnic American Literature: Comparing Chicano, Jewish, and African American Writing* (Virginia University Press, 2006).

6. Cynthia Ozick has described Roth's novel as his "*Moby-Dick.*" Elaine Kauvar, "An Interview with Cynthia Ozick," *Contemporary Literature* 34.3 (Autumn 1993): 370.

7. Jonathan Freedman, *Klezmer America: Jewishness, Ethnicity, Modernity* (New York: Columbia University Press, 2009); and Benjamin Schreier, "Jew Historicism: Delmore Schwartz and Overdetermination," *Prooftexts* 27.3 (2007): 500–530.

8. Robert Young, *White Mythologies: Writing History and the West* (New York: Routledge, 1990); and Homi Bhabha, "The Postcolonial and the Postmodern: The Question of Agency," in *The Location of Culture* (New York: Routledge, 1994).

9. Derrida, "Circumfession"; Jean-Francois Lyotard, *Heidegger and "the Jews."* (Minneapolis: Minnesota University Press, 1990); Edward Said, "Reflections on Exile," in *Reflections on Exile and Other Essays* (Cambridge, MA: Harvard University Press, 2002); Paul Gilroy, *Black Atlantic: Modernity and Double-Consciousness* (Cambridge, MA: Harvard University Press, 1993); and Gilroy, *Against Race: Imagining Political Culture beyond the Color Line* (Cambridge, MA: Harvard University Press, 2000).

10. Aamir Mufti, *Enlightenment in the Colony: The Jewish Question and the Crisis of Postcolonial Culture* (Princeton, NJ: Princeton University Press, 2007); Michael Rothberg, Multidirectional Memory: Remembering the Holocaust in the Age of Decolonization (Stanford: Stanford University Press, 2009).

11. Jonathan Boyarin and Daniel Boyarin, "Diaspora: Generation and the Ground of Jewish Identity," *Critical Inquiry* 19.4 (1993): 693–725.

12. Riv-Ellen Prell, "Disappearing Jews and the Challenge of Cultural Studies" Annual Association of Jewish Studies Conference, American Jewish Studies Annual Conference, UCLA, December 13, 2009.

13. "Identity Crisis," Inside Higher Ed, March 9, 2006. Available at www.insidehighered.com/news/2006/03/09/oberlin, accessed August 24, 2011.

14. Kushner, *Homebody/Kabul,* 17.

15. Jake Tapper, "Senate Democratic Leadership Will Pass Health Care Reform 'By Any Legislative Means Necessary,'" ABCNews.com, August 19, 2009. Available at http://blogs.abcnews.com/politicalpunch/2009/08/senate-democratic-leadership-will-pass-health-care-reform-by-any-legislative-means-necessary.html, accessed August 24, 2011.

16. Roth, *Human Stain,* 329.

17. Jean-Paul Sartre, "Dirty Hands," *Three Plays,* trans. Lionel Abel (New York: Knopf, 1949).

18. Malcolm X, *By Any Means Necessary* (New York: Pathfinder, 1998).

19. Steve Clark, "Introduction," *By Any Means Necessary,* Malcolm X, vii–xix.

20. Moya, *Learning from Experience.*

21. Americo Paredes, *With His Pistol in His Hand: A Border Ballad and Its Hero* (Austin: University of Texas Press, 1956).

22. Teresa McKenna, "On Chicano Poetry and the Political Age: *Corridos* as Social Drama," in *Criticism in the Borderlands,* ed. Hector Calderon and José David Saldívar (Durham, NC: Duke University Press, 1994), 188–202.

23. See, for example, Walter Benn Michaels, *Our America: Nativism, Modernism, and Pluralism* (Durham, NC: Duke University Press, 1995); and Michaels, *The Trouble with Diversity: How We Learn to Love Identity and Ignore Inequality* (New York: Holt, 2007).

24. Christopher Douglass, *A Genealogy of Literary Multiculturalism* (Ithaca, NY: Cornell University Press, 2009); and Hungerford, *Holocaust of Texts.*

25. Teresa McKenna, *Migrant Song: Politics and Process in Contemporary Chicano Literature* (Austin: University of Texas Press, 1997); José David Saldívar, *Border Matters: Remapping American Cultural Studies* (Los Angeles: University of California Press, 1997); Ramón Saldívar, *Borderlands of Culture: Americo Paredes and the Transnational Imaginary* (Durham, NC: Duke University Press, 2006); John-Michael Rivera, *The Emergence of Mexican America: Recovering Stories of Mexican Peoplehood in U.S. Culture* (New York: New York University Press, 2006); and José Limón, "Imagining the Imaginary: A Reply to Ramon Saldivar," *American Literary History* 21.3 (2009): 595–603.

26. Ramon Saldívar, "Asian Américo: Paredes in Asia and the Borderlands: A Response to José E. Limón," *American Literary History* 21.3 (2009): 584–94; and Limón, "Imagining the Imaginary."

27. Irena Klepfisz, acknowledgements, *Dreams of an Insomniac: Jewish Feminist Essays, Speeches, and Diatribes* (Portland, OR: Eight Mountain Press, 1990), xv.

28. Hungerford, *Holocaust of Texts.*

29. Sundquist, *Strangers in the Land;* Freedman, *Klezmer America;* and Caroline Rody, "Letters from Camp Guglestein: Interethnicity and Jewishness in Gish Jen's *Mona in the Promised Land,*" in *The Interethnic Imagination: Roots and Passages in Contemporary Asian American Fiction* (New York: Oxford University Press, 2009).

30. Bellow, *Adventures of Augie March.*

31. See Michael Galchinsky, "Scattered Seeds: A Dialogue of Diasporas," in *Insider/Outsider,* ed. Biale, Galchinksy, and Heschel, 185–211.

32. The artist is Todd Levin. Other choice lines, indicating New Mexico ("Are you kidding? The Mexicans will kill you for sure. I read an article about it"), Utah ("Personally I think the Mormons are sick but it's none of my business what they do, as long as they are not hurting anyone"), and the Midwest ("Where the nice people live") cover most of the bases. Though I can no longer find my copy of *Heeb,* the map can be found online at Levin's website: http://www.tremble.com/scribblins/meet021027.html.

33. Peter Beinart, "The Failure of the American Jewish Establishment," *New York Review of Books,* June 10, 2010. Available at www.nybooks.com/articles/archives/2010/jun/10/failure-american-jewish-establishment/, accessed August 24, 2011.

7. Epilogue

1. Rachel Calof, *Rachel Calof's Story: Jewish Homesteader on the Northern Plains,* ed. J. Sanford Rikoon (Bloomington: Indiana University Press, 1995).

2. Willa Cather, *My Antonia,* ed. Joseph R. Urgo (New York: Broadview, 2003), 158.

3. Jacob Calof, epilogue, *Rachel Calof's Story,* 99–104. Less formally, when I discussed the novel with academic and lay readers shortly after its publication, it seemed that all anyone wanted to discuss were the sumptuous descriptions of halvah at the end.

4. Frederick Jackson Turner, *The Frontier in American History* (New York: Holt, 1920).

5. Brodkin, *How Jews Became White Folks.*

6. Norman Podhoretz, *Making It* (New York: Random House, 1967).

7. Harriet Rochlin, *The Reformer's Apprentice: A Novel of Old San Francisco* (Santa Barbara: Fithian, 1997); Rochlin, *The First Lady of Dos Cacahuates* (Los Angeles: Roots West, 1998); Rochlin, *On Her Way Home* (Santa Barbara: Fithian, 2001); and Harriet Rochlin and Fred Rochlin, *Pioneer Jews: A New Life in the Far West* (New York: Houghton, 2000).

8. Harriett Rochlin, personal conversation, Westwood, California, June 15, 2004.

9. Rochlin, personal conversation.

10. Rochlin, personal conversation.

11. T. Coraghessan Boyle, *The Tortilla Curtain* (New York: Viking, 1995); and Irving Howe, *World of Our Fathers* (New York: Harcourt, 1976).

12. Leon Uris, *Exodus* (New York: Doubleday, 1958).

13. Rochlin, personal conversation.

14. Horace M. Kallen, "Democracy Versus the Melting-Pot: A Study of American Nationality," *The Nation,* February 18 and 25, 1915, p. 220.

15. Kallen, "Democracy Versus the Melting-Pot."

16. Among the most recent versions of the question was at the panel titled "Does the English Department Have a Jewish Problem?" at MLA's annual convention, Philadelphia, Pennsylvania, December 27, 2009.

17. Freedman, *Klezmer America;* Rachel Rubinstein, *Members of the Tribe: Native America in the Jewish Imagination* (Detroit: Wayne State University Press, 2010); and Dalia Kandiyoti, *Migrant Sites: America, Place, and Diaspora Literatures* (Hanover, NH: Dartmouth University Press, 2009).

Bibliography

"Afghan Girl Revealed." Audio recording. Available at ngm.nationalgeographic.com/2002/04/afghan-girl/sight-and-sounds-interactive.

Alter, Robert. "Jewish Dreams and Nightmares." *Commentary,* January 1968, 48–54.

Anderson, Carol. *Eyes off the Prize: The United Nations and the African American Struggle for Human Rights: 1944–1955.* New York: Cambridge University Press, 2003.

Anidjar, Gil. "On the (Under)Cutting Edge: Does Jewish Memory Need Sharpening?" In *Jews and Other Differences: The New Jewish Cultural Studies,* ed. Jonathan Boyarin and Daniel Boyarin. Minneapolis: Minnesota University Press, 1997, 360–96.

Appiah, Kwame Anthony. *Cosmopolitanism: Ethics in a World of Strangers.* New York: Norton, 2007.

Arendt, Hannah. "Reflections on Violence." *New York Review of Books,* February 27, 1969. Available at www.nybooks.com/articles/archives/1969/feb/27/a-special-supplement-reflections-on-violence/, accessed June 15, 2011.

———. *The Origins of Totalitarianism.* New York: Harcourt, 1951.

Arnold, Matthew. *Culture and Anarchy.* New York: Oxford University Press, 2006.

Baldwin, James. *The Fire Next Time.* New York: Vintage, 1992.

Balibar, Etienne. *We the People of Europe?: Reflections on Transnational Citizenship.* Trans. James Swenson. Princeton, NJ: Princeton University Press, 2004.

Barry, Brian. *Culture and Equality: An Egalitarian Critique of Multiculturalism.* Cambridge, MA: Harvard University Press, 2001.

Beinart, Peter. "The Failure of the American Jewish Establishment." *New York Review of Books.* June 10, 2010.

Bellow, Saul. *The Adventures of Augie March.* New York: Viking, 1953.

———. "Mr. Sammler's Planet." *New York Review of Books,* November 1969: 95–150, December 1969: 99–142.

———. *Mr. Sammler's Planet.* New York: Viking, 1970.

Benjamin, Gerald. *Race Relations and the New York City Commission on Human Rights.* Ithaca, NY: Cornell University Press, 1974.

Berger, Peter. *The Sacred Canopy: Elements of a Sociological Theory of Religion.* New York: Doubleday, 1967.

Berkson, Isaac. *Theories of Americanization: A Critical Study, with Special Reference to Jewish Groups.* New York: Arno, 1969.

Bhabha, Homi. "The Postcolonial and the Postmodern: The Question of Agency." In *The Location of Culture.* New York: Routledge, 1994.

Biale, David, Michael Galchinksy, and Susannah Heschel, eds. *Insider/Outsider: Jews and Multiculturalism.* Berkeley: University of California Press, 1995.

Bloom, Harold. "Introduction." *Cynthia Ozick: Modern Critical Views.* Ed. Harold Bloom. New York: Chelsea, 1986.

Boas, Franz. *Anthropology and Modern Life.* New York: Norton, 1928.

———. *Race, Language, and Culture.* Chicago: Chicago University Press, 1995.

Boyarin, Daniel, and Jonathan Boyarin. "Diaspora: Generation and the Ground of Jewish Identity." *Critical Inquiry* 19.4 (1993): 693–725.

Boyarin, Jonathan. "Circumscribing Constitutional Identities in *Kiryas Joel.*" In Daniel Boyarin and Jonathan Boyarin, *Powers of Diaspora: Two Essays on the Relevance of Jewish Culture.* Minneapolis: Minnesota University Press, 2002, 103–27.

———. *Thinking in Jewish.* Chicago: Chicago University Press, 1996.

Boyle, T. Coraghessan. *The Tortilla Curtain.* New York: Viking, 1995.

Braun, David. "How They Found National Geographic's 'Afghan Girl.'" *National Geographic News,* March 7, 2003. Available at http://news.nationalgeographic.com/news/2002/03/0311_020312_sharbat.html, accessed August 24, 2011.

Brodkin, Karen. *How Jews Became White Folks and What That Says about Race in America.* Newark: Rutgers University Press, 1998.

Brooks, David. "The Underlying Tragedy." *New York Times,* January 15, 2010.

Brown, Wendy. "'The Most We Can Hope For': Human Rights and the Politics of Fatalism." *South Atlantic Quarterly* 103.2/3 (2004): 451–63.

———. *Regulating Aversion: Tolerance in the Age of Identity and Empire.* Princeton, NJ: Princeton University Press, 2006.

Butler, Judith. "Giving an Account of Oneself." *Diacritics* 31.4 (2001): 22–40.

———. *Precarious Life: The Powers of Mourning and Violence.* New York: Verso, 2004.

Cadava, Eduardo, and Ian Balfour. "The Claims of Human Rights: An Introduction." *South Atlantic Quarterly* 103 (Spring/Summer 2004): 277–96.

Calof, Jacob. Epilogue. *Rachel Calof's Story: Jewish Homesteader on the Northern Plains.* Ed. J. Sanford Rikoon. Bloomington: Indiana University Press, 1995, 99–104.

Calof, Rachel. *Rachel Calof's Story: Jewish Homesteader on the Northern Plains.* Ed. J. Sanford Rikoon. Bloomington: Indiana University Press, 1995.

Caruth, Cathy. *Unclaimed Experience: Trauma, Narrative, and History.* Baltimore: Johns Hopkins University Press, 1996.

Cather, Willa. *My Antonia.* Ed. Joseph R. Urgo. New York: Broadview, 2003.

Cavanaugh, Philip G. "The Present Is a Foreign Country: Lore Segal's Fiction." *Contemporary Literature* 34.3 (Autumn 1993): 474–511.

Cayton, Horace. "Any Negro Delegate to the United Nations Must Follow Policy of State Department." *Pittsburgh Courier,* February 23, 1953.

———. *Long Old Road: An Autobiography.* Seattle: University of Washington Press, 1963.

Clark, Steve. "Introduction." *By Any Means Necessary.* Malcolm X. New York: Pathfinder, 1998, vii–xix.

Cleaver, Eldridge. *Soul on Ice.* New York: Delta Press, 1999.

Cohler, Deborah. "Keep the Home Front Burning: Renegotiating Gender and Sexuality in U.S. Mass Media after 9-11." *Feminist Media Studies* 6.3 (2006): 245–61.

Connolly, William. *Pluralism.* Durham, NC: Duke University Press, 2005.

Crouch, Stanley. "Foreword: An American First." *Her First American.* New York: New Press, 2004.

de Man, Paul. "Autobiography as Defacement." *Modern Language Notes* 94.5 (1979): 919–30.

de Sade, Marquis. *Justine, Philosophy in the Bedroom, and Other Writings.* Trans. Richard Seaver. New York: Grove, 1990.

Denker, Debra. "Along Afghanistan's War-Torn Frontier." *National Geographic* 167.6 (1985): 772–97.

Derrida, Jacques. "Circumfession." *Jacques Derrida.* Ed. Geoffrey Bennington. Chicago: University of Chicago Press, 1991.

———. *The Gift of Death.* Trans. David Willis. Chicago: Chicago University Press, 1992.

———. "Structure, Sign, and Play in the Discourse of the Human Sciences." *Writing and Difference.* Trans. Alan Bass. London: Routledge, 1967, 278–94.

Dershowitz, Alan. *The Case for Israel.* New York: John Wiley and Sons, 2004.

Diamond, Larry. "Universal Democracy?" *Policy Review.* 119. June 1, 2003, available at http://www.hoover.org/publications/policy-review/article/8078, accessed September 19, 2011.

Dollinger, Marc. *Quest for Inclusion: Jews and Liberalism in Modern America.* Princeton, NJ: Princeton University Press, 2000.

Domke, David. "George W. Bush and the Gospel of Freedom and Liberty." *Seattle Times,* May 1, 2005.

Douglass, Christopher. *A Genealogy of Literary Multiculturalism.* Ithaca, NY: Cornell University Press, 2009.

Ellison, Ralph. *Invisible Man.* New York: Vintage, 1995.

———. "The World and the Jug." *Shadow and Act.* New York: Vintage, 1995.

Embassy of Afghanistan, "Business and Investment in Afghanistan: A Resource Guide." Washington, D.C. Available at http://www.embassyofafghanistan.org/resourceguide.html., accessed, September 19, 2011.

Felman, Shoshana, and Dori Laub. *Testimony: Crises of Witnessing in Literature, Psychoanalysis, and History.* New York: Routledge, 1992.

Fish, Stanley. "Boutique Multiculturalism, or Why Liberals Are Incapable of Thinking about Hate Speech." *Critical Inquiry* 23.2 (1997): 387–95.

Franco, Dean. *Ethnic American Literature: Comparing Chicano, Jewish, and African American Writing*. Charlottesville: Virginia University Press, 2006.

Freedman, Jonathan. *Klezmer America: Jewishness, Ethnicity, Modernity*. New York: Columbia University Press, 2009.

Freud, Sigmund. "The Economic Problem of Masochism," *The Standard Edition of the Complete Psychological Works of Sigmund Freud, Vol. 19*. Ed. James Strachey. New York: W. W. Norton, 1976.

——. *Interpreting Dreams*. Trans. and ed. James Strachey. New York, Avon Books, 1965.

Galchinsky, Michael. "One Jew Talking: Jacob Glatstein's Diminished Imperative Voice." *Prooftexts* (September 1991): 241–57.

——. "Scattered Seeds: A Dialogue of Diasporas." In *Insider/Outsider: American Jews and Multiculturalism,* ed. David Biale, Michael Galchinksy, and Susannah Heschel. Berkeley: University of California Press, 1995, 185–211.

Gates, Henry Louis, Jr. *In Search of Our Roots: How Nineteen Extraordinary African Americans Reclaimed Their Past*. New York: Crown Publishers, 2009.

——. *"Race," Writing, and Difference*. Chicago: Chicago University Press, 1986.

Geertz, Clifford. *The Interpretation of Cultures: Selected Essays*. New York: Basic Books, 1973.

Gilroy, Paul. *Against Race: Imagining Political Culture beyond the Color Line*. Cambridge: Harvard University Press, 2000.

——. *Black Atlantic: Modernity and Double-Consciousness*. Cambridge: Harvard University Press, 1993.

Gollnick, Donna. *Multicultural Education and Ethnic Studies in the United States: An Analysis and Annotated Bibliography of Selected ERIC Documents*. Washington, DC: American Association of Colleges for Teacher Education, 1976.

Goodman, Allegra. *Kaaterskill Falls*. New York: Delta, 1999.

Goren, Arthur. *The Politics and Public Culture of American Jews*. Bloomington: Indiana University Press, 1999.

Gourevitch, Philip. "The Abu Ghraib We Cannot See." *New York Times,* May 24, 2009. Available at www.nytimes.com/2009/05/24/opinion/24gourevitch.html, accessed August 24, 2011.

Greenberg, Cheryl. *Troubling the Waters: Black-Jewish Relations in the American Century*. Princeton, NJ: Princeton University Press, 2006.

Gross, Barry. "American Fiction, Jewish Writers, and Black Characters: The Return of 'The Human Negro' in Philip Roth." *MELUS* 11.2 (1984): 5–22.

Hegel, G. W. F. *The Phenomenology of Spirit*. Trans. A. V. Miller. London: Clarendon Press, 1977.

Herberg, Will. *Protestant, Catholic, Jew: An Essay in American Religious Sociology*. New York: Doubleday, 1955.

Heschel, Susannah. "Jewish Studies as Counter-History." In *Insider/Outsider: Jews and Multiculturalism,* ed. David Biale, Michael Galchinksy, and Susannah Heschel. Berkeley: University of California Press, 1995.

Hough, Joseph. *Black Power and White Protestants: A Christian Response to the New Negro Pluralism*. New York: Oxford University Press, 1968.

Howe, Irving. *World of Our Fathers*. New York: Harcourt, 1976.

Hungerford, Amy. *The Holocaust of Texts: Genocide, Literature, and Personification.* Chicago: Chicago University Press, 2003.

Hunt, Lynn. *The Invention of Human Rights: A History.* New York: Norton, 2007.

"Identity Crisis." Inside Higher Ed, March 9, 2006. Available at www.insidehighered.com/news/2006/03/09/oberlin, accessed August 24, 2011.

Ignatieff, Michael. *Human Rights as Politics and Idolatry.* Princeton, NJ: Princeton University Press, 2001.

Jacobson, Matthew Frye. *Whiteness of a Different Color: European Immigrants and the Alchemy of Race.* Cambridge: Harvard University Press, 1998.

Kallen, Horace. *Culture and Democracy in the United States.* New York: Transaction, 1998.

———. "Democracy Versus the Melting-Pot: A Study of American Nationality." *The Nation,* February 18, 190–94, and February 25, 1915, 217–20.

Kandiyoti, Dalia. *Migrant Sites: America, Place, and Diaspora Literatures.* Hanover, NH: Dartmouth University Press, 2009.

Kaplan, Carla. *The Erotics of Talk: Women's Writing and Feminist Paradigms.* New York: Oxford University Press, 1996.

Kaplan, Fred. "Was George Bush Right about Freedom and Democracy?" *Slate,* March 2, 2005.

Kauvar, Elaine. *Cynthia Ozick's Fiction: Tradition and Invention.* Bloomington: Indiana University Press, 1993.

———. "An Interview with Cynthia Ozick." *Contemporary Literature* 34.3 (Autumn 1993): 358–94.

Klepfisz, Irena. Acknowledgments. *Dreams of an Insomniac: Jewish Feminist Essays, Speeches, and Diatribes.* Portland, OR: Eight Mountain Press, 1990, xv.

Kramer, Michael. "Race, Literary History, and 'the Jewish Question.'" *Prooftexts* 21.3 (Fall 2001): 287–321.

Kushner, Tony. *Homebody/Kabul.* New York: Theatre Communications Group, 2004.

———. Interview. "All Things Considered." National Public Radio. December 3, 2001.

Kymlicka, Will. *Multicultural Citizenship: A Liberal Theory of Minority Rights.* New York: Oxford University Press, 1995.

La Belle, Thomas, and Christopher Ward. *Ethnic Studies and Multiculturalism.* Albany: State University of New York Press, 1996.

Lacan, Jacques. "Kant avec Sade." *October* (Winter 1989): 55–75.

Levinas, Emmanuel. *The Levinas Reader.* Ed. Sean Hand. Cambridge, MA: Blackwell Publishers, 1994.

———. "Peace and Proximity." In *Emmanuel Levinas: Basic Philosophical Writings,* ed. Adriaan T. Peperzak, Simon Critchley, and Robert Bernasconi. Bloomington: Indiana University Press, 1996.

Levitt, Laura. "Impossible Assimilations, American Liberalism, and Jewish Difference: Revisiting Jewish Secularism." *American Quarterly* 59.3 (2007): 807–32.

Limón, José E. "Imagining the Imaginary: A Reply to Ramon Saldivar." *American Literary History* 21.3 (2009): 595–603.

Lyotard, Jean-Francois. *Heidegger and "the Jews."* Minneapolis: Minnesota University Press, 1990.

Mahmood, Saba, and Charles Hirschkind. "Feminism, the Taliban, and the Politics of Counter-Insurgency." *Anthropological Quarterly* 75.2 (2002): 339–54.

Malamud, Bernard. "Angel Levine." *The Magic Barrel.* New York: Farrar Straus Giroux, 2003.

Mann, Vivian B., Thomas F. Glick, Jerrilynn D. Dodds, eds. *Convivencia: Jews, Muslims, and Christians in Medieval Spain.* New York: George Braziller, 1992.

McClintock, Ann. "Paranoid Empire: Specters from Guantanamo and Abu Ghraib." *Small Axe* 28 (March 2009).

McKenna, Teresa. *Migrant Song: Politics and Process in Contemporary Chicano Literature.* Austin: University of Texas Press, 1997.

——. "On Chicano Poetry and the Political Age: *Corridos* as Social Drama." In *Criticism in the Borderlands,* ed. Héctor Calderón and José David Saldívar. Durham, NC: Duke University Press, 1994, 188–202.

Michaels, Walter Benn. *Our America: Nativism, Modernism, and Pluralism.* Durham, NC: Duke University Press, 1995.

——. *The Trouble with Diversity: How We Learn to Love Identity and Ignore Inequality.* New York: Holt, 2007.

Miller, Emily Budick. *Blacks and Jews in Literary Conversation.* New York: Cambridge University Press, 1998.

Moya, Paula M. L. *Learning from Experience: Minority Identities, Multicultural Struggles.* Los Angeles: University of California Press, 2002.

Mufti, Aamir. *Enlightenment in the Colony: The Jewish Question and the Crisis of Postcolonial Culture.* Princeton, NJ: Princeton University Press, 2007.

Nall, Al. "King Says More Interest in Hungarians Than Al. Negroes." *Amsterdam News,* December 22, 1956.

Newman, Cathy. "A Life Revealed." *National Geographic,* April 2002.

Newton, Adam Zachary. *Facing Black and Jew: Literature as Public Space in Twentieth-Century America.* New York: Cambridge University Press, 1999.

Obama, Barack. *Dreams from My Father: A Story of Race and Inheritance.* New York: Crown, 2007.

Okin, Susan Moller, ed. *Is Multiculturalism Bad for Women?* Princeton: Princeton University Press, 1999.

Omer-Sherman, Ranen. *Diaspora and Zionism in Jewish-American Literature.* Hanover, NH: Brandeis University Press, 2002.

O'Neill, Daniel. "Multicultural Liberals and the Rushdie Affair: A Critique of Kymlicka, Taylor, and Walzer." *Review of Politics* 61 (1999): 219–50.

Ozick, Cynthia. *Bloodshed and Three Novellas.* Syracuse, NY: Syracuse University Press, 1995.

——. "The Dock-Witch." *The Pagan Rabbi and Other Stories.* New York: Knopf, 1971, 173–206.

——. *Heir to the Glimmering World.* New York: Houghton, 2004.

——. "Letter." *Commentary,* September 1976, 8–10.

——. "Literary Blacks and Jews." *Art and Ardor,* New York: Dutton, 1984.

——. *The Messiah of Stockholm.* New York: Knopf, 1987.

——. "Metaphor and Memory." *Metaphor and Memory.* New York: Vintage, 1991, 265–83.

——. "The Pagan Rabbi." *The Pagan Rabbi and Other Stories.* New York: Knopf, 1971, 1–38.

——. "Toward a New Yiddish." *Art and Ardor.* New York: Dutton, 1984.

——. "Usurpation (Other People's Stories)." *Bloodshed and Three Novellas.* Syracuse, NY: Syracuse University Press, 1995, 129–78.

Palumbo-Liu, David. *The Ethnic Canon: Histories, Institutions, and Interventions.* Minneapolis: Minnesota University Press, 1995.

Paredes, Americo. *With His Pistol in His Hand: A Border Ballad and Its Hero.* Austin: University of Texas Press, 1956.

Parker, Robert Dale. *The Invention of Native American Literature.* Ithaca: Cornell University Press, 2003.

Parrish, Timothy. "Creation's Covenant: The Art of Cynthia Ozick." *Texas Studies in Language and Literature* 43 (2000): 440–64.

——. "Ralph Ellison: *The Invisible Man* in Philip Roth's *The Human Stain,*" *Contemporary Literature* 45 (2004): 421–59.

Parrish, Timothy, ed. *Cambridge Companion to Philip Roth.* New York: Cambridge University Press, 2007.

Podhoretz, Norman. *Making It.* New York: Random House, 1967.

——. "My Negro Problem—and Ours." In *The Commentary Reader,* ed. Norman Podhoretz. New York: Athenaeum, 1966, 376–87.

Povinelli, Elizabeth. *The Cunning of Recognition: Indigenous Alterities and the Making of Australian Multiculturalism.* Durham, NC: Duke University Press, 2002.

Raab, Earl. "Review of the Year: Intergroup Tension and Relations in the United States." In *American Jewish Yearbook,* Vol. 71 (1970), ed. Morris Fine and Martin Himmelfarb. Prepared by the American Jewish Committee, 191.

Raab, Jennifer. "Frederic Church and the Culture of Detail." Ph.D. Dissertation. Yale University, 2009.

Rancière, Jacques. *Disagreement: Politics and Philosophy.* Trans. Julie Rose. Minneapolis: Minnesota University Press, 1999.

——. "Who is the Subject of the Rights of Man?" *South Atlantic Quarterly* 103.2/3 (2004): 297–310.

Reed, William. "The Census Form: Send it Back!" *San Francisco Bay National Black Newspaper,* March 2010.

Rivera, John-Michael. *The Emergence of Mexican America: Recovering Stories of Mexican Peoplehood in U.S. Culture.* New York: New York University Press, 2006.

Rochlin, Fred, and Harriet Rochlin. *Pioneer Jews: A New Life in the Far West.* New York: Houghton, 2000.

Rochlin, Harriet. *The First Lady of Dos Cacahuates.* Los Angeles: Roots West, 1998.

——. *On Her Way Home.* Santa Barbara, CA: Fithian, 2001.

——. *The Reformer's Apprentice: A Novel of Old San Francisco.* Santa Barbara: Fithian, 1997.

Rody, Caroline. *The Interethnic Imagination: Roots and Passages.* New York: Oxford University Press, 2009.

Roth, Philip. *The Counterlife*. New York: Vintage, 1986.

——. *The Ghost Writer*. New York: Farrar Straus Giroux, 1979.

——. "How Did You Come to Write That Book, Anyway?" *Reading Myself and Others*. New York: Vintage, 1985.

——. *The Human Stain*. New York: Vintage, 2001.

——. *Operation Shylock: A Confession*. New York: Vintage, 1993.

——. *Portnoy's Complaint*. New York: Vintage, 1994.

Michael Rothberg, *Multidirectional Memory: Remembering the Holocaust in the Age of Decolonization*. Stanford: Stanford University Press, 2009.

Rubin-Dorsky, Jeffrey. "Philip Roth and American Jewish Identity: The Question of Authenticity." *American Literary History* 13 (2001): 79–107.

Rubinstein, Rachel. *Members of the Tribe: Native America in the Jewish Imagination*. Detroit: Wayne State University Press, 2010.

Said, Edward. "Reflections on Exile." In *Reflections on Exile and Other Essays*. Cambridge: Harvard University Press, 2002.

Saldívar, José David. *Border Matters: Remapping American Cultural Studies*. Los Angeles: University of California Press, 1997.

Saldívar, Ramon. "Asian Américo: Paredes in Asia and the Borderlands: A Response to José E. Limón." *American Literary History* 21.3 (2009): 584–94.

Sartre, Jean-Paul. "Dirty Hands." *Three Plays*. Trans. Lionel Abel. New York: Knopf, 1949.

Savran, David. *Taking It Like a Man: White Masculinity, Masochism, and Contemporary American Culture*. Princeton, NJ: Princeton University Press, 1998.

Schreier, Benjamin. "Jew Historicism: Delmore Schwartz and Overdetermination." *Prooftexts* 27.3 (2007): 500–530.

Segal, Lore. *Her First American*. New York: New Press, 2004.

——. *Other People's Houses*. New York: Harcourt, 1963.

Shechner, Mark. *After the Revolution: Studies in Contemporary Jewish American Literature*. Bloomington: Indiana University Press, 1987.

Shteyngart, Gary. *Absurdistan*. New York: Random House, 2007.

Sieberg, Daniel. "Iris Recognition at Airports Uses Eye-Catching Technology." CNN. com, July 24, 2000. Available at http://archives.cnn.com/2000/TECH/computing/07/24/iris.explainer/, accessed August 24, 2011.

Sollors, Werner. *Beyond Ethnicity: Consent and Descent in American Culture*. New York: Oxford University Press, 1987.

Spivak, Gayatri Chakravorty. "*Frankenstein* and a Critique of Imperialism." In *Frankenstein: A Norton Critical Edition,* ed. J. Paul Hunter. New York: Norton, 1996, 262–70.

St. Claire, Drake, and Horace Cayton. *Black Metropolis: A Study of Negro Life in a Northern City*. New York: Harcourt, 1945.

Stockton, Kathryn. *Beautiful Bottom, Beautiful Shame: Where Black Meets Queer*. Durham, NC: Duke University Press, 2006.

Stoddard, Lotharp. *The Rising Tide of Color against White World-Supremacy*. New York: Scribner, 1921.

Strandberg, Victor. *Greek Mind/Jewish Soul: The Conflicted Art of Cynthia Ozick*. Madison: Wisconsin University Press, 1994.

Sundquist, Eric. *Strangers in the Land: Blacks, Jews, and Post-Holocaust America.* Cambridge, MA: Harvard University Press, 1995.

Taylor, Charles. "The Politics of Recognition." In *Multiculturalism: Examining the Politics of Recognition,* ed. Amy Gutman. Princeton, NJ: Princeton University Press, 1994, 25–74.

Travis, Jennifer. *Wounded Hearts: Masculinity, Law, and Literature in American Culture.* Chapel Hill: University of North Carolina Press, 2009.

Trigano, Shmuel. "The French Revolution and the Jews." *Modern Judaism* 10.2 (1990): 171–90.

Turner, Frederick Jackson. *The Frontier in American History.* New York: Holt, 1920.

Uris, Leon. *Exodus.* New York: Doubleday, 1958.

van den Haag, Ernest. *The Jewish Mystique.* New York: Stein and Day Press, 1969.

Walzer, Michael. "Multiculturalism and the Politics of Interest." In *Insider/Outsider: Jews and Multiculturalism,* ed. David Biale, Michael Galchinksy, and Susannah Heschel. Berkeley: University of California Press, 1995.

Warner, Michael. *Publics and Counterpublics.* Brooklyn: Zone Books, 2002.

Wright, Richard. *Black Boy.* New York: Harper Perennial Classics, 2008.

X, Malcolm. *By Any Means Necessary.* New York: Pathfinder, 1998.

Young, Robert. *White Mythologies: Writing History and the West.* New York: Routledge, 1990.

Žižek, Slavoj. *Tarrying with the Negative: Kant, Hegel, and the Critique of Ideology.* Durham, NC: Duke University Press, 1993.

INDEX

Baldwin, James, 118
Barry, Brian, 210n12
Barth, John, 59
Barthelme, Donald, 59
Bellow, Saul, 6, 43; *Adventures of Augie March,*
    189; *Mr. Sammler's Planet,* 1–3, 6–8, 10–11,
    43, 74, 76
Berger, Peter, 172–73
Berkson, Isaac, 63
Bhabha, Homi, 174
bildungsroman, 9, 48, 120
Bill of Rights, 183
Black Panthers, 18, 19, 38–39, 65, 124–25, 181
Blake, William, 136
"Bloodshed" (Ozick), 18, 22, 69, 71, 73–79,
    92–93, 184
Boas, Franz, 14, 16, 66, 187, 189
Booth, William, 36
Boyarin, Daniel, 173
Boyarin, Jonathan, 15, 77, 173, 215n28
Boyle, T. Coraghessan, 200
Bradley, David, 211n6
Brodkin, Karen, 67, 133, 199, 214n8
Brooks, David, 153, 218n19
Brown, Wendy, 95–96, 153, 210n2
Buddick, Emily Miller, 209n5, 213n7
burkhas, 142, 149, 155–57, 165
Bush, George W., 12, 14, 178
Bush, Laura, 150, 151
Butler, Judith, 15, 20, 144–45, 159

Cahan, Jacob, 171, 194
Cain, mark of, 159, 218n23
Calof, Abraham, 194, 197–99
Calof, Jacob, 198
Calof, Rachel, 15, 25, 193–202
Canada, Québec separatists in, 69
Carmichael, Stokely, 65, 138, 181
Caruth, Cathy, 145, 154
Cather, Willa, 196, 199
Cavanaugh, Philip, 128–29
Cayton, Horace, 19, 23, 118–19, 124–26,
    130–33, 198
Cheyette, Brian, 215n28
Chicanas/Chicanos, 84, 187; civil rights
    movement of, 17, 60, 70, 185; and
    Mexicans, 11, 185–87, 190, 201–4; and
    multiculturalism, 71, 173–74
Chicana/o Studies, 174, 185–86, 206
Church, Frederic, 89–90

circumcision, 35–36, 176, 211n9
Civil Rights Act (1964), 120
civil rights movement, 4–6, 32–33, 181; and
    affirmative action programs, 5–6, 8, 60, 112;
    Chicana/o, 17, 60, 70, 185; communitarian
    rights of, 60; Jews in, 14, 30–34, 37–38,
    65–66, 75, 121; Roth on, 21–22. *See also*
    African Americans
Cleaver, Eldridge, 19, 138; and Cayton, 127;
    on rape, 40–42, 45; and Roth, 21, 38–45, 52,
    53; *Soul on Ice,* 21, 34, 39–42, 51–52
Clinton, Bill, 139–40
Cohen, Lillian, 38, 39, 54
Cold War, 30; and human rights, 32–33,
    123–24; and McCarthyism, 33, 204
Cole, Thomas, 89, 91, 105
colonialism, 60. *See also* decolonization
Commentary (journal), 17–18, 43; on black-
    Jewish alliance, 38; Ozick in, 60–61;
    Podhoretz in, 65–66, 214n10; Raab in, 75
commodification, of diversity, 62–63, 85, 147,
    150–51, 176–79
Commonweal (journal), 60
Connolly, William, 20, 61; on "creedal
    ventilation," 78, 203; and Goodman, 22–23;
    on pluralism, 17–18, 99–101; and Taylor,
    215n26
Constitution, U.S., 77, 183
consumerism, 62–63, 140–42, 151, 171, 179
Cortez, Gregorio, 186, 187
cosmopolitanism, 137–38; Ellison's view
    of, 104; and immigrants, 146, 165; and
    nationalism, 125–26, 140–41; Shteyngart's
    view of, 171, 172, 179
Counterlife (Roth), 54, 169
counterpublics, 97–98
Crouch, Stanley, 128
cultural pluralism. *See* pluralism

Danticat, Edwidge, 59
Darfur crisis, 160–61
Daugman, John, 149
*Declaration of the Rights of Man and of the
    Citizen* (1791), 32, 48–50, 95–96
decolonization, of Africa, 71, 110, 112, 123–25,
    144, 172–74, 218n19
de Man, Paul, 129–30
Derrida, Jacques, 15, 20–21, 144, 163–64; and
    Bhabha, 174; and Levinas, 168; and Lévy-
    Strauss, 172; on logocentrism, 173